MAJOR-GENERAL SIR JAMES K. TROTTER, K.C.B., C.M.G.,
who raised the 62nd (W.R.) Division in 1914, and commanded
it until 24th December, 1915.

Frontispiece.

THE HISTORY OF THE 62nd (WEST RIDING) DIVISION
1914—1919

MILITARY HISTORIES BY THE SAME AUTHOR

The History of the
2nd DIVISION, 1914-1918

The
WEST YORKSHIRE REGIMENT
IN THE WAR,
1914-1918

The History of the
SOMERSET LIGHT INFANTRY
1914-1918
[*In Preparation.*]

The History of the
MIDDLESEX REGIMENT,
1914-1919
[*in Preparation.*]

The History of the
EAST YORKSHIRE REGIMENT
1914-1918
[*In Preparation.*]

The History of the
30th (HOW.) BATTERY, R.F.A.
1914-1918
[*In Preparation.*]

THE HISTORY OF THE 62nd (WEST RIDING) DIVISION 1914—1919

*

By
EVERARD WYRALL

Author of " Europe in Arms—A Concise History of the Great War ":
" The History of the 2nd Division, 1914—1918 ":
" The West Yorkshire Regiment in
the War, 1914—1918,"
Etc., Etc.

VOLUME I

WITH 40 PHOTOGRAPHIC ILLUSTRATIONS
AND 23 COLOURED BATTLE PLANS.

JOHN LANE THE BODLEY HEAD LIMITED
VIGO STREET, LONDON, W.

CONTENTS.

		PAGE
I.	The Raising and Training of the Division	1
II.	The Division leaves England	9
III.	The First Sector—Beaumont Hamel	15
IV.	The Advance to the Hindenburg Line	31
V.	The First Attack on Bullecourt	37
VI.	The Battle of Bullecourt	45
VII.	Trench Warfare: 29th June—19th November, 1917	59
VIII.	The Battle of Cambrai, I.	69
IX.	,, ,, ,, II.	79
X.	,, ,, ,, III. The Taking of Anneux	95
XI.	,, ,, ,, IV. The Capture of Bourlon Wood	111
XII.	From the Battle of Cambrai, 1917, to the Great German Offensive, 21st March, 1918	123
XIII.	The Greatest German Effort: The Offensive of 21st March, 1918	129
XIV.	The Defence of Bucquoy	143
XV.	The Period of Active Defence	165
XVI.	The Division moves down to the Marne	169
XVII.	The Battle of Tardenois: Capture of Marfaux	175
XVIII.	The Capture of Bligny and Montaigne de Bligny	209
XIX.	The Advance to Victory	221
XX.	Mory	229

LIST OF MAPS

VOLUME I.

		facing PAGE
I.	The First Sector: Beaumont Hamel..	15
II.	The Advance to the Hindenburg Line. I. ..	31
III.	The Advance to the Hindenburg Line. II. ..	36
IV.	The Battle of Bullecourt	45
V.	The Noreuil—Lagnicourt Sector	59
VI.	The Battle of Cambrai, 1917: Havrincourt before capture by the 62nd Division on 20th November, 1917	69
VII.	The Battle of Cambrai, 1917: The Capture of Havrincourt	79
VIII.	„ „ „ The Taking of Anneux	95
IX.	„ „ „ The Capture of Bourlon Wood ..	111
X.	The Defence of Bucquoy	143
XI.	The Division moves down to the Marne	169
XII.	The Battle of Tardenois: Capture of Marfaux ..	175
XIII.	The Capture of Bligny and Montaigne de Bligny ..	209
XIV.	Mory	229

ILLUSTRATIONS

VOLUME I.

	PAGE
Major-General Sir James K. Trotter, K.C.B., C.M.G.	*frontispiece*
Lieut-General Sir Walter P. Braithwaite, K.C.B. .. *facing*	6
In Beaumont Hamel, 1917 .. .. „	16
Near Beaumont Hamel in 1917 .. .. „	19
A Wiring Party moving up to the Front Line .. .. „	22
The Old German Front Line, Beaumont Hamel .. „	26
The German Retreat to the Hindenberg Line .. .. „	34
An Advanced Dressing Station, Ecoust, 1917 .. .. „	41
Aeroplane Photographs showing the Destruction of Bullecourt by the Guns.. .. .. „	46
The Slag Heap near Havrincourt in 1917 .. .. „	82
Divisional Machine Gunners at Graincourt .. .. „	88
Bourlon Wood in November, 1917 .. .. .. „	112
Bourlon Wood: The Chalet .. .. „	114
The Tile Factory in Bourlon Village .. .. .. „	116
Bucquoy: The Ruined Church .. .. „	144
Private Thomas Young, V.C., 9th Bn. Durham Light Infantry .. .. „	152
The late Lieut.-Colonel O. C. S. Watson, V.C., 5th K.O.Y.L.I. .. .. „	156
The 1/5th Devons resting in the Forest of Rheims .. „	182
A British Sentry in the Forest of Rheims .. .. „	190
"Then began an extraordinary man hunt in the depths of a Forest" .. .. „	196
Capturing a Hun .. .. „	201
Men of the Duke of Wellington's Regt. resting in a shell hole .. .. „	202
The 8th West Yorkshires moving back from the Front Line after the capture of the Montaigne de Bligny „	214
Ervillers .. .. „	232

Chapter I.

RAISING AND TRAINING OF THE DIVISION

> Come, join in the only battle,
> Wherein no man can fail,
> Where whoso fadeth and dieth,
> Yet his deed shall still prevail.
>
> William Morris.

THE sturdy patriotism and fighting qualities of the Yorkshireman figure largely in the military history of Great Britain. Of the six northern counties of England, Yorkshire has in past ages witnessed many desperate struggles: her wild moors, steep hills and deep valleys have many times been drenched with blood. Cæsar's legions knew full well the stubborn resistance offered by the men of the north: Royalist and Roundhead troops fought many a sanguinary battle for the possession of Yorkshire towns, whilst abroad in the Napoleonic wars and the numerous struggles in which the Nation has in the past been engaged, thousands of Yorkshiremen have stoutly upheld the honour of the British Empire.[1] Thrifty and industrious in peace, brave and enduring in war, these are the inherent qualities of the men of the County.

Of such a race it was only natural that when the peace of the world was rudely disturbed in 1914, Yorkshiremen from all parts of the County flocked to the colours and, whilst the old Regular Army was fighting in France and Flanders in the early months of the war, were fitting themselves for the hour in which they, too, would take their places in the trenches.

---

[1] No less than five regular infantry regiments of the British Army, take their names from the County: The West Yorkshire Regiment (The Prince of Wales's Own)—14th Foot: The East Yorkshire Regt.—15th Foot: The Green Howards (Alexandra, Princess of Wales's Own Yorkshire Regt.)—19th Foot: The King's Own Yorkshire Light Infantry—51st and 105th Foot: and the York and Lancaster Regt.—65th and 84th Foot. The Duke of Wellington's Regt. (West Riding)—33rd and 76th Foot—takes its title both from the County and the Great Duke.

When war was declared the Territorial troops in the West Riding of Yorkshire were mobilized as the West Riding (Territorial) Division. Later, on arrival in France this division was re-named the 49th (West Riding) Division.

Within a few weeks of the outbreak of war the Army Council had decided to raise reserve or second line units from which reinforcements for the first line could be drawn. Thus in October, 1914, recruiting began for the new reserve battalions of the West Riding Territorial Division, which, as already stated, afterwards became the 49th (West Riding) Division. But long before the first line Division crossed over to Flanders, the formation of a second line Division was begun. This second line Division was destined to become the 62nd (West Riding) Division, a division which had an extraordinary record of achievements, for, with one exception, in the battles in which it took part (and they were many) it always won through to its objectives.

The early days of this Division were fraught with troubles and difficulties, which to those who were responsible for raising and training the newly enlisted troops seemed at times almost unsurmountable. The first line Division naturally claimed precedence. In pre-war days the West Riding Territorial Association of which Lord Scarbrough and Brig.-Gen. H. Mends, C.B., were the moving spirits, had done its work well : it had carried out faithfully a precept which Continental Powers had long observed :

" In times of peace, prepare for war."

In consequence the first line Division was well equipped and trained. But at the close of 1914, when the second line Division was being formed there were no trained officers or N.C.O.'s, surplus to the establishment who could take over and immediately begin the training of the raw recruits.

Detailed records of the strenuous efforts put forward by those who were responsible for raising and training these new Territorial troops are scanty, but from the information which does exist, it is clear that the Honorary Colonels of the first line Battalions, who had been asked by the Territorial Force Association of the West Riding of Yorkshire at York to raise units in their respective recruiting areas, set to work whole-heartedly and soon men from all parts of the county were pouring in and attesting.

From that great area of mills and furnaces and mines—the West Riding—which includes the cities of Leeds, Sheffield and Bradford and the towns of Doncaster, Halifax, Huddersfield, Dewsbury,

Skipton, Rotherham, Keighley, Pontefract, Barnsley, Castleford, Ossett and Normanton and the wide agricultural area between Leeds and York, and from the capital itself, men of all conditions of life joined up, casting aside (for the nonce) their civil employment and civilian clothes to undergo the vigorous training and don the uniform of a soldier.

The West Riding of Yorkshire is almost a county in itself, attracting and creating in the different industrial centres, different types of men. And as one Commanding Officer said " The stranger coming amongst them found new and strange variations of the English language peculiar to small districts from which the units were recruited."

The men who formed the 2/1st West Riding Infantry Brigade (subsequently the 185th Infantry Brigade) were drawn mainly from the cities of York, Leeds and Bradford. This Brigade consisted of four Battalions of the West Yorks. Regiment, *i.e.*, the 2/5th, 2/6th, 2/7th and 2/8th,[1] In their ranks were clerks and warehousemen from the big banks and merchant houses, skilled and unskilled artisans from the great combing, spinning and weaving works, and from the big engineering plants of which Yorkshire is justly proud.

The 2/2nd West Riding Infantry Brigade (afterwards the 186th Infantry Brigade) consisting of the 2/4th, 2/5th, 2/6th and 2/7th Battalions of the Duke of Wellington's Regiment, was largely formed of men who had hitherto spent most of their lives in the local woollen, worsted and cotton mills : the 2/4th from the area round Halifax, the 2/5th from about Huddersfield, the 2/6th of men from the Skipton district, and the 2/7th from the Colne Valley as far as the borders of Lancashire, near Todmorden. A fair number of men of these battalions came also from the stone quarries, engineering works and offices in their respective districts.

Two Battalions of the 2/3rd West Riding Infantry Brigade, the 2/4th King's Own Yorkshire Light Infantry from the district of which Wakefield is the centre, including the " Heavy Woollen " districts of Dewsbury and Batley and the mining areas between the latter towns, and the 2/5th K.O.Y.L.I. from Doncaster and district, mostly miners and men from the farms and railway works, and two Battalions of the York and Lancaster Regt., the 2/4th (The Hallamshires) from Sheffield, and the 2/5th from the district about Rotherham, were destined to become the 187th Infantry Brigade.

[1] The 7th and 8th were the " Leeds Rifles."

Men for the 2/1st and 2/2nd Field Ambulance were recruited in Leeds and the surrounding district, and for the 2/3rd Field Ambulance, in the Sheffield area: Lieut.-Col. Lister commanded the 2/1st., Lieut.-Col. C. W. Eames, the 2/2nd and Lieut.-Col. Kerr, the 2/3rd.

The first A.D.M.S. of the Division was Col. de Burgh Birch, C.B., who in 1908, on the formation of the Territorial Force had been appointed A.D.M.S. of the 1st (M.R.) Territorial Division. Colonel de Burgh Birch had already served for a very long period in the old Volunteer Brigade, and not only was he the original founder of the Volunteer Medical Staff Corps in Leeds many years ago, but the development of the R.A.M.C. in the West Riding was due to his untiring efforts, for he organized the first Field Ambulance under the Territorial Force scheme. When war broke out in 1914, however, he had already retired, but his services were too valuable to be spared and he was asked to command the Medical units of the new second line West Riding Division.

There was no lack of skilled men for the Field Companies of the Royal Engineers, or for the Machine Gunners: nor were horsemen wanting for the Artillery, the Brigades of which were formed of men drawn mainly from Leeds, Bradford, Sheffield and Huddersfield. But " a man did not always get into his right berth " said an officer of the Division, "for there is a tale told of one spinner who when asked his trade replied that he 'tended a mule.' Whereupon he was immediately sent to the horse lines as an expert in the care of a difficult animal, to find out from bitter experience that the care of a spinning mule is a trivial, childish task compared with the stern realities of the charge of the real article."

The men were of good physique and keen sportsmen, the townsmen were of average height, but the dalesmen were taller: stout fellows all, who stripped well, of a surprising toughness, used to hard work and long hours, who in a fight could be trusted to give (as indeed later on they did most worthily give) a good account of themselves. Of such was this new second line Territorial Division formed.

The command of the Division was given to Major Gen. Sir J. K. Trotter, K.C.B., C.M.G. He had, as Chief of the Staff, Col. H. S. Sloman, D.S.O., Colonel J. H. Balguy as C.R.A., and the three Infantry Brigades (2/1st, 2/2nd and 2/3rd) were commanded respectively by Col. H. W. Guinness, C.B., late Royal Irish Regt., Col. H. G. Mainwaring, late S. W. Borderers, and Col. H. B.

Lassetter, C.B., late S. Staffordshire Regt. and Australian Light Horse.

Divisional Headquarters were established at Doncaster, on February 17th, 1915, the 1st West Riding Division (49th) being then at the same place. The units of the Division were at that time at their own regimental stations, where recruiting was being carried on with all vigour possible. In order that the Staff might get into touch with and exercise control over them, it was decided to remove Headquarters to Matlock Bath, where they arrived on March 1st, and within a week or so the Brigades and independent units were brought into billets in Matlock, Derby, Belper, Nottingham and Bakewell.

The R E. Headquarters and the Field Companies were at Sheffield, where they had a very complete and well-found depot with especially good mobilization stores and a riding school.

It was now possible to take stock of the Division. It was found to consist of a mass of men, partly clothed in uniform, untrained, unarmed, having for instruction purposes a few d.p. rifles, without equipment, horses or waggons, with practically no officers or N.C.O.'s competent to train and discipline, and without one of the many small customs and traditions which influence the regular recruit from the moment of his enlistment. At this time, it should be noted, the Territorials were competing with the units of the Kitchener Divisions, and these latter having found favour with those in high places swept into their own ranks all the training ability of this country. In these conditions the work of the Staff was arduous and often disappointing.

The Divisional Train experienced many obstacles to efficiency : " Everybody was new to the job, including officers. The first few months were spent in teaching the men drill and waggon drill (without waggons, as few vehicles were available) : also route marching and physical drill. Then orders were received to disband the M.T men and some were drafted to the first line M.T. Column at Doncaster : also drafts were sent to the first line H.T......In February, 1915, the train went to Derby, and one Company to Matlock. We had just a few old civilian carts at that period and the supply question was difficult. In the case of one of our Companies we had to divide the rations up for each man, as they were billeted in separate houses, two in some houses, and only one in others."

Difficulties were increased by frequent changes of plan, for which, no doubt, the authorities cannot be blamed. During the month of March, 1915, orders came to embark the 49th Division for service in France, and the 2nd West Riding Division was ordered back to Doncaster to take its place there. Headquarters reached Doncaster on April 8th, and the troops moved into the town and neighbourhood shortly afterwards, excepting the 3rd Brigade, which went to Strensall Camp, near York.

On April 13th, the 49th Division left for France, and the 2nd W.R. Division then became a training and reinforcing formation to supply it with recruits. The artillery received an armament of old French guns, and twenty rounds per gun of ammunition which had remained in store for some thirty years. The guns were equipped with sights graduated in inches, and the fuzes with divisions no one could interpret. Nevertheless the Division was instructed to be prepared to entrain at any moment to meet a possible invading force on the east coast, and trains to move it were held in readiness day and night.

The Ist, IInd, IIIrd and IVth Artillery Brigades were commanded respectively by Lieut.-Colonels Beever, Gadie (afterwards Lord Mayor of Bradford), Mackenzie Grieve and Molesworth.

Arrangements were made to encamp the Division during the spring and summer in the Dukeries. On May 1st, Headquarters were installed in Edwinstowe, the 1st and 2nd Brigades encamped in Thoresby Park, two battalions being detached to Babworth Park to be in readiness to entrain for the coast, the Artillery were in Welbeck Park, the Engineers at Southwell. The 3rd Brigade moved fr m Strensall to camp at Beverley, having with it a proportion of R.A., Medical units and transport.

During the summer months the equipment of the Division with everything except guns for the R A. was completed. Training was carried out day and night under schemes initiated and supervised by the Chief of the Staff, Colonel Sloman, who had gained a reputation as a battalion commander, and progress towards efficiency was marked. Methods adopted in France and Belgium were practised, and lectures were given to officers by experts in various subjects.

All this time the Division was supplying its most efficient officers and men to fill the gap in the 49th Division. Then in the autumn a change of organization was made. A third line was formed at Clipstone Camp, the establishment of the Division was reduced, and the excess numbers became the nucleus of third line units. To these units was assigned the duty of finding drafts for the Division abroad and the 2nd W.R. Division was henceforth an

LIEUT.-GENERAL SIR WALTER P. BRAITHWAITE, K.C.B.,
who commanded the 62nd (W.R.) Division from 24th December, 1915,
to 28th August, 1918.

independent formation. Its title was changed. It was now the 62nd Division, its Infantry Brigades were numbered 185, 186 and 187, its Artillery Brigades 310, 311, 312, the Royal Engineer Companies 457, 460, 461, the Divisional Train Companies 525, 526, 527 and 528.

The Division was moved in the late autumn from the Sherwood Forest to quarters and billets in and around Retford, where the Headquarters were established on October 15th. From Retford it moved to Newcastle, on November 28th, exchanging quarters with the 2nd Northumberland Division. The 187th Brigade from Beverley joined the Division there. At Newcastle the artillery at last received its equipment of modern guns (18 pr.) and howitzers, and during the month of December instructions were received that the Division had been selected for service abroad.

On December 24th, Major-General W. P. Braithwaite, C.B., succeeded Major-General Sir James Trotter as G.O.C. Division. A new C.R.A. arrived on the 1st April—Brigadier-General A. T. Anderson, who relieved Brigadier-General J. A. Balguy, and by that date several other changes had taken place in the staff and commands.

Early in 1916, the Division found itself in camp on Salisbury Plain, for the purpose, as one of the Brigadiers said, of having "the finishing touches put to our training." By this time the 62nd had been organized, equipped and trained out of all resemblance to its former state in 1914, and presented an excellent appearance on parade.

To the average soldier who usually prefers town life, Salisbury Plain is not a very attractive place, even in the summer time, and when the Division took up its abode in hutments the mud was even worse than at Newcastle-upon-Tyne. But the 62nd had yet to experience a winter in the front line trenches in France.

In June, the Division moved up to Norfolk with great expectations of proceeding overseas at an early date, but again these expectations were not realized, though the Division had a certain amount of mild excitement during the Zeppelin raids of the late summer and early autumn of that year. On the 26th July, 1916, the Division was inspected at Gillingham by His Majesty the King, who expressed his pleasure at the soldierly bearing of the men.

In October, the Division moved further inland to Bedford, Wellingborough and Northampton, and in these areas completed its final training.

Chapter II.

1917.

THE DIVISION LEAVES ENGLAND

"YOUR period of training has been very long and arduous, but the time has now come for you to put the results of your instruction to the test, and, with your comrades now in the field, to maintain the unceasing efforts necessary to bring the War to a victorious ending. Good Luck, and God Speed."

"George R. I."

FOR a little over two years the 62nd (W.R.) Division had worked and had waited for embarkation orders: they came at the close of December, 1916. And when on 4th January, the above gracious message was received from His Majesty the King, all ranks knew that at last the moment was at hand when artificialities were to give place to the grim realities of War.

Divisional Headquarters left Bedford, and arrived at Southampton on 9th January, embarking at 9-30 p.m. About 7 a.m. on the 10th, the transport arrived off Havre and disembarkation began soon after 12 noon. At 3 p.m. on the 11th, Divisional Headquarters left Havre, detrained at Auxi-Le-Chateau about 4 p.m. on the 13th, and marched to Frohen-le-Grand, then in the Third Army Area; Third Army Headquarters were at St. Pol.[1]

9TH JAN.

The Divisional Artillery (R. A. Headquarters, 310th, 311th and 312th Brigades, R.F.A.) left Northampton on the 5th, 6th and 7th January, and travelling *via* Southampton and Havre were concentrated about Wavans by the 11th, establishing communications with Divisional Headquarters at Frohen-le-Grand on the arrival in that place of General Braithwaite and his Staff.

Of the three Infantry Brigades, the 185th embarked at Southampton on the 8th, the 186th Brigade (less the 2/6th Duke of Wellington's Regt.) on the 10th, and the 187th Brigade on the 12th January All three Brigades disembarked at Havre and within the next few

[1] For the Order of Battle of the 62nd (W. R.) Division on arrival in France, *see* Appendix I.

9TH JAN.

days arrived at Frévent in the Divisional area. The 2/6th Duke of Wellington's Regt. had been detained in Bedford owing to an outbreak of scarlet fever.

13TH JAN.

The Divisional Engineers and the Divisional Troops had by this time also arrived in France, the concentration of the whole Division being practically complete by the 13th January.[1]

Two days later the 62nd was transferred to the Vth Corps of the Fifth Army, and received orders to march on the 22nd, 23rd and 24th January to Beauval and Bus.

January was at its worst when the Division arrived in France, and heavy rain, sleet and snow, with occasional hard frosts welcomed the Yorkshiremen in their new training area behind the front lines. Here at last within measurable distance was the real thing. The holocaust of War had not as yet passed over the villages in which the troops were billeted, but the roads were inches deep in mud, and broken by abnormal traffic, and men moved to and from their drill and duties, wallowing perforce in slush and across sodden ground. For on the 18th and 20th, four officers and sixteen N.C.O.'s per Battalion were sent to the trenches of the 19th and 32nd Divisions, in order to receive their first introduction to trench warfare. Four hundred gunners (including officers) were also attached to the Artilleries of the 19th and 32nd Divisions for training purposes.

21ST JAN.

On the 21st, under Vth Corps orders, the Divisional Field Companies of Royal Engineers marched to Authie in order to construct a system of practice trenches for the Infantry Brigades when they should arrive in the Bus area. The Heavy, Medium and Light

---

[1] The Divisional Artillery, however, did not complete concentration until the 18th, as No. 1 and No. 4 sections of the Divisional Ammunition Column did not arrive in the Divisional area until that date.

Shortly after its arrival in France the 62nd Divisional Artillery received orders to reorganize under a new reorganization scheme. Army Field Artillery Brigades were then in the process of formation and the 311th Brigade, R.F.A., and the 62nd Divisional Ammunition Column were reconstituted for this purpose. D/311 Battery of the 311th Brigade was broken up to bring D/310 and D/312 Batteries up to six-gun Battery strength. To complete the reorganization B/308 Battery (18-Pdrs. Q. F.) from the 61st Divisional Artillery and half of 517th Battery (4·5 Q.F.) from the 31st Divisional Artillery joined the 311th Brigade. B/308 Battery then became C/311 and the half of 517th Battery with the remaining section of C/311 became D/311 Battery.

The Divisional Ammunition Column was apportioned similarly. The 311th Field Artillery Brigade then became an Army Artillery Brigade, but was ordered for the present to remain with its Division. Each Artillery Brigade under the new organization consisted of three six-gun 18-Pdr. Batteries and one six-gun 4·5 Howitzer Battery. The Batteries in the Brigades were usually known as A, B, C or D Battery.

Trench Mortar Batteries were also instructed on this date to join 21ST JAN. the Fifth Army School at Valheureux, for a fortnight's course beginning on the 23rd.

The march to Beauval was carried out on the 22nd without incident, and at nightfall on the 23rd, the Division reached Bus and was located in that town and area. Only the Artillery, the 525th Company, A.S.C. and the T.M.B.'s (seven in number) were not with the Division: the Artillery and Army Service Corps were in billets in Authie and Amplier and the Trench Mortar Batteries had left for Valheureux. On the 24th, Headquarters, R.A., the Divisional Artillery and the Divisional Ammunition Column marched to the Bus area, the former taking up quarters in the town, the guns to Vauchelles (310th Brigade R.F.A.), Acheux Wood (311th Brigade R.F.A.) and Louvencourt (312th Brigade R.F.A.) and the D.A.C. to Thievres and Couin: the 525th Company A.S.C. also marched to the Bois du Warnimont.

From the 25th January onwards, the Division furnished parties 25TH JAN. of officers and men—infantry, gunners and sappers—for attachment to the 19th and 32nd Divisions for instructional purposes.[1] Sniping, the handling of Lewis Guns and Trench Mortars, Intelligence duties, Gas and Bombing became part of their daily instruction. It was well that all ranks were kept busy, for hard work counteracts ills not only of the body, but of the mind. The conditions under which the Division now lived and prepared for active work in the front line, were far different from the comfortable life in billets in England. From the 20th, a hard frost had settled upon the ground which was still covered with snow. Little wonder that some of the men (especially those out in tents) fell ill. But on the whole the Division was wonderfully healthy and above all the men retained their cheerfulness under most depressing conditions.

Apart from "Courses" and tours of instruction in the front line[1] there was an enormous amount of work to be carried out behind the lines, on roads, the construction of ammunition dumps, and in burying cables. Close on 2,500 men from the 185th and 186th Infantry Brigades were employed on this work daily, and towards the close of January it became necessary to employ the whole of the 187th Infantry Brigade (less a few officers and specialists who were undergoing training) on railway construction, the Brigade being

---

[1] A few casualties (the first) were suffered by the 62nd Division during these tours of instruction in the front line trenches—two other ranks being killed and eleven wounded.

25TH JAN. struck off all instruction in the trenches. Work on the railway necessitated a redistribution of the 187th and portions of the 185th and 186th Brigades, but not beyond the Bus area.

January closed dry, but still bitterly cold. Fuel, both coal and wood, was scarce. In spite of these discomforts, however, the Divisional G. S. Diary closes with these words : " The men are keeping very well and cheery." It was a good augury for the future.

The beginning of the year 1917 was an anxious period, not only for the enemy, but for the Allies also.

The Battles of the Somme, 1916, had scarcely ended when the 62nd Division landed in France. As a result of those costly operations the offensive had passed to the Allies and the enemy was hard put to it to maintain his line. His huge losses in men and material had not yet been made good, his exhausted divisions still held the line with greatly diminished *morale*. And he was nervous lest the Somme Battles should again break out.

On the other hand the position of the Allies was not too favourable. Both France and Britain had lost very heavily during the campaign of 1916, and the capture of large tracts of the enemy's positions necessitated a vast amount of labour and preparation which entailed the employment of troops which should have been available for offensive purposes. Moreover, thousands of casualties had to be replaced, the new arrivals trained, and the huge stocks of ammunition which had been collected for, and used in, the Somme Battles, replenished. And yet, so far as circumstances and the weather would allow, the enemy could not be allowed to re-organize, refit and strengthen his positions : he was to be given no respite. The pendulum had swung towards the Allies and they could not afford to let it go from them.

The dawn of 1917, therefore, heralded plans for an Allied offensive on an extensive scale. They were the continuation and elaboration of a scheme of operations which had been decided upon at a conference of military representatives of all the Allied Powers, held at French General Headquarters, at Chantilly, in November, 1916. At this conference Sir Douglas Haig and General Joffre, representing Great Britain and France, respectively, formulated their plans to begin a series of offensives on all fronts, timed to assist each other by depriving the enemy of the power of weakening any one of his fronts in order to re-inforce another.

Upon the British Front, Arras and the Ypres Salient had been selected as the points from which these offensives should take place: the French were to launch offensives in Champagne and North of the Aisne.

Just south of Arras, the salient between the Scarpe and the Ancre into which the enemy's troops had been forced as a result of the Somme Battles, was to be the first point of attack. Later, the Vimy Ridge was to be assaulted and captured, then, before the enemy had time to realize Sir Douglas Haig's intention, the offensive was to be transferred to Flanders.

When these operations were decided upon the enemy still held the whole of the Ancre Valley, from Le Transloy to Grandcourt, including the lower northern slopes of the Thiepval Ridge. Across the river he held the greater part of the spur about Beaumont Hamel, and north of the latter point still clung to his positions in front of Serre, Gommecourt, Monchy-au-Bois and Ransart, the line running thence north-east to east of Arras. Behind this front line were second and third lines strongly fortified, consisting, in places, of double lines of trenches heavily wired.

The first position to be assaulted was the Le Transloy—Loupart Line which ran from Saillisel, past Le Transloy to the Albert— Bapaume Road, where it turned west past Grévillers and Loupart Wood, then north-west again in front of Achiet-le-Petit to Bucquoy. The enemy's third line of defence was known as the Rocquiguy— Bapaume—Ablainzevelle Line.

West of the Le Transloy—Loupart Line were the villages of Beaumont Hamel, Miraumont, Petit Miraumont, Serre, Puisieux-au-Mont, Achiet-le-Petit, Irles and Bucquoy, and the Beauregard Dovecote—all names which in time became terribly familiar to the troops of the 62nd Division. Many of these places were in ruins —mere naked, scorched walls, and battered masses of brick and stone, whilst the ground round about was pock-marked by shell holes, full of water, and on all sides viscous mud and slush abounded from inches to feet in depth: terrible country in which to live and wage constant warfare.

Below the surface of these slimy morasses lay many a brave man—friend and foe—their poor remains at times torn rudely from their unnamed graves by the blast of shells. An unholy and unsavoury place to come to rest!

Before the end of November, 1916, an attack on the German trenches overlooking the villages of Pys and Grandcourt had taken place, resulting in the gain of positions on a front of 5,000 yards.

North of the Ancre, a simultaneous attack improved the situation of the troops in the Beaucourt Valley. But winter had set in and a further advance was practically impossible. All that could be done up to the close of the year until the weather improved, was to improve the trenches and repair and construct roads and communications.

By the end of January, 1917, however, the whole of the high ground north and east of Beaumont Hamel had been captured from the enemy, and British troops had pushed into the Beaucourt Valley, 1,000 yards north of Beaucourt Village. Early in February (on the 7th), owing to the continued advance north of the Ancre, Grandcourt was evacuated by the enemy and on the same night Baillescourt Farm, halfway between Beaucourt and Miraumont, fell into the hands of the 63rd Division (Vth Corps). An advance towards Serre was then begun and it was at this stage of the operations that the 62nd (W. R.) Division was ordered forward into the front-line trenches.

The foot of the Pelican was raised.[1]

---

[1] A Pelican was the 62nd Divisional sign.

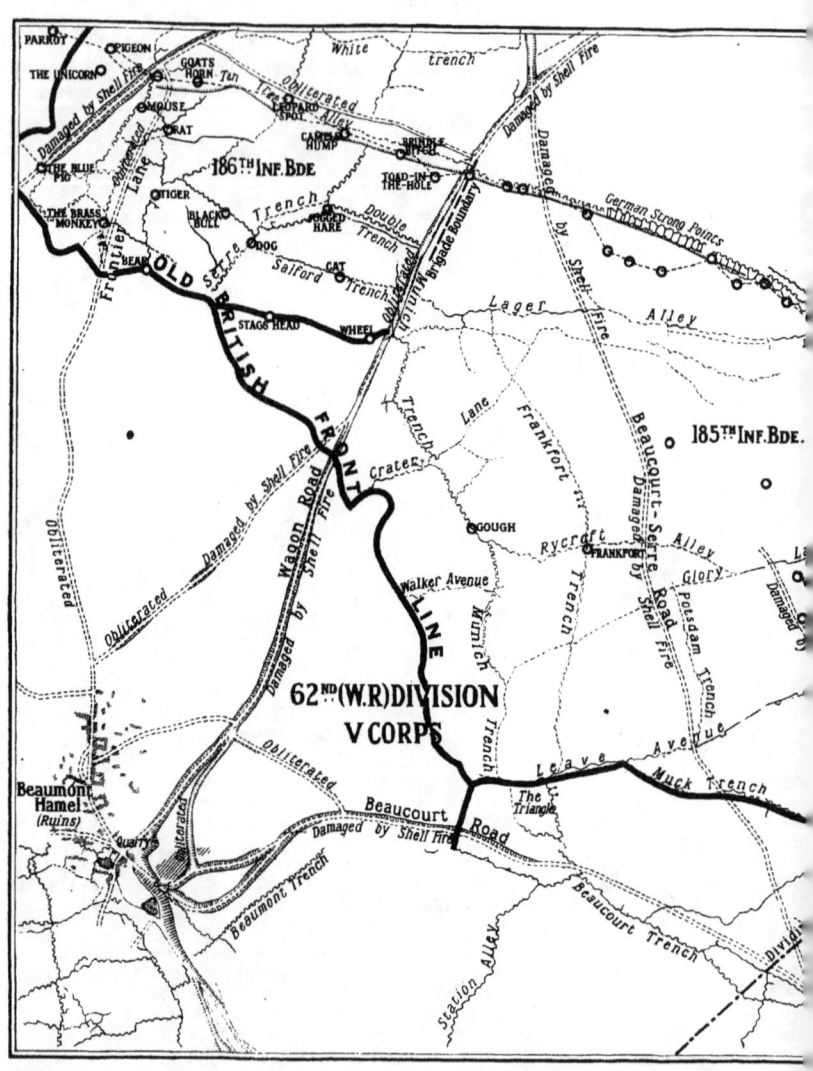

THE FIRST SECTOR—BEAUM

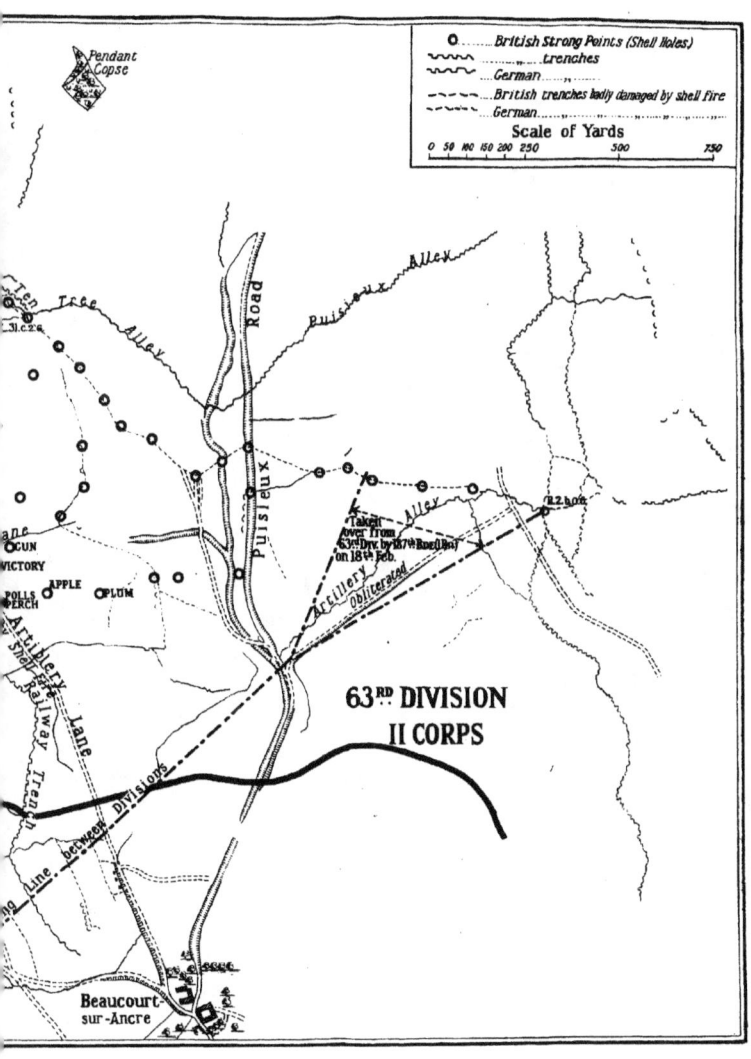

Chapter III.   1917.

THE FIRST SECTOR—BEAUMONT HAMEL

" Endless lanes sunken in the clay,
  Bays, and traverses, fringed with wasted herbage;
  Seed-pods of blue scabious, and some lingering blooms;
  And the sky, seen as from a well,
  Brilliant with frosty stars."
                                        Frederick Manning.

THE guns were first into the line. One Brigade (the 310th) 1ST FEB. and a Battery of the 311th Brigade—A/311—relieved the XXIInd Brigade, R.F.A., and "T" Battery, R.H.A. (both of the 7th Division), on the night of 1st February, and occupied positions west of Auchonvillers and east of Engelbelmer respectively. The Divisional Ammunition Column relieved the 7th Division D. A. C. along the Bertrancourt—Acheux road on the 5th. The 310th Brigade, R.F.A., and A/311 Battery came into action on the 10th and 11th, and assisted the 32nd Division in its attack on Ten Tree Alley, south-west of Serre : this operation being the first of a series designed to drive the enemy from the Beaucourt Valley.

On the nights of the 11th/12th and 12th/13th February, the 13TH FEB. remainder of the guns completed the relief of the 7th Divisional Artillery, and by the morning of the 13th, all units of the 62nd Divisional Artillery were in action.

During the early days of February, the Infantry battalions of the Division[1] were still engaged alternately in work behind the lines, and by daily tours of instruction in the forward areas of the 19th and 32nd Divisions, gaining further insight into trench warfare. On the 2nd February, the 62nd had received warning that it was to relieve the 32nd Division in the line north and north-east of Beaumont Hamel on or about the 12th, but the exact position to be taken over could not be defined, as it depended upon the result of the operations to be carried out during the next few days.

---

[1] On 8th February, the 2/6th Duke of Wellington's Regt. arrived from England and marched to billets in Louvencourt.

13TH FEB. It was during one of the above-mentioned instructional tours in the front line that 2nd Lieut. N. E. Bentley, of the 2/5th Duke of Wellington's Regt. was reported missing. A and B Companies of the Battalion were in the trenches opposite Hebuterne with the 56th and 58th Infantry Brigades (19th Division). During the night, 5th/6th February, Lieut. Bentley went out into No Man's Land with a patrol of the 7th East Lancashires. The patrol stumbled upon a party of Germans in a trench and a fight ensued, during which a prisoner was taken by the patrol. A retirement was then ordered, but on getting through the German wire an N.C.O. belonging to the East Lancashires became entangled and Lieut. Bentley returned to help him out. This was the last seen of him. On the way back the German prisoner was shot dead by a bullet from the enemy's trenches. This appears to be the first officer casualty suffered by the 62nd Division.

The 97th Infantry Brigade (32nd Division) attacked the enemy on the night 10th/11th, and gained all its objectives—some 1,500 yards of a strong line of trenches lying on the southern part of the Serre Hill—with the exception of two strong points. Heavy counter-attacks, supported by artillery and machine-gun fire, were launched by the enemy on the 11th and 12th, but they were broken up and repulsed with considerable loss. The 32nd Division was, however, ordered to capture the two strong points still holding out before handing over the line to the 62nd Division.

SEE MAP NO. 1. The relief of the 32nd by the 62nd was finally carried out on the nights of 13th/14th and 14th/15th February, the 186th Infantry Brigade relieving the 14th Infantry Brigade in the left sub-sector, the 185th Infantry Brigade relieving the 97th Infantry Brigade in the right sub-sector : the 187th Infantry Brigade was in Divisional reserve.

15TH FEB. The reliefs were completed without a hitch by 2-40 a.m. on the 15th, and at 9 a.m. General Braithwaite (G.O.C. 62nd) assumed command of the sector, the first front-line sector held by the Division after its arrival in France.

The conditions prevailing in the front line (and indeed in all the forward areas) almost baffle description. Trenches as such did not exist, for they had been obliterated by the concentrated fire of the guns previous to the attack which took place on the 10th/11th of the month. The front line was held in a series of posts and dug-outs, which somewhat resembled islands in a sea of mud. Shell-holes pock-marked the ground, often overlapping one another, and where pathways existed between them they were but a few inches

IN BEAUMONT HAMEL, 1917.
GERMAN GRAVES AND MONUMENT: CHURCH IN BACKGROUND.
"The village church . . . was no more distinguishable, other than by a tumbled heap of white stone."

wide. The holes were full of water and more than one man lost his 15TH FEB. life through slipping off the narrow pathway into the slimy mass which engulfed him. In daylight it was difficult enough to pick a way safely across such ground, but in the darkness of the night, when most of the reliefs had to take place, it was a miracle if the relieved or relieving troops escaped without at least one casualty—through mud. So terrible had been the holocaust which passed over this part of the line that even the villages of Beaumont Hamel and Beaucourt-sur-Ancre had practically ceased to exist. The village church of the former was no more distinguishable, other than by a tumbled heap of white stone which looked for all the world as if it had been dumped on the ground by a builder.

Even in the rear positions of the Divisional area where the guns were situated, conditions were appalling. The gun-pits were unavoidably dug amidst awful surroundings. Some of them—about Beaumont—were on the site of the Ancre Battlefield, and the guns had to be dragged across ground full of shell-holes, thick in viscous mud. Horses, gun-carriages and limbers slipped about and stuck fast, and more than one animal sank deep into the spongy morass and disappeared entirely. In the trench-maps of this area, almost all the roads which once existed are marked "obliterated."

Such was the sector over which General Braithwaite assumed command on the morning of the 15th February. He had on his right the 63rd (Naval) Division, and on his left the 19th Division.

The intention of the Vth Corps Commander[1] (in which the 62nd Division was now contained) was to advance on Miraumont and Serre, and for this purpose the troops holding front-line posts were ordered to push out patrols for the purpose of testing the enemy's strength. The 185th and 186th Infantry Brigades were therefore hardly settled in their shell-hole posts when active patrolling began.

The 185th Infantry Brigade holding the right sub-sector had in the front line posts, the 2/5th West Yorks. (right), 2/7th West Yorks. (centre) and 2/6th West Yorks. (left), the 2/8th West Yorks. being held in reserve. Each Battalion disposed two Companies in the line of posts allotted to it, one Company in support and one in reserve. The 186th Infantry Brigade, on the left of the Divisional front, disposed the 2/5th Duke of Wellington's Regt. in the right sub-sector, and the 2/4th Duke of Wellington's in the left sub-sector:

[1] The Vth Corps on 15th February, formed part of the Fifth Army (General Sir H. Gough).

15TH FEB. the 2/6th and 2/7th Duke of Wellington's were in Brigade reserve in Mailly Maillet.

The 187th Infantry Brigade in Divisional reserve was engaged in railway construction, the formation of dumps and the laying of cables.

The reliefs, which were completed by 2-40 a.m. on the morning of the 15th, were carried out without a hitch, reflecting great credit upon troops, who, with the exception of instructional tours of very short duration, had never been in the front line, much less taken charge of a sector.

Patrol work began immediately. But the enemy's machine-guns and snipers were extremely active and movement by daylight was exceptionally dangerous. From Serre the enemy had a fine field of view, of which he took full advantage—his machine-guns sweeping the left Brigade area and Wagon Road intermittently. The forward posts in this Brigade sector were also heavily shelled about mid-day, but little damage was done, only the troubled earth being still further churned up, mud-pools becoming deeper and more loathsome.

Throughout the 15th and 16th, the Division was chiefly employed in settling down in its new area, and in improving the battered position won by, and taken over from the 32nd Division. But early on the morning of the 17th, the Divisional Artillery co-operated in an attack by the 63rd, 18th and 2nd Divisions—the first of the actions of Miraumont in the advance to the Hindenburg Line.

At this period, owing to the successful British attack which had recently taken place north of the River Ancre, the village of Serre formed a very pronounced salient, and to force the enemy to relinquish his hold upon it, a further advance along the Ancre Valley was ordered. The operations, which began at 5-45 a.m. on the 17th, were designed to seize the spur which ran northwards from the main Morval—Thiepval Ridge, about Corcelette, and a portion of the sunken road which ran along the eastern crest of the second spur, north of the Ancre, which would secure the approaches to Miraumont from the west. The possession of these two spurs, besides assuring the British command of the approaches to Pys and Miraumont, would afford observation over the upper valley of the Ancre, where many hostile batteries were situated in such positions as enabled them to defend the Serre sector.

From the position already won on the right bank of the Ancre, the artillery observers were able to direct the fire of the guns, and

NEAR BEAUMONT HAMEL IN 1917.

"So terrible had been the holocaust which passed over this part of the line that the villages of Beaumont Hamel

the attack north of the River (by the 63rd Division) was immediately 17TH FEB.
successful. South of the river, however, the 18th Division progressed well, but the 2nd Division was for a while held up by shell fire on its flanks, the enemy having put down a barrage just before the hour of assault. Good progress was, however, eventually made both by the 18th and 2nd Divisions, and at nightfall on the 17th, the line had been pushed forward to within a few hundred yards of Petit Miraumont.

The Artillery support lent by the 311th Brigade, R.F.A., of the 62nd Division, was so successful as to draw a letter of thanks from the General Officer Commanding IInd Corps.

But along the 62nd Divisional front no action took place. On two occasions parties of the enemy attempted to approach advanced posts held by the 186th and 185th Infantry Brigades : the first party was wiped out by rifle fire, and of the second party every man was hit, and one was killed. Shoulder straps and identity discs were obtained from the dead man's uniform.

The inevitable counter-attack took place at 11-30 a.m. on the 18TH FEB.
18th, but was repulsed with very heavy losses—the enemy's advancing waves coming under the concentrated fire of the artillery of four Divisions. The 63rd Division sent up an S.O.S. call to the 62nd Divisional Artillery, whose guns opened promptly.

On the night of 18th/19th, the 2/5th West Yorks. (under orders of the 185th Infantry Brigade) took over a further 500 yards of frontage from the left flank of the 63rd Division, but there was no depth in the new area—the line consisting only of seven posts, placed approximately along Artillery Alley, and held by one Company.

In the early hours of the 19th, a post manned by A Company of the 2/5th West Yorks. was raided—the first hostile raid on the 62nd Division. The raid was observed and reported by an N.C.O. belonging to B Company of the same Battalion, holding No. 1 Post on the right of the post raided. This N.C.O. stated that at 6-15 a.m., a German bombing party of ten men approached A Company's post under cover of the uncertain morning light and fog. Bombs were thrown into the post, the enemy jumped in and shouted " Hands up," all commands being given in English. Three men were killed and six men were taken away as prisoners, one of whom was evidently wounded, as two of the enemy were seen helping the man out of the post. As the raiders retired to a trench some 200 yards away, the post held by B Company opened fire, and three of the enemy were seen to fall. A hostile trench mortar then threw ten bombs which,

18TH FEB. however, did no damage. Rifleman P. Bottomley (of No. 1 Post) now volunteered to go to No. 2 Post and ask for the assistance of the Lewis guns. Bottomley crawled out and safely delivered his message, though sniped at by the enemy as he pluckily made his way across the open. On his return, however, he was again sniped at and killed. As no help was forthcoming, Rifleman S. Preval volunteered to take another message, and started out. But owing to the enemy's fire he was ordered to return. B Company's Post then kept up continuous rifle-fire and the enemy withdrew.

The conditions prevailing in and about these posts were truly appalling. Men who had been in the line appeared, on relief, to be absolutely exhausted. Some had been long periods without food, owing to the ration parties not being able to find them. "The ground," reported one diary, "is getting softer every day and conditions more difficult." Enough to demoralize any but the stoutest hearted troops. But fortunately these conditions were but temporary, for the Division was soon to move forward rapidly from position to position until stopped by the formidable Hindenburg Line.

The Hindenburg (or Siegfried) Line had been prepared by the enemy for the following reasons : " The general situation made it necessary for us to postpone the struggle in the West as long as possible, in order to allow the submarine campaign to produce decisive results. Tactical reasons and a shortage of ammunition provided additional reasons for delay. At the same time it was necessary to shorten our front in order to secure a more favourable grouping of our forces and create larger reserves. In France and Belgium we had 154 divisions facing 190 divisions, some of which were considerably stronger than ours.[1] In view of our extensive front this was an exceedingly unfavourable balance of forces. Moreover, we had on certain sectors of our line to endeavour to avoid enemy attacks as long as possible, by preventing adversaries from concentrating strong forces in front of them......These conditions, taken in close connection with the opening of the submarine campaign, led to the decision to straighten our front by withdrawing to the Siegfried Line which was to be in a state of defence by the beginning of March, and methodically to carry out the work of demolition over an area of 15 kilometres in breadth in front of our new position."[2]

[1] Ludendorff's estimate of the Allied Forces on the Western Front at this period cannot be accepted : a year later the Allied Forces numbered only about 155 Divisions. Early in 1917 also, many of the Allied Divisions were much weaker than the Divisions opposed to them.

[2] Ludendorff.

This new powerful system of defences occupied a line approxi- 18TH FEB.
mately from just east of Crouay (north of the River Aisne), through
La Fere, north again, skirting the western exits of St. Quentin,
thence to about 10 kilometres west of Cambrai, and on to St. Laurent,
east of Arras. The whole of the ground between this new line and
the old German front line, was to be laid waste and the inhabitants
removed. The work of demolition was to occupy five weeks, to
begin on the 9th February. The German retirement was to begin
on the 16th March.

" The decision to retreat," said Ludendorff, " was not reached
without a painful struggle. It implied a confession of weakness
bound to raise the *morale* of the enemy and lower our own. But it
was necessary for military reasons : we had no choice : it had to
be carried out.... Our first object was to avoid a battle, our second
to effect the salvage of all our raw material of war and technical
and other equipment that was not actually built into the positions,
and finally the destruction of all high roads, villages, trees and wells,
so as to prevent the enemy establishing himself in the near future
in front of our new position."

In such terms did the Chief of the German General Staff state
the intentions of the enemy.

The positions won by the 63rd, 18th and 2nd Divisions, north
and south of the River Ancre, on the 17th and 18th February, had
left Serre a very pronounced salient. Complete command had now
been obtained over the enemy's artillery positions in the upper Ancre
Valley, and over his defences in and around Pys and Miraumont.
The evacuation of the latter villages, therefore, was to be expected.

Accordingly, everywhere along the Vth and IInd Corps front,
north and south of the Ancre, the troops were warned of the enemy's
probable action.

On the 19th, the 7th Division was ordered to take over the left 19TH FEB.
flank of the frontage held by the 62nd Division, from a point approximately where Lager Alley cut across Ten Tree Alley, thence northwards. The relief was carried out on the nights 21st/22nd and
22nd/23rd, and at 10 a.m. on the 23rd, the General Officer Commanding 7th Division assumed command of that portion of the line.

The much-shortened front of the 62nd Division was now held
by the 187th Infantry Brigade, which on the night 20th/21st had
relieved the 185th Infantry Brigade. The 2/4th York and Lanc.
Regt. held the front line, the remaining battalions of the 187th
Brigade being in support and reserve. The 185th and 186th Infantry

19TH FEB. Brigades were now located in the Forceville and Mailly areas, respectively.

At this period the enemy's intentions had already been discovered. At certain places along the whole front he had neglected to mend his wire—sure signs of an impending retirement. Moreover, his front line trenches were but lightly held and these seemed to be rear-guards only. Machine-guns and trench mortar batteries were, however, everywhere evident. Aerial reports contained information of abnormal activity behind the enemy's front lines.

24TH FEB. The beginning came on the 24th, when patrols pushed out, found the enemy's positions before Pys, Miraumont and Serre evacuated. At 11-55 p.m. the 187th Infantry Brigade received orders from Divisional Headquarters to push patrols out immediately, and supporting troops were ordered to be ready to move at short notice. The Brigade was also instructed to send out strong advanced guards at 9 a.m. on the 25th towards Beauregarde Dovecote and Puisieux. The 186th Infantry Brigade in the Mailly area was to be ready to move at thirty minutes' notice from 5 a.m. on the 25th, and the 185th Brigade at Forceville, at one hour's notice from the same hour on the same date.

In conjunction with the advance of the 62nd Division, the 7th Division on the left was pushing out advanced guards to Pendant Alley and Wing Trench, and if these were found unoccupied, on to Puisieux. The 63rd Division on the right of the 62nd Division was to patrol Miraumont, Beauregarde Dovecote and Beauregarde Alley. These orders were, however, in confirmation of telephone orders, which had been issued during the afternoon of the 24th; for about mid-day Vth Corps Headquarters reported the enemy's withdrawal from Petit Miraumont, patrols of the IInd Corps having found that place evacuated.

The front line of the 62nd Division—as already stated—was held by the 2/4th York and Lancs. Regt. (The Hallamshires), and at 3-15 p.m. the C.O. was instructed by telephone from Divisional Headquarters to move his troops forward at 4 p.m. Owing to the advanced posts and Company Headquarters being situated some distance from Battalion Headquarters, these orders did not reach the former until about 3-50 p.m. But shortly afterwards the Battalion advanced—D Company on the right, C on the left, and two platoons of B Company in the centre : A Company was in support behind C Company. " I wish to record," said the Commanding Officer of the Battalion, " that at this time the men holding advanced

Near Beaumont Hamel.
A Wiring Party Moving up to the Front Line.

Face p. 22.

posts had been without food or water in many cases from twelve to 24TH FEB. twenty-four hours, which was due to the great difficulty in getting to them and getting forward supplies."

Orders had been given that as posts were established they would form patrols, all posts to move forward simultaneously.

Cautiously the troops moved forward, having to pick their way between the shell holes, across sunken roads and ditches and old trenches full of mud and water. The "going" was appalling. Things seemed suspiciously quiet, for contact with the enemy was not obtained. By the time the troops had covered about 500 yards darkness had fallen. A halt was then called, and the line consolidated. Touch on the left had been obtained with the Staffords of the 7th Division, but on the right the line was out of touch with the 63rd Division.

During the night the 2/4th K.O.Y.L.I. were ordered to take over the ground won by the 2/4th York and Lancs. In a heavy mist the relief began at 5 a.m., and was completed by 6-30 a.m. on the 25th, the relieved battalion marching back to "Y" Ravine, south-west of Beaumont Hamel. "It is only fair to record the splendid spirit," said Colonel Blacker, commanding the Hallamshires, "in which the men moved forward on receiving orders to do so. No direct information was to hand that the enemy had totally vacated his previous line and this unit has the honour of being the first Battalion in the 62nd Division to be sent forward against the enemy."

The relief had hardly been completed when the 2/5th K.O.Y.L.I. passed through the 2/4th Battalion with orders to advance towards Puisieux, keeping touch with units on either flank. The 2/4th Battalion K.O.Y.L.I. was, however, ordered to push a Company forward towards Beauregarde Dovecote, whilst the 2/5th York and Lancs. Regt. was to conform to the movement and be prepared to advance in the direction of Bucquoy, at three hours' notice if Puisieux was won: the 2/4th York and Lancs. Regt. was to support the advance on Beauregarde Dovecote.

At 9-40 a.m. Divisional Headquarters received information from the 7th Division that the latter was pushing on towards the second objective—Wing Trench. Machine-gun fire, but not of a heavy nature, had been heard coming from the direction of Serre. A patrol of the 63rd Division had reached as far as the mill west of Miraumont and had found it unoccupied: the 190th Infantry Brigade of the 63rd Division was moving forward to a line from the northern portion of Miraumont to Beauregarde Dovecote.

24TH FEB.

By this time the 187th Infantry Brigade was well advanced, when orders came to hand cancelling the previous instructions to push on to Puisieux, and to consolidate on the line Beauregarde Dovecote—Wund Werk—L. 25. b. 5.2., and to reinforce the line with one battalion.

25TH FEB.

At nightfall on the 25th, the Brigade reported its dispositions thus : 2/5th Y. and L.—Beauregarde Dovecote inclusive, and Beauregarde Alley ; 2/4th K.O.Y.L.I.—the Wund Werk to Puisieux Road ; thence the 2/5th K.O.Y.L.I. up to L.25 b.5.2. Touch with the 7th Division on the left and with the 63rd Division on the right had been maintained.

All along the line on the 25th, an advance had been made, and by the evening the enemy's front line system of defences from north of Gueudecourt to west of Serre and including Luisenhof Farm, Warlencourt, Encourt, Pys, Miraumont, Beauregarde Dovecote and Serre had been occupied by British troops.

In accordance with the enemy's plans, machine-gun opposition was experienced at certain points, and his artillery shelled the vacated areas, but casualties were negligible and the steps taken to minimize them were effective. From a captured German it was learned that the enemy was withdrawing generally to the Bucquoy—Achiet-le-Petit—Loupart Line.

The rapid retirement of the enemy had necessitated a corresponding advance of the troops behind the front line. The 185th and 186th Infantry Brigades were moved forward to support and reserve positions in rear of the 187th Brigade. But for the Artillery and Divisional troops to get their guns and transport forward was no light matter. The gunners had a terrible time. " Strenuous efforts " said the C. R. A. of the Division,[1] " which none who took part in them are likely to forget, were now made to push forward the guns, although the one road through Beaucourt to Miraumont was all but impassable." The Divisional Sappers at once set to work to repair the roads, but still the mud impeded the advance. It was mud, mud everywhere ! The Signal Section found that to maintain communications was only really possible by runners and visible means. To lay cables with the ground in places feet deep in slime was an impossibility. Under such conditions the Divisional Pack Transport was invaluable and supplies and ammunition were carried up to the front areas into which it was not possible to move wagons.

[1] Brigadier-General A. T. Anderson, R.A.

At a conference held at Vth Corps Headquarters on the night 25TH FEB. 25th/26th February, it was decided that the 62nd Division should take over the left Brigade sector held by the 63rd Division. And before it was light on the morning of the 26th, the 185th Infantry Brigade was ordered to relieve the 190th Infantry Brigade (63rd Division) on the line L.30.a.1.0. to L.28. central : the 186th Infantry Brigade, to relieve the 187th Infantry Brigade which held the line Beauregarde Dovecote—Wund Werk—to L. 26.c. central, the 7th Division taking over the remainder of the line held by the 187th : the latter on relief, marching back to Mailly Wood Camp.

The morning of the 26th was misty, but as soon as it was light 26TH FEB. the 187th Brigade pushed out patrols, and by 9 o'clock had reported to Divisional Headquarters that a Company of the 2/4th K.O.Y.L.I. had occupied Gudgeon Trench from L.21.c.0.6. to L.21.d.1.1. with two posts forward in the sunken road immediately north of the Trench. Patrols were then sent forward, but no further advance could be made. A, B and D Companies of the Battalion were then moved up to Gudgeon Trench : C Company, with Battalion Headquarters remaining at Wund Werk.

This advance reflected great credit upon the 187th Infantry Brigade. The enemy's machine-guns and snipers and his artillery kept the area under continuous fire and the 2/4th King's Own Yorks. Light Infantry were fortunate in having only two other ranks killed and nine wounded. Several officers, N.C.O.'s and men were mentioned for gallant conduct, especially No. 4018, Lance/Cpl. J. Barker, who was sent forward to take charge of a small party of men who were under a galling fire from machine-guns. This N.C.O. was himself sniped from the moment he left the trench, but succeeded in reaching the men and in keeping them in a shell-hole all day, until he was able to bring them back under cover of darkness. The steadying influence exercised by this N.C.O. was of considerable value in setting an example to his comrades.

On the left and right flank of the 2/4th K.O.Y.L.I., the 2/5th K.O.Y.L.I. and the 2/5th York and Lancs. Regt. respectively, maintained their positions until the 187th Infantry Brigade was relieved in the evening by the 186th Brigade. The 185th Infantry Brigade, as ordered, relieved the 190th Infantry Brigade, the front held by the 63rd Division being taken over later by the 18th Division.

Thus on the night of the 26th/27th February, the front line of the 62nd Division was held by the 185th Infantry Brigade on the

26TH FEB.   right, and the 186th Infantry Brigade on the left, the 187th having marched back to Mailly Wood Camp for a well-earned rest in reserve.

27TH FEB.   Soon after 9 o'clock on the morning of the 27th, a message reached Divisional Headquarters stating that patrols of the 7th Division had reached the western edges of Puisieux without encountering the slightest opposition. The 186th Infantry Brigade was therefore ordered to push on to, and occupy as quickly as possible, the sunken road at the north-eastern corner of the village. But although the enemy had seemingly evacuated Puisieux, the sharp sounds of bursts of machine-gun fire soon established the fact that he intended holding up any advance as long as possible, until forced to retire to his next rear position—the Bucquoy—Achiet-le-Petit line. This was in accordance with Ludendorff's plan of operation, for behind the German lines the work of demolition had already begun and the Hindenburg Line was fast approaching completion. From just east of Arras to east of Soissons, the ruthless hand of the enemy had been turned to the destruction of whole villages, the blowing up of roads, tearing down of trees, the ruination of orchards of fruit trees, the forcible abduction of the civil population and the destruction (and poisoning) of wells. Seldom has the hand of the invader been laid more heavily upon a fair country. If, for military purposes, much of this destruction was necessary, a great deal of purposeless damage and inhuman conduct towards the defenceless civil population was carried out.

Under the rubric of " Alberic " this dastardly work had been begun on 9th February : the German retirement to the Hindenburg Line was to begin on 16th March. But the retreat as Ludendorff stated : " Under enemy pressure, might start at any earlier date." Caution, as the British line advanced, was therefore necessary. The machine-gun posts which the enemy everywhere along the front left behind to cover the general retirement of his troops as the work of destruction proceeded, made progress slow and toilsome.

At 11 a.m. a flying officer reported to Divisional Headquarters that the Division held Gudgeon Trench which ran approximately from immediately south of Puisieux, in L.20. c. 1.0., through L.21. c. and d., L.27.b., L. 28 a. and b. and L.29 a. and b. to the line of the Achiet-le-Grand—Miraumont railway.

The 186th Infantry Brigade had, however, been unable to get on as far as the sunken road, N.E. of Puisieux. Four hostile machine-guns held up any attempt to advance. But at 3 p.m. urgent orders arrived from Division Headquarters to attack and

Beaumont Hamel : The Old German Front Line.

capture Orchard Alley, as it was essential to push on. The organiza- 27TH FEB.
tion of an attack was immediately begun. The 2/5th Duke of
Wellington's Regt. was detailed for the assault, and three fighting
patrols each consisting of one officer and fifteen other ranks, with a
Lewis Gun, were formed. Two parties were furnished by D
Company, and a third by A Company. Lieut. Ridley, as senior
officer, was in command of all three parties : he placed his party in
the centre and took charge of the compass bearing.

At 5-30 p.m. the three parties advanced cautiously towards
Orchard Alley, but the enemy's troops, of whom only a small number
held the trench, after firing a few shots at the assaulting parties,
bolted. By 6-10 p.m. Orchard Alley was occupied. One German
was killed and another taken prisoner. The assaulting parties had
three men slightly wounded. On word being sent back that Orchard
Alley had been captured, D Company of the 2/5th Dukes advanced
from Gudgeon Trench and consolidated the position won. Orchard
Alley ran almost due east from Puisieux, through L.20 b., L.21 a. and
b. and L.22 a. and b.

An attempt was then made to push out patrols from the newly-
won position to cover the exits from the village, but a strong party
of the enemy appeared and after a fight lasting half-an-hour the
patrols were forced to return to Orchard Alley. No casualties were
suffered in this affair. At midnight another attempt was made and
the Battalion succeeded in establishing posts in the sunken road in
L. 15.c. and d.

Meanwhile the 185th Infantry Brigade—the right flank—had
been unable to make progress, as Goods Trench (a system of trenches
on the right front of the West Yorkshiremen) was held by the enemy
in strength. The 18th Division on the right of the 62nd Division
had also been unable to advance, and the attack on Goods Trench was
therefore postponed until the following day.

Throughout the 27th February, the Divisional Artillery was
engaged in moving the guns forward. Strenuous efforts were
needed, the one road from Beaucourt to Miraumont having been
badly cut up by motor lorries. But eventually new positions were
taken up near Bois d'Hollande and Baillescourt Farm. A section
of the Divisional Ammunition Column was also moved forward to
near Hamel. In the whole course of the history of the 62nd Division
in France no period was fraught with more discomfort or extraordinary difficulties than those early days of the advance to the Hindenburg Line, for not only did the men suffer, but the horses had a

27TH FEB. terrible time. There was mud and slush everywhere, but hardly a drop of water for the horses. The poor animals did their work nobly and when wheeled transport was impossible they were used as pack transport.

28TH FEB. Early on the morning of the 28th, patrols from the 186th Infantry Brigade went out, and by 9 a.m. reported touch with the 7th Division in Puisieux itself. But before touch was established a regular man-hunt had taken place in the village, the enemy disputing possession until, seeing further resistance hopeless, he withdrew northwards to the Bucquoy—Achiet-le-Petit defences. A report " Puisieux is in our hands," was sent back to the troops in the Divisional front line, at 11-10 a.m. On the right of the Divisional front, the enemy still held Irles.

Late in the afternoon, the 185th Infantry Brigade reported the occupation of Goods Trench and patrols were being pushed out to the Ditch, north and north-west and had gained touch with the 186th Brigade at L. 16. c. The latter Brigade, under Divisional orders, had continued to press forward and at this period occupied the sunken road, north-east of Puisiuex to L. 16. c. where touch was established.

During the night 28th February/1st March, the enemy shelled Goods Trench heavily, while hostile machine-guns south of Achiet-le-Petit, kept the West Yorkshiremen under continual fire, though fortunately casualties were negligible.

The Divisional Artillery had also come into action on this day and fired with excellent effect on the enemy's positions between Bucquoy and Achiet-le-Petit. Unfortunately the Battery Commander of C/310, Major R. C. Williams, was wounded and had to be evacuated.

From a captured prisoner, information was gathered that the enemy intended holding the line Bucquoy—Achiet-le-Petit : this statement was confirmed by the enemy's attitude and by Vth Corps Intelligence. Arrangements were accordingly pushed forward in order to attack that line, though before a further advance could be undertaken a vast amount of work on the roads and communications was necessary. The guns had again to be moved forward and dumps of ammunition established. The retirement of Ludendorff's rear-guards had been more rapid than he had intended and in consequence, the British troops, who had to move forward without their transport and in many instances without the support of their guns, were now forced to wait until they came up and complete touch was established with all units. When all was ready Irles was to be 28TH FEB. attacked, as a preliminary to the larger operations against the Bucquoy —Achiet-le-Petit—Loupart—Le Transloy Line, which formed a part of the German Third Line system. It will thus be seen that though the enemy's retirement to the Hindenburg Line had been ordered to begin on 16th March, he had in point of fact been forced back a considerable distance before that date arrived.

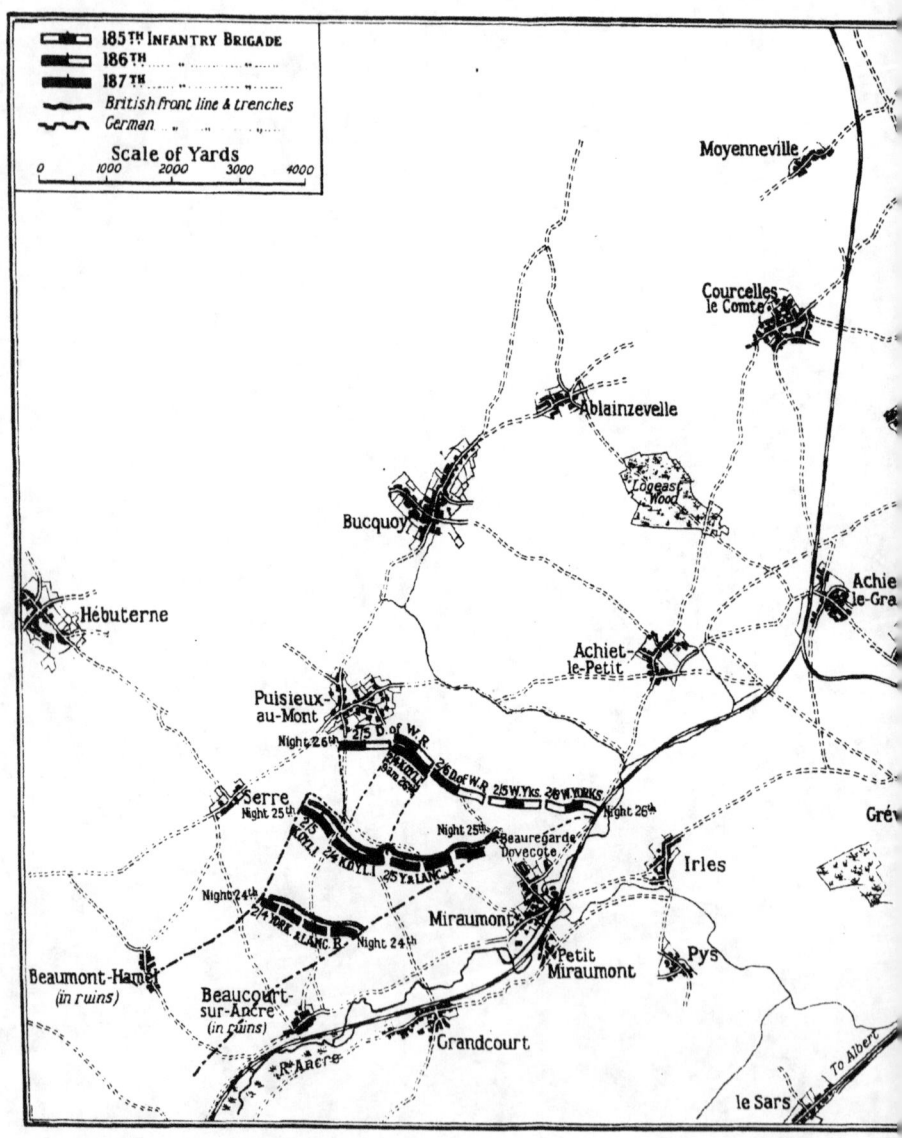

The Advance to

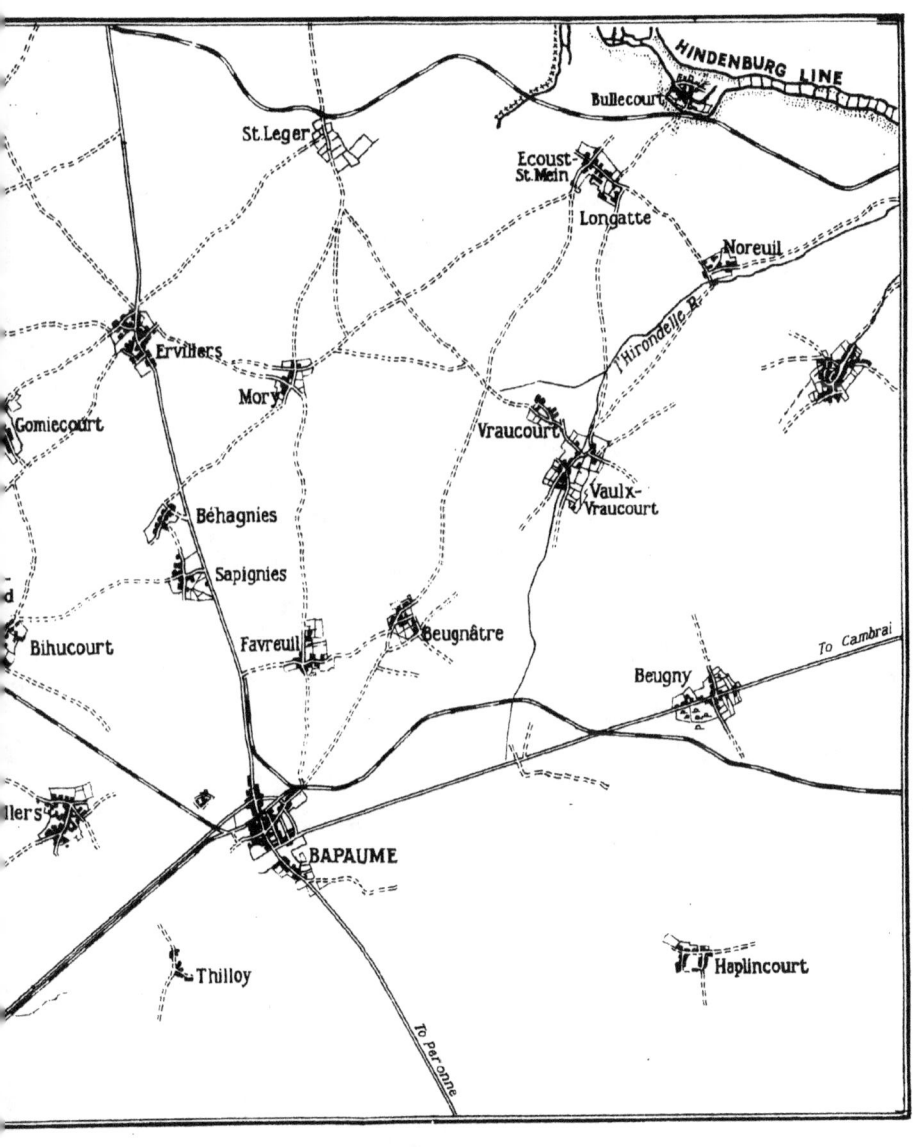

THE HINDENBURG LINE, I.

Chapter IV.   1917.

THE ADVANCE TO THE HINDENBURG LINE

"And it shall come to pass in that day, that his burden shall be taken away from off thy shoulder, and his yoke from off thy neck."—Isaiah.

EARLY on the morning of the 1st March, the 186th 1ST MARCH. Infantry Brigade, holding the left sub-sector of the 62nd Divisional front, was relieved by the 7th Division, the SEE MAP Brigade moving back to Englebelmer. With the 187th No. 2. Infantry Brigade in Mailly Maillet Woods (in Divisional Reserve), the 62nd Division now held the line on a one Brigade frontage—a line running through L.22.b. L.23.a., L.23.d. and L.30.a., which the 185th Infantry Brigade was holding when night set in.

There was no doubt that the enemy was retiring. He had been observed during the day burning his dug-outs, and frequent explosions behind his front line denoted the blowing up of roads and houses. But he still continued to shell with varying degrees of intensity the evacuated ground. Miraumont and Beauregarde Dovecote in particular and the gun positions near the former village and back at Baillescourt Farm came in for a good deal of attention and throughout the day the 185th Infantry Brigade suffered a number of casualties.[1] Patrols reported numbers of machine-guns left behind with small detachments of the enemy, who entirely prevented anything in the nature of a rapid advance. Indeed at this period it was a question of feeling the way forward, and considerable vigilance was necessary in order to maintain touch with an enemy whose movements were uncertain. Moreover, those deadly pests—snipers— were very active and any movement towards the enemy's trenches

---

[1] 2/5th West Yorks.: Major Alwyne Percy Dale and two other ranks killed, one other ranks wounded: 2/6th West Yorks.: 2nd Lieut. E. S. Smith, missing, two other ranks killed, one wounded, one missing: 2/7th West Yorks, five other ranks wounded: 2/8th West Yorks., two other ranks wounded.

drew bursts of machine-gun fire and the sharp report of rifle-fire from concealed posts.

2ND MARCH.   On the 2nd March orders for preparations to be made for an early attack on Achiet-le-Petit were issued. To the 62nd Division had been assigned the task of capturing the village which lay about midway between Bucquoy and Logeast Wood, in the Le Transloy—Loupart Line. Here, the enemy had well-constructed and thickly wired trenches and the orders for the attack were somewhat intricate. The attack was originally designed for the 10th March, when the flanking Divisions—the 7th and 18th—were also to assault the enemy's position. Practice for the attack began at once—two Brigades, the 185th and 187th, having been detailed for the operation. But " Z " day was postponed, as the 18th and 2nd Divisions had received orders to attack and capture Irles on the 10th. In this attack, which was entirely successful, the 62nd Divisional Artillery co-operated. The attack on Achiet-le-Petit was then ordered for the 13th. But the artillery preparation which began on the 11th was too much for the enemy, who, on the night 12th/13th, once more evacuated his positions and fell back, leaving behind only small detachments of Infantry with machine-guns to cover the retirement of his main body. The villages of Irles and Grevillers, and Loupart Wood were then occupied by the 18th and 2nd Divisions.

Into all the details of that terribly difficult advance over devastated country, it is impossible to go, but the 62nd Division during the whole of its service in France, had not a more difficult task than in following up the enemy's retirement during those hard days of March, 1917. For as the troops advanced the roads had to be rebuilt, which necessitated the accommodation of large numbers of working parties close up to the front line. At night-time it was impossible to find shelters for all of them, and many had perforce to sleep in hastily erected shelters, which in many places consisted of tarpaulins stretched above excavations in the muddy ground, or over piles of stones : some men were in tents. The weather was abominable—sometimes cold and frosty and at other times wet and muggy, which impeded progress and called forth superhuman effort in moving up guns and stores and all the impedimenta of a division on the advance. But the stout Yorkshiremen were equal to the occasion ; their hardy lives in the north of England had well fitted most of them for their tasks, whilst two years of training had produced that spirit which refuses to be depressed even under the most depressing circumstances.

Between the 1st and 13th March, the enemy's shell-fire 1ST—13TH took heavy toll of all units. Hostile artillery and machine-gun fire MARCH. and the persistent efforts of snipers had claimed no less than fifteen officers and 400 other ranks, killed, wounded and missing, the loss in officers being especially serious : sickness claimed many more.

Of all the unhealthy spots behind the front line (and there were many) Miraumont was the worst. At this period the village had been almost entirely demolished, but had not yet quite disappeared—a few walls and ruins standing to mark the site of a once charming Picardy village. There was only one road which ran up from Beaucourt, and this the enemy shelled heavily and intermittently, so that death or mutilation haunted those who lingered in the vicinity. Yet in a sunken road an Infantry Brigade had its Headquarters, whilst not far off the commanding officers of three Battalions lived in precarious shelters. All that was alive in Miraumont lived underground, in deep cellars and dug-outs. " Almost unceasingly in one part or another of the skeleton village, shells scream and crash, raking the streets with bullets and splinters and hurling bricks and beams in every direction. Here are to be found Swain's, Foot's, Bigg's, Arnold Forster's, Hudson's and Robinson's batteries, the others being outside in the scarcely less dangerous outskirts of the village."[1] The gunners alone in Miraumont lost six officers and seventy other ranks, whilst nine guns were knocked out of action, and many horses and mules killed.

Casualties were also suffered from enemy " booby-traps." One officer had a fortunate escape. When his battery entered Miraumont he had taken up his quarters in a German dug-out which boasted a fire-place. His batman was about to light a fire when his officer told him he need not bother until the morning. Next morning as the man was laying the fire he noticed a piece of wire and on close examination found a length of quick match fastened to the wire leading to a hole under the dug-out in which was packed sufficient explosive to send the whole place sky high.

A further postponement of the attack on Achiet-le-Petit was made until the 18th March, but before that date the enemy had again retired, for the guns had begun the preliminary bombardment on the 16th, and on the morning of the 17th, patrols entering the village found it deserted. The enemy was now making his way back to the Hindenburg Line with all possible speed.

[1] War Service of the 62nd Divisional Artillery " : Col. A. T. Anderson.

17TH MARCH   News was received at Divisional Headquarters during the 17th March, that Chaulnes and Bapaume had fallen, and with Bucquoy, Bienvillers and the Bihucourt Line in British hands, the enemy's positions at all points in the line from Damery to Monchy-au-Bois had been entered. Peronne was entered on the 18th, and Mont St. Quentin, north of the town, occupied.

The 186th Infantry Brigade had taken over the front line from the 187th Brigade on the night 16th/17th March, the latter moving back to Engelbelmer : the 185th Brigade was then employed chiefly on road making in the Beaucourt area.

The relief had been completed by 3 a.m., and the West Riding Battalions set to work immediately to reconnoitre the line in front of them. But although the enemy was still retiring, his artillery continued to shell his evacuated positions. The 2/4th Duke's, on the line of the Railway, south—south-east of Achiet-le-Petit were particularly unfortunate and suffered from thirty to forty casualties during the day. Forward movement was therefore stopped until nightfall when patrols were to be pushed out. When darkness had fallen three officers' patrols were sent forward. Only one of these, that on the right, experienced opposition and that of a slight nature— a hostile machine-gun firing down a sunken road. But as the patrol advanced the gun was withdrawn, and unmolested the three patrols pushed up into a communication trench. None of the enemy was encountered and a further advance was made. Step Trench and Quick Trench were each entered and occupied and a message sent back to the Officer Commanding 2/4th Duke's giving the situation. Other patrols drawn from the 2/5th Duke's were pushed up into the village of Achiet-le-Petit, and at 3-30 a.m. on the 18th, it was ascertained that none of the enemy was in the village.

Meanwhile the 2/7th Duke's had also pushed out patrols and had obtained touch with the left of the 2/5th Battalion. Three battalions of the 186th Brigade were thus in line—2/4th on the right, 2/5th in the centre and 2/7th on the left : the 2/6th was in Miraumont in Brigade Reserve.

By 11-50 p.m. the 2/5th Batt. Duke of Wellington's Regt. had occupied the Bihucourt Line between Logeast Wood and Achiet-le-Grand, having cut a passage through five belts of wire each ten feet thick, and about 30 yards apart, for the cavalry to pass through. Three Companies of the Battalion—A, C and B—had been allotted this task and right well had they carried out their instructions : the remaining Company—D—had pushed on to Gomiecourt and at

The German Retreat to the Hindenburg Line.
Trees were Felled by the Enemy and placed across the Road to Obstruct the Advance of the British.

4-30 a.m. on the 18th, the Company Commander reported that he 17TH MARCH
held the village.

Throughout the 17th, the flanking Divisions (7th on the left and 18th on the right) had advanced in touch with the 62nd Division, and at 3 p.m. on the 18th D Company of the 2/5th Duke's (still in Gomiecourt) reported touch with the 7th Division at Courcelles, and with the 54th Brigade of the 18th Division at about 1500 yards due west of Béhagnies.

At 8 o'clock in the morning Indian Cavalry had passed through the Logeast Wood—Achiet-le-Grand line and orders had been received (subsequently cancelled) for the 62nd Division to form an advanced guard.

But at this period the advance of the 62nd Division to the Hindenburg Line ends, for the flanking Divisions were advancing on a converging front, and by the 19th March had squeezed the 62nd 19TH MARCH out of the line. On the morning of the 19th, the 7th and 18th Divisions were in touch at St. Leger. Thus the 186th Infantry Brigade no longer held the front line and the troops were withdrawn and concentrated, the 2/5th Duke of Wellingtons in the sunken road (G. 14.b.), the Bihucourt Line (three Companies) and Gomiecourt (D Company): the 2/7th in Logeast Wood, the 2/4th in Achiet-le-Petit and the 2/6th in Miraumont.

After something less than three months' service in France the 62nd Division had again demonstrated the sterling qualities of Territorial troops. The advance to the Hindenburg Line was a difficult operation: it was not (as may be supposed) a straightforward march in rear of retiring troops. Some idea of the conditions along the line of advance is given in an officer's diary— an officer belonging to the 2/5th Duke of Wellingtons, the Battalion which had the honour of pushing forward at the head of the Division : " There were many fires burning when we occupied the village (Gomiecourt) and as they were still burning we tried to put them out. The junction of every road in the village had been mined and blown up and everything of value had been destroyed. All fruit trees had either been pulled down or an incision made round the barks so that the sap could not rise. All wells had been blown in and one had been poisoned with arsenic, so the R.E. officer told me. The only buildings left standing were the Chateau and the billets with fifty wire beds in it. The Chateau had been mined, but the charge had failed to explode fully and the only damage done was that the entrance hall had a big hole in the floor and the first stairway

19TH MARCH. had fallen in. The Royal Engineers with a party of our men took 700 pounds of unexploded charge out of the cellars of this place.... Found a German whip with six lashes in it."

SEE MAP No. 3.

Every road over which the advancing troops had to pass had either been blown up, or else huge trees had been felled and placed across the roadway : devastation and desolation was on every side. The ground, soft and muddy, pitted with gaping mine-craters, the thick belts of uncut wire, rows of wrecked dug-outs with here and there a " booby-trap " in the form of an intact shelter heavily mined and fitted with a delay fuse : inclement weather and above all the constant activities of the enemy's artillery, machine-guns and snipers, combined to make that advance one of the most difficult operations which could befall a Division new to active warfare.

It is impossible to read the official diaries during this strenuous period without feeling a deep sense of admiration for all ranks of all units: the patient infantry, the hard-working gunners, the sappers, the tireless energies of the Divisional Train in its efforts to keep the troops supplied with the necessaries of life : the Divisional Ammunition Column, whose devoted efforts in carrying ammunition to the forward dumps as the Division moved forward, will never be forgotten, and last of all to the constant and tender care of the R.A.M.C. in tending the sick and wounded.

Between the 1st and the 31st March, 1917, the Division suffered the loss of no less than thirty-five officers and 300 other ranks killed, wounded and missing ; and an interesting point concerning these casualties was the large proportion of senior officers.

Following a retreating enemy is not always a bloodless victory !

THE ADVANCE TO THE HINDENBURG LINE II.

Chapter V.   1917.

THE FIRST ATTACK ON BULLECOURT

THE Capture of Bapaume on the 17th March, and the occupation of Peronne on the following day, were the final tactical incidents in the British Advance to the Hindenburg Line.

On the morning of the 20th March, the 186th Infantry Brigade still held the Logeast Wood—Achiet-le-Grand line, with three Companies of the 2/5th Duke of Wellington's Regt. and Battalion Headquarters in the vicinity of the sunken road in G.14.b. and the Bihucourt Line, and one Company at Gomiecourt: the 2/7th Duke's were in Logeast Wood, the 2/4th at Achiet-le-Petit and the 2/6th at Miraumont.   20TH MARCH

For the next few days little fighting was done, and all Brigades found large working parties to repair the roads and communications. The enemy had indeed devastated the area from which he had been forced to withdraw. All around the Division there was desolation and it was extremely difficult to find accommodation for the troops as they moved forward. Only the gunners took an active part in the operations which were still going on, on the northern flank of the 62nd Division—D/312 Battery moving forward at dawn on the 21st to assist the 7th Division advanced guard at Ervillers in an attack on Croisilles. In this attack the Divisional Artillery lost Lieut. C. W. Pullan, who was killed as he was gallantly directing the fire of his battery from an observation post near St. Léger, a shell falling and bursting in the post. A/312 and C/312 were also in action on the same day, between Ervillers and St. Léger. The 310th Brigade R.F.A. remained in readiness near Logeast Wood.

To the general regret of all ranks of the Division, the 311th Brigade, R.F.A., which, shortly after the arrival of the 62nd Division in France, had become an Army Artillery Brigade, but allowed to stay with its Division for the time being, was withdrawn from the line to Englebelmer on the 23rd March. On the following day, Lieut.-Colonel A. Gadie (Commanding the Brigade) marched his guns out of Englebelmer, *en route* for an area in the north. The 311th Brigade, R.F.A., was the first unit to leave the 62nd Division after its arrival in France.

20TH MAR. For several more days large parties of men were at work upon the roads between Miraumont and Gomiecourt, and the Puisieux—Achiet-le-Grand, and Miraumont—Achiet-le-Grand railways, but rumours were in the air of an attack upon the Hindenburg Line. The three Infantry Brigades had been ordered to withdraw the *personnel* of their Machine Gun Companies from all working parties, in order to train and re-equip, with a view to going into the line at an early date.

26TH MARCH. Instructions for the attack on the Bullecourt—Fontaine line (in the Hindenburg Line) were received from Vth Corps Headquarters on the 26th, and the Divisional Staff after working out the necessary plans issued preliminary orders on the 30th March. The 186th Infantry Brigade was ordered to concentrate in the area Ecoust St. Mein (exc.)—Mory—Béhagnies—Sapignies; the 187th in the area St. Léger (exc.)—Ervillers—Gomiecourt; and the 185th Brigade, in the area Achiet-le-Petit—Achiet-le-Grand. Both the 186th and 187th Brigades after reconnaissance were to move forward to their new areas accompanied by their Machine Gun Companies[1] and affiliated Companies of Royal Engineers.

4TH/5TH APRIL. On the night of the 4th/5th April, the 185th Infantry Brigade took over the front line from the 22nd Infantry Brigade (7th Division), the General Officer Commanding 62nd Division assuming command of the sector on the morning of the 5th.

The front line of the sector now held by the 62nd Division ran from the Bullecourt—Longatte road, thence in a north-westerly direction partly along the railway, and then along the sunken road to the right bank of the River Sensee: this was the main defence line. The flanking divisions were the 4th Australian on the right and the 21st (which had just relieved troops of the 7th) on the left.

In front of the main defence line was an outpost-line, and behind the former, in support, a line of companies and platoons at points varying from 500 to 2000 yards in rear of the railway.

On completion of the relief the 2/7th West Yorks. held the right sub-sector, the 2/8th (Leeds Rifles) the centre, and the 2/5th West Yorks. the left. The 2/6th Battalion West Yorks. was in Brigade reserve in St. Léger. The 212th Machine Gun Company

---

[1] The Machine Gun Companies had but recently arrived in France. The 208th Company arrived at Forceville on the 2nd March, and was attached to the 187th Brigade. The 213th Company (ten officers and 177 other ranks) reported to Divisional Headquarters on the 9th March, and was attached to the 186th Infantry Brigade. The 212th Company arrived on the same day and was affiliated to the 185th Brigade.

relieved the 22nd Machine Gun Company in the front line. The 186th Infantry Brigade (less one Battalion in Mory) with the 213th Machine Gun Company was in Divisional Reserve at Ervillers, Béhagnies and Sapignies, while the 187th Infantry Brigade was at Achiet-le-Petit. 4TH/5TH APRIL

The relief of the 7th Division passed without incident, but the bitterly cold and wet weather and the condition of the ground caused great discomfort and fatigue. The enemy's guns fired into Ecoust intermittently during the night, but his machine-guns and snipers were inactive.

The second sector held by the 62nd Division, was not unlike the first: there was much that resembled the old line of posts in front of Beaumont Hamel. But the enemy's position in front of the Division was much more powerful. The Hindenburg Line was a prepared position which the enemy could be counted upon to defend with the utmost stubbornness. His trenches were deep and dry: his machine-gun positions were strong and thick belts of wire out in No Man's Land prevented surprise. Ludendorff certainly expected that his opponents would be occupied in repairing the roads, building dug-outs, digging new trenches and wiring the front of them, as well as in carrying up stores and ammunition, before any attack on his new line could be made : " The country we had traversed," he said, " was devastated, and before military operations could be made possible over it, a certain amount of restoration was essential. For an attack to be launched over it an infinite amount of road and bridge building would have to be done." Admittedly ! But the Chief of the German General Staff was wrong in his estimation of the amount of time required before an offensive was again possible. For up and down the line the Royal Engineers, assisted by Pioneers and large working parties of infantrymen had in a short space of time wrought a marvellous change in that devastated area. In particular, the splendid work and devotion of the Sappers under Lieut. Col. F. Gillam (the C.R.E.) was beyond all praise.

The General Officer Commanding 62nd Division had hardly taken over command of the new sector when orders were issued to the 185th Brigade to push forward their posts gradually towards the Hindenburg Line, so that by the 9th April they would be within 300 yards of the enemy's front line. But in order that they should not interfere with the wire-cutting operations of the Artillery, the posts for the present were to stop short at about 500 yards from the German wire.

D

4TH/5TH APRIL.

Besides the Heavy Artillery of the Vth Corps, five groups of Horse and Field Artillery covered the front.

At a conference held at Chantilly, in November, 1916, the Military representatives of all the Allied Armies decided upon a definite plan of campaign during 1917 : a series of offensives on all fronts, timed to assist each other and so deprive the enemy of the power of weakening any one of his fronts in order to reinforce another. In the spring, the British Army was to begin operations by an attack launched at the salient between the Scarpe and the Ancre : the Fifth Army was to operate against the Ancre, whilst the Third Army attacked simultaneously from the north-west about Arras. The front of attack on the Arras side was to include the Vimy Ridge. The objectives between the Ancre and the Scarpe having been obtained, the offensive was to be transferred to Flanders. The German Retreat to the Hindenburg Line and a change in the Command of the French Armies[1] necessitated slight modifications in the plans formulated by the British Commander-in-Chief, but the offensive on the Arras front was timed to begin on 9th April. Sir Douglas Haig's attack was to be preparatory to a more decisive operation to be undertaken a little later by the French Armies. He was, in the first instance, to attract as large hostile forces as possible to his front, before the French offensive was launched. If the First and Third Armies could capture Vimy Ridge and Monchy-le-Preux respectively, and the Fifth Army in the south could exercise considerable pressure on the Hindenburg Line, the enemy would be forced to employ and use up many of his Divisions, and reinforce largely his threatened front. In this scheme of operations the northern flank of the Hindenburg Line was involved, an outcome of which were the flanking operations round Bullecourt which began on the 11th April and ended on the 16th June.[2]

The village of Bullecourt formed a strong salient in the Hindenburg Line. A well-constructed trench ran round three sides of it—west, south and east—protected by three formidable belts of wire, each from 10 to 15 yards wide. Machine-gun emplacements had been built in such positions as to afford an almost perfect field of enfilade fire along the whole length of the wire ; a second trench ran from west to east through the village itself, whilst a third line heavily wired lay immediately north of it, along the outskirts of the

[1] In December, 1916, General Nivelle succeeded Marshal Joffre as Commander-in-Chief, and new plans were made and adopted by the French.
[2] The dates fixed by the Battles Nomenclature Committee.

An Advanced Dressing Station, Écoust, in 1917.

village. At this period—early in April—Bullecourt had not been 4TH/5TH subjected to heavy shell fire, but just in front of the enemy's wire APRIL. mines had been exploded under the two roads leading from Ecoust—Longatte, and two huge craters were the result.

When darkness fell on the 5th April, the three Battalions of the 5TH APRIL 185th Infantry Brigade in the front line, *i.e.*, 2/7th, 2/8th and 2/5th West Yorks. (in the order given from right to left) had taken stock of their surroundings. The Battalions were disposed in depth in the outpost line, the main line of defence, and the support line.[1] All three had been ordered to establish forward posts during the night. The 2/5th and 2/8th West Yorks. found little difficulty in pushing their posts out to a distance of 500 yards from the enemy's wire, but the 2/7th Battalion had to attack the enemy in order to eject him from the line of the railway north-east of Ecoust—Longatte. The attack was made at 3 a.m. on the 6th April, under a barrage, and was successful. Later, however, the enemy counter-attacked and a party of Germans succeeded in getting in between the right of the 2/7th West Yorks. and the left of the 13th Australian Infantry Brigade. The enemy was ultimately beaten off and the West Yorkshiremen established posts well in advance of those taken over from the 7th Division.

The guns continued to pound the enemy's trenches, but according to patrol reports little impression had as yet been made on his formidable wire entanglements.

In the forward area the Battalions in the line lived as best they could—in ruins, and extemporized shelters : but many men were forced to live in the open. In the back areas, tents and improvised shelters " housed " the supporting and reserve troops.

On the morning of the 9th April, the general attack on the 9TH APRIL Arras front from just north of Croisilles to (and including) the Vimy Ridge, was launched by the Third and First Armies, and was completely successful. " Closely following the track of our shell-fire " the official despatches stated, " our gallant infantry poured like a flood across the German lines, overwhelming the enemy's garrisons," and by nightfall the British line had jumped forward to include St. Martin-sur-Cojeul, Feuchy, Fampoux, Point du Jour, just north of Farbus and most of the Vimy Ridge to just west of Givenchy-en-Gohelle.

Originally the 62nd Division had been ordered to attack

---

[1] The three sub-sectors were (right) from C.3.d.2.2. to U.26.c.6.3. (centre) U.26.c.6.3. to U.19.c.9.5. (left) U.19.c.9.5. to the Sensee River.

9TH APRIL. Bullecourt on the 9th, but the attack was cancelled and the 185th Infantry Brigade received instructions to push out strong patrols at 4-30 a.m. on the 10th, under an artillery barrage, and occupy the enemy's front line and support trenches if he had vacated them. Tanks and the Australian Brigade on the right of the 2/7th West Yorks. were to co-operate.

Three strong patrols were made up from each of the 2/7th and 2/8th West Yorks., and were formed up ready for the attack.

At 4-35 a.m. they went forward, and ten minutes later the 2/7th had passed through the enemy's first belt of wire. No signs of Tanks or any advance by the Australians on the right had, however, been observed, and at 4-50 a.m. the enemy's machine-guns from both flanks opened a murderous fire on the patrols. It was evident the Hindenburg Line was still held in considerable force.

At 5-10 a.m. as Tanks and Australians still failed to appear the patrols began to withdraw, but the withdrawal was as dangerous as the advance and it was not accomplished without severe losses, two Lewis Gun teams of the 2/7th having to be left on the enemy's side of the wire.

The 2/5th West Yorks. (Lieut.-Col. J. Josselyn) on the left of the 2/8th Battalion were also ordered to occupy the Hindenburg Line, and they co-operated accordingly, with several small battle patrols which got into the wire where possible. They were, however, heavily fired on and suffered some loss : the Companies in support of the battle patrols were therefore not advanced for the occupation of the Hindenburg Line as had been intended.

Finally, the survivors of all patrol parties reached their own positions, where it was learned that the supporting attack by the Tanks and Australians had been postponed, though it was not until 4-55 a.m., when the patrols of the 185th Infantry Brigade were already within the enemy's wire, that the 62nd Division received notice of the cancellation.[1]

10TH APRIL. About 3 o'clock on the afternoon of the 10th orders for another attack on Bullecourt by the 62nd and 4th Australian Divisions were received. Zero hour was at 4-30 a.m. the following morning, at which hour the Australians were to attack the enemy's line between U.30. a. and U.28. b. and clear Bullecourt as far west as the western exits of the village. The 185th Infantry Brigade was then to

[1] The 2/7th West Yorks. upon whom fell the brunt of this unfortunate attack, lost as a result of the operations on the 10th April, one officer wounded, and in other ranks, nineteen killed, seventy-two wounded and nineteen missing.

advance one Battalion from the south-west into Bullecourt, and, supported by Tanks, clear and occupy the Hindenburg Line as far as U.20. b. Riencourt and Hendecourt were the final objectives of the Australian and 62nd Divisions respectively.

The 2/6th West Yorks. (Lieut-Col. J. Hastings) supported by the 2/8th Battalion (Lieut.-Col. A. H. James) had been detailed to occupy Bullecourt and clear the Hindenburg Line in the vicinity as soon as the Australians had cleared the village. The 2/6th Battalion was then at St. Léger, but during the night moved up to its assembly position, and when zero hour arrived, A and D Companies were on the railway—the former at U.26.d. and D Company from C.2.b.7.9 to C.2.b.5.9.; B Company was in support and C Company in reserve.

Gas was discharged into the village during the night, but it did not seem to have had much effect on the enemy, who was in considerable strength, and it was not until 7-30 a.m. that 62nd Divisional Headquarters received a report that the Australians had captured their first objective. The Officer Commanding 2/6th West Yorks. had previously reported that no Tanks had arrived, and that nothing was known of the results of the Australian attack, and they had certainly not entered Bullecourt. In spite of this unsatisfactory situation, however, orders were issued to push forward patrols immediately, to be followed by the Battalion.

A patrol report on the south-west portion of the village stated that snipers and machine-guns were active in Bullecourt where men could be seen moving about among the houses : that the wire was practically uncut and that any attempt to storm the village would entail very great sacrifice. On the other hand a patrol which reconnoitred the south-east and eastern roads of Bullecourt reported no movement and no resistance and that the Corps on the right was advancing and that the enemy was shelling the northern edges of the village.

Apparently the Australians attacked their objective and overpowered the enemy, then pushed on towards Riencourt and Hendecourt, but were counter-attacked and the majority of the Tanks having been put out of action, the Colonials were forced back to their own original trenches.

At 8 p.m. the 2/6th Battalion relieved the 2/7th Battalion in the right sub-sector of the Divisional front.[1]

[1] The 2/6th West Yorks. had two officers killed and sixty-one other rank casualties during the 11th April.

11TH APRIL. Meanwhile general progress along the front of the Arras offensive was not entirely satisfactory: the Third Army had indeed captured Monchy, but the resistance of the enemy at Héninel and Wancourt prevented a junction between that Army and the Australian troops of the Fourth Army at Hénencourt, the latter having to withdraw to their own trenches.

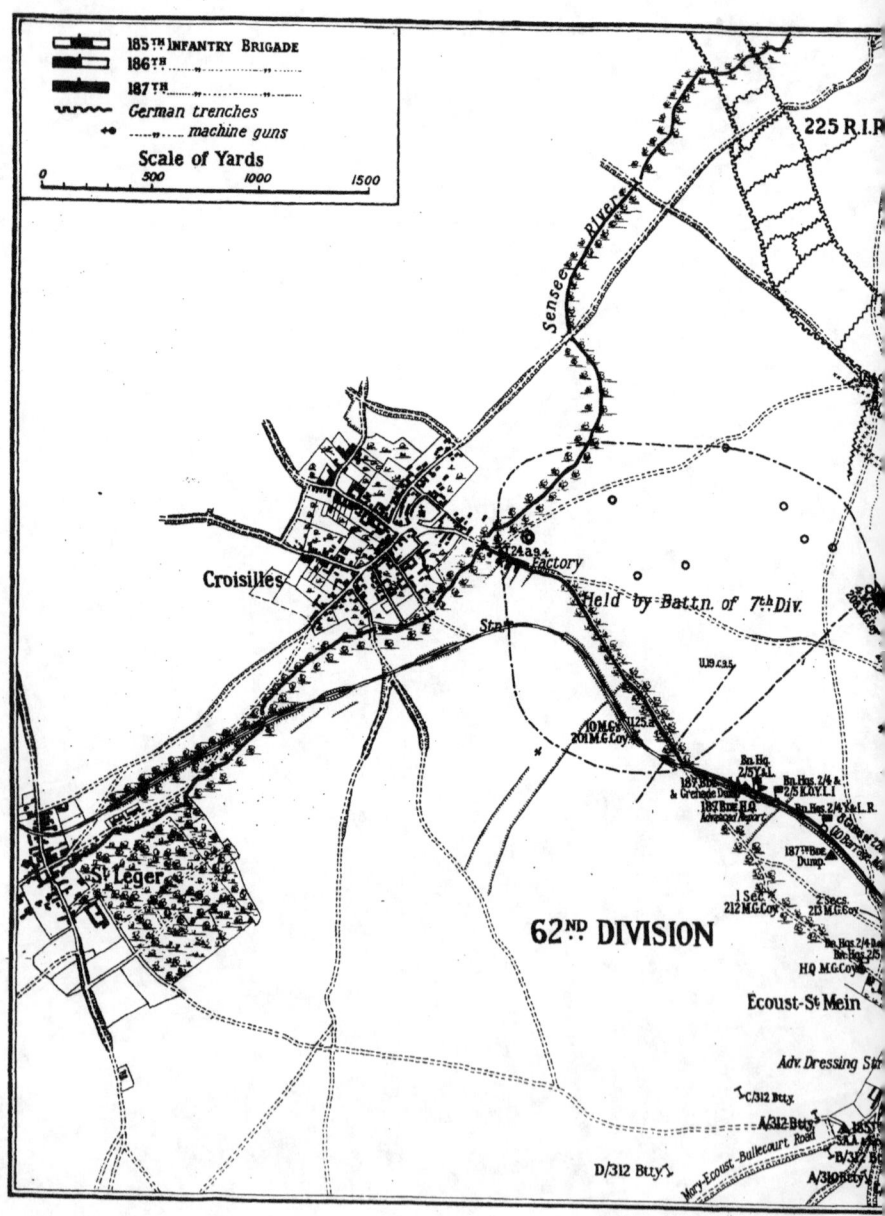

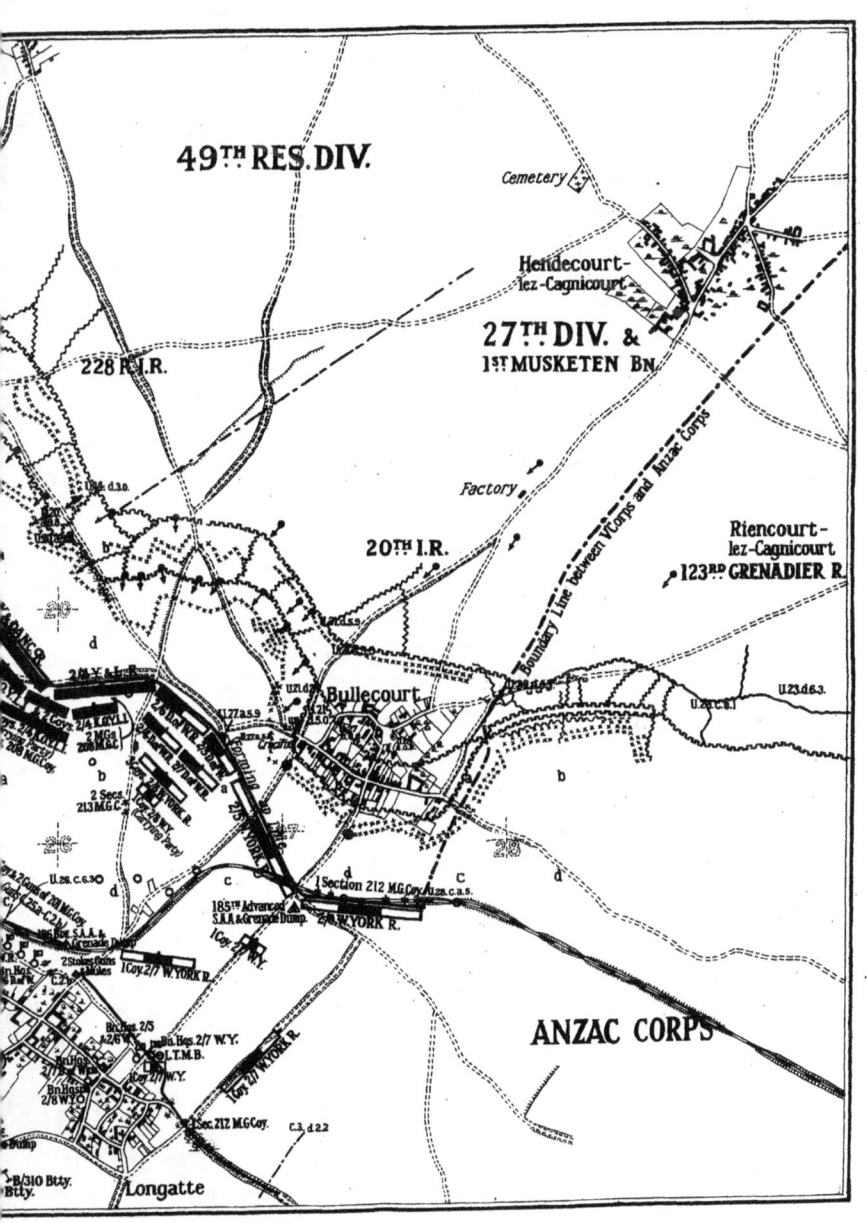

Chapter VI. 1917.

THE BATTLE OF BULLECOURT:
3rd—17th May, 1917.

" Fight on, my men," says Sir Andrew Barton,
" I am hurt, but I am not slaine,
I'll lie me down and bleed awhile
And then I'll rise and fight againe."

DURING the three weeks following the first attack on Bullecourt on 11th April, the 62nd Division was engaged in trench warfare, and in preparing for another attack on the Hindenburg Line which had been ordered to take place on various successive dates and subsequently postponed, until finally it was definitely decided that Bullecourt should again be attacked on the 3rd May. SEE MAP No. 4.

The Arras offensive had gone well: the First and Second Battles of the Scarpe and the Battle of Arleux, which included as tactical incidents the Captures of Monchy-le-Preux, Wancourt Ridge, Guémappe, Gavrelle and the subsidiary attack on La Coulette, had yielded considerable gains in enemy positions, as well as large numbers of prisoners and much war material. But the Russian Revolution early in the year had robbed the Allies of the full advantage of their strenuous efforts: the enemy's resistance was hardening for he had been able to reinforce his front with troops brought back from the Eastern theatre of War.

The Battle of Bullecourt was destined to be the last of the major operations of the Allied Offensive of the Spring of 1917, and formed part of a battle front which extended from Bullecourt through Fontaine-lez-Croisilles to Fresnoy, a distance of 16 miles. On the 3rd May, the Third and First Armies attacked from Fontaine and Fresnoy, and the Fifth Army, in the neighbourhood of Bullecourt. But whereas the operations of the Third and First Armies practically finished at nightfall of the 3rd, those by the Fifth Army against Bullecourt dragged on for no less than fourteen days.

For a week the 185th Infantry Brigade had held the front line of the Division, suffering many casualties from the enemy's persistent shell-fire, and leading a life (which can only be described as abominable) in shell-holes and ruined buildings, frequently without any shelter whatsoever: and the men were exhausted. On the night

12TH/15TH APRIL. of the 12th/13th April, the 187th and 186th Infantry Brigades took over the front line and the 185th Brigade was withdrawn to Gomiecourt, Ervillers, Sapignies and Béhagnies, in support, for a much needed rest and " clean up."

The 186th Brigade was on the right and the 187th on the left. On the night of the 13th/14th, the former Brigade extended its right as far as U.28.c.2.5., taking over a portion of the front line held by the 13th Australian Infantry Brigade. On the same night also, and again on the night of the 14th/15th, the Division had its first experience with Bangalore Torpedoes—tubes of iron tightly rammed with Ammonal, fired by fuse, which specially trained men carried across No Man's Land and flung on top of the enemy's wire. These torpedoes exploded and caused gaps in the entanglements.

15TH APRIL. Early on the morning of the 15th, the enemy made a determined attack on the Australians and the right flank of the 62nd Division, and for a time the situation caused considerable anxiety. The Germans broke through as far as Noreuil and Lagnicourt, and penetrated as far as (and captured) two Brigades of Australian Artillery. But about 8 a.m. the Colonials made a splendid counter-attack and clearing the enemy out of the two villages, recaptured the guns and chased the Germans back to their own original lines. A thousand German dead lay on the field and 400 prisoners were left behind in the hands of the furious, but victorious Australians.

As already stated frequent orders announced the attack on Bullecourt, only to be cancelled subsequently. But through all, the methodical preparations continued and all ranks were eager for that first battle to take place which was to test the fighting qualities of the Division. Only a little more than two months had elapsed since the 62nd (W. R.) Division took over its first front-line sector in France, and despite the strenuous times through which it had passed and a heavy casualty list, it had not been engaged in any big attack.

Whilst the infantry were practising and preparing for the battle, the guns seldom ceased wire-cutting operations. The systematic shelling of Bullecourt and the defences in and about the village had gone on for many days and towards the end of April the whole form

BULLECOURT IN 1917.

1

On 3rd April, showing the Village almost untouched by Shell-Fire.

The triangular markings are thick belts of wire entanglements protecting the village.

3

On 25th April: the Village gradually disappearing.

BULLECOURT IN 1917.

2

ON 14TH APRIL, AFTER THE GUNS
HAD GOT TO WORK.

4

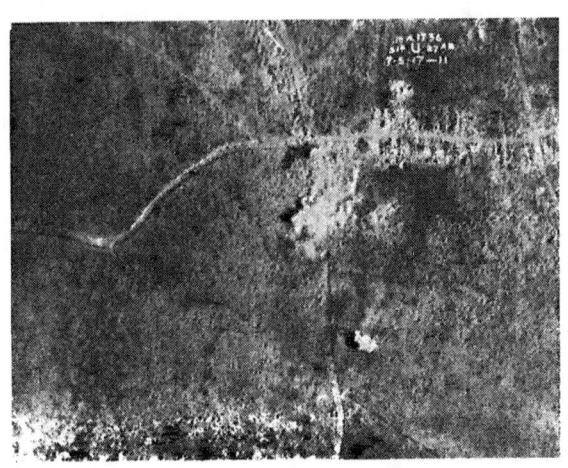

ON 7TH MAY: BULLECOURT HAD PRACTICALLY
CEASED TO EXIST.

of the village had changed, since the day on which the Division had made its first reconnaissance. An aeroplane photograph taken on the 3rd of the month showed the village practically untouched, with only a very few shell holes, the broad belts of thick wire uncut, the roads, buildings and formidable trenches clearly defined. Eleven days later, after the guns had got to work, the whole area had become pock-marked, the buildings tumbled and broken and the roads through the village partially obliterated. By the 23rd of the month Bullecourt was almost on the verge of utter extinction, only a few bare walls and tumbled masses of bricks and stone, inter-mixed with shell-holes and craters remaining to mark the place which once had been a village wherein men lived and led a peaceful life before the coming of war. But through all, the enemy kept his trenches in a fair state of repair, and his wire still presented formidable obstacles; many a shell-hole and crater was a hidden machine-gun nest, capable of dealing death whenever a living target presented itself.

15TH APRIL.

This continuous bombardment of the enemy's defences necessitated much work for the gunners and Divisional Ammunition Column. Strenuous as well as perilous were those days of preparation : " The men fell asleep whilst working the guns. For nine or ten weeks now they have worked without a rest, and it is a question whether human endurance can go much further. They fire day and night, and when not firing they are struggling through the mud carrying up ammunition : they have no shelter except what they can dig in the ground, and no sooner have they dug a resting place than the batteries have to move to fresh positions. And the weather is beyond words abominable. If it is not raining, it's snowing, and it's impossible to keep anything dry : nothing but cold, squallor and hideous discomfort. And yet they stick it out with the utmost courage and cheerfulness and fight splendidly : "

"We are the guns. Saw ye our flashes ?
Heard ye the scream of our shells in the night, and the shuddering crashes ?
Saw ye our work by the roadside, the grey wounded lying,
Moaning to God that He made them—the maimed and the dying ?
Husbands or sons,
Fathers or lovers, we break them ! We are the guns ! "

Spinners and combers from the mills, clerks and warehousemen,

15TH APRIL. men from the steel works and mines, engineers, artisans and agriculturalists—they had been in private life, and now with indescribable pluck they faced the grim and awful things which War enforces upon all—and how finely they did it ! Those men from the West Riding of Yorkshire were amongst the finest who served their country with unselfish devotion. Perhaps at present they were somewhat new at the game, but the time would come when having again and again paid in blood as the price of victory, many would say " I should be proud to command the 62nd West Riding Division."

Towards the end of April the date of the attack on Bullecourt became certain—it was fixed for the 3rd May.

27TH APRIL. At 11-30 p.m. on the night of the 27th, Divisional Headquarters received notification from Vth Corps Headquarters that simultaneously with an attack by the Third Army on the left and the 2nd Australian Division on the right, the Hindenburg Line at Bullecourt would be attacked on the 3rd May.

The 62nd Division was ordered (I.) to capture the Hindenburg Line from U.22. d.o.3. to U.14.d.3.0. including the village of Bullecourt. (II.) To capture the village of Hendecourt and (III.) form a defensive flank from the west of Hendecourt to the Hindenburg Line in U.20.a.9.6. The attack was to be carried out under a creeping barrage beginning at Zero hour on the line of the enemy's wire, and advancing approximately at the rate of 100 yards in three minutes. The weather had become warm and dry, and the ground had dried hard so that in crossing No Man's Land on the heels of the barrage the troops would be better able to keep to the time table.

For many days and nights the infantry had been practising the attack and every detail to assure success had been thought out.

1ST/2ND MAY. During the night of the 1st/2nd May, the three Infantry Brigades moved up and took over their battle-positions from the 91st Infantry Brigade (7th Division), which for several days had held the Divisional front (under orders of the General Officer Commanding 62nd Division) in order to allow the assaulting troops time in which to rest and train for the attack.

The 185th Infantry Brigade was on the right, the 186th in the centre and the 187th Brigade on the left : one Battalion of the 7th Division held the left flank of the Divisional sector. To the first-named Brigade (185th) had been assigned the task of capturing Bullecourt, including the front and support trenches of the Hindenburg Line from U.22.d.o.3. to U.21.d.5.5. The 186th Brigade was to secure the front and support trenches of the Hindenburg Line *on its front* and then push on and capture the village of Hendecourt. The 187th Brigade was ordered to form a defensive flank from about the cemetery in Hendecourt to about U.20.a.9.8. The Third Army on the left and the 2nd Australian Division on the right were attacking simultaneously.

1ST/2ND MAY.

Zero hour was 3·45 a.m.

At dusk on the 2nd May, the 2/7th West Yorks. began taping out the lines on which the troops of the 185th Infantry Brigade were to form up for the attack, and had finished their task by 11·45 p.m. This Battalion then held a line of posts in front of the forming-up line. The day had been hot, with good visibility, but the moon was approaching its fulness and the early hours of the night which followed were clear—not the best conditions for an attack. But towards midnight the assembling troops moved forward to their taped lines, the 2/6th Battalion West Yorks. (Lieut.-Col. J. Hastings) on the right, the 2/5th Battalion (Lieut.-Col. J. Josselyn) on the left, the 2/7th Battalion (Lieut.-Col. C. K. James) in support. The 2/8th Battalion (Lieut.-Col. A. H. James) had been lent to the 186th Brigade. The 212th Machine Gun Company supported the 185th Brigade.

2ND MAY.

In the centre of the Divisional front, the troops of the 186th Infantry Brigade reached their allotted places by 3·30 a.m., though during the evening of the 2nd, the enemy's artillery had caused considerable trouble—all forward telephone and telegraph wires having been cut and communication interrupted. The Signallers, however, repaired them and communication was re-established. The 2/5th Duke of Wellington's (Lieut.-Col. F. W. Best) were on the right, the 2/6th (Lieut.-Col. S. W. Ford) on the left : the 2/7th Battalion (Lieut.-Col. F. G. C. Chamberlin) was in rear of the 2/5th and the 2/4th (Lieut.-Col. H. E. Nash) in rear of 2/6th.

3RD MAY

Three Companies of the 2/8th West Yorks. were formed up in rear of the 2/4th and 2/7th Battalions Duke of Wellington's Regt., the remaining Company of the 2/8th having been detailed as a carrying party was in rear of the three Companies. The 213th Machine Gun Company supported the 186th Brigade.

On the left of the Divisional front, held by the 187th Infantry Brigade, the 2/4th Battalion York and Lancs. Regt. (Lieut.-Col. F. St. J. Blacker) was on the right, the 2/5th York and Lancs. Regt. (Lieut.-Col. L. H. P. Hart) on the left, the 2/5th King's Own Yorks. Light Infantry (Lieut.-Col. W. Watson) with two Companies of the 2/4th Battalion (Lieut.-Col. R. E. Power) of the same Regiment

3RD MAY. in rear of the two front line battalions, and the remaining two Companies of the 2/4th K.O.Y.L.I. were in rear of the 2/5th Battalion, detailed for " carrying " duties. The 208th Machine Gun Company was in support.

The taping and forming up operations were carried out without serious casualties and were completed by 3-30 a.m., but Lieut.-Col. F. St. J. Blacker, D.S.O., commanding the Hallamshires, was wounded on the forming up line.

Shortly after two o'clock in the morning the moon disappeared and the night turned to inky blackness, but fifteen minutes before Zero all was ready for the attack. At this period the enemy put down a very heavy barrage on the 185th Infantry Brigade, which gradually spread along the whole front.

At Zero the creeping barrage opened on the enemy's position and the assaulting troops began to move forward immediately. But now an unexpected difficulty presented itself : the warm weather had baked the ground hard and as the shells fell, churning it up, clouds of dust filled the air, and with the smoke from the guns, and the smoke bombs, the objectives were hidden from the advancing troops, and there was much loss of direction.

The 2/5th West Yorks. on the left of the 185th Brigade front speedily captured the enemy's first line trench, the wire entanglements having been well cut. The 2/6th Battalion, however, was not as fortunate : Colonel Hastings' Battalion had been met by very heavy machine-gun fire which caused many casualties, and in the smoke and confusion sheared off towards the left, overlapping the right of the 2/5th Battalion. Meanwhile the latter had pushed on towards the centre of the village and had established two posts, one at U.27.b.6.8. and the other at U.21.d.5.0. At this point touch was lost with the 2/6th Battalion, though it was eventually established about the church. A pigeon message timed 5-15 a.m. from an officer of the left Company of the third and fourth waves of the 2/5th Battalion which reached Divisional Headquarters stated that the writer was in the communication trench at U.21.d.5.5. with about forty of his men.

On the left of the 185th Infantry Brigade, the 186th had accomplished only part of its task. The 2/5th Duke of Wellington's found the wire cut and no difficulty was experienced in reaching the second German trench of the first objective. Here touch was obtained with the left of the 185th Brigade, and maintained for several hours until broken by enfilade machine-gun fire from both flanks. But the 2/6th Duke of Wellington's found the wire uncut and their attack was held up. Hostile shell-fire and the rear waves closing in on the leading waves, added to the confusion and all that could be done was to occupy some shell holes in front of the enemy's wire. An attempt was then made to cut the second belt of wire, but again machine-gun fire from the north, and the enemy's activity with bombs frustrated this endeavour and finally the shell-holes were established as posts.

3RD MAY.

The 2/5th Duke's had by this time established themselves in the enemy's front line trench from U.21.d.1.0. to U.21.d.2.4. and had been reinforced by the 2/8th West Yorks.

Similarly on the left of the 186th Brigade, the 187th had met with success—and failure. The 2/5th York and Lancs. Regt. reached its first objective without difficulty, but the 2/4th Battalion was hung up by the thick wire entanglements which were insufficiently cut. In seeking to find a way through the Battalion moved off to its left and became interminged with the 2/5th Battalion, whose right flank was " in the air." At about 4-20 a.m. Lieut.-Col. W. Watson, commanding the 2/5th K.O.Y.L.I. was killed as he was gallantly rallying his men and leading them forward.

For a while no reports from the right flank of the attack were received at Divisional Headquarters, and nothing could be ascertained as to what was taking place in the village of Bullecourt. At 6-50 a.m. the situation was so obscure that the protective barrage was ordered to remain on the second objective until a further advance could be organized. A little later (at 7 a.m.) the situation of the 185th Brigade appeared to be as follows : Posts had been established at U.21.d.5.5. with a certain number of men further east along the Support line at U.21.d.5.9., U.27.b.6.8. and at the church (U.28.a.0.9.) : the whole of the German front line trench as far east as U.27.b. had been occupied. Touch was maintained with the 2/5th Duke of Wellington's Regt., on the western side of the village and in the trench running south from the Crucifix. But of the 2/6th West Yorks. little was known, and all attempts to communicate with or reach the probable position of the Battalion, failed. Large numbers of men of the battalion—dead and wounded—were found in front of the German wire. A Company of the 2/7th West Yorks. was sent forward to try to reach their comrades of the 2/6th, but the men were met by a murderous machine-gun fire which swept the line of the advance and after having suffered heavy casualties the Company withdrew to the Railway Embankment.

3RD MAY.

Repeated attempts by the 186th and 187th Brigades to penetrate the enemy's positions were frustrated, and at noon the little party of 2/5th Duke's and 2/8th West Yorks., were bombed out of their portion of the trench and were forced to take shelter in shell holes south and south-west of Bullecourt. The advance by the 2/5th K.O.Y.L.I., under Major O. C. Watson, at first progressed, but was eventually checked by heavy machine-gun fire and a continuous H.E. barrage.

At mid-day the situation was as follows: about fifty men per battalion of the 186th Infantry Brigade had found shelter on the Railway Line U.26.c. and d., the remainder of the Brigade was in the Sunken Road in U.27.a.5.8. and U.20.d.9.4.: of the 187th Brigade elements were in the Sunken Road in U.20.b. and in shell holes in U.20.c. and d.: the Company of 2/5th West Yorks. (185th Brigade) which had been driven out of the western side of Bullecourt, had also reached the Railway Line, the 2/7th West Yorks. were also at U.27 c. and d., on the Railway Line: but there was still no news of the 2/6th West Yorks.

Just after 5 o'clock in the evening orders from Divisional Headquarters to the three Infantry Brigades contained instructions to the Brigadiers to make every effort to reorganize their battalions on the line of their original fronts, in their own sectors: the 7th Division was to take over the front held by the 185th Infantry Brigade as soon as possible. The same orders stated that the VIIth Corps had taken Chérisy and the 2nd Australian Division (on the right of the 62nd Division) was in occupation of the Hindenburg Line from U.23.c.8.1. to U.22.d.6.3.

The failure of the 62nd Division to capture Bullecourt was due largely to a fault which certainly cannot be charged to the gallant troops who stormed the village and the Hindenburg Line in the vicinity. Neither could the Divisional Staff, which had laboured to make all arrangements as complete as possible, be blamed. It was due principally to an error in tactics which had so often failed in the earlier years of the war—notably at Festubert in 1915. The Australian Division on the right of the 62nd Division did not launch its attack *side by side* with the 2/6th West Yorks., the flanking battalion of the West Riding Division. There was a gap—a fatal gap— in the line of attack between the Colonials and the Yorkshiremen, the former having decided to attack the first objective frontally, only as far to the left as U.23.d.6.3., and then bomb down the Hindenburg Line westwards to the left boundary where touch was to be gained with the 185th Infantry Brigade. Thus some hundreds of yards of the enemy's positions (unfortunately that portion which was very strongly defended by machine-guns) was left free to enfilade the 2/6th West Yorks. as that Battalion advanced : which indeed happened. In all justice to the Australian troops it must be noted that they reached their objective, but before they got there the West Yorkshiremen had been cut up and of those brave fellows who had penetrated the village the greater number had either been killed, wounded, or taken prisoner, only a hundred survivors getting back to their own trenches.

The inky blackness of the night, which caused much confusion during the forming-up operations, also contributed to the failure of the assault, many of the troops losing themselves and being entirely ignorant of the direction of the enemy's trenches.

The enemy was in considerable strength, the 49th Reserve Division and the 27th Division was holding the Hindenburg Line between Fontaine and Riencourt (inclusive). The latter had with it the 1st Musketeen (Automatic Rifle) Battalion.[1]

Many deeds of gallantry were witnessed during that attack, and the Division emerged from its first set battle sorely tried and tested and badly mauled, but with many proofs of its fighting qualities.[2]

Two incidents will suffice to show the spirit which animated the attacking troops. In one part of the line a young subaltern led his platoon forward with great dash and determination against a murderous machine-gun and rifle fire. He fell wounded, but jumping to his feet went on until wounded again more severely and in no less than fourteen places. But in spite of his wounds he still kept up in the enemy's wire with his men, encouraging them to hold on to the position they had won, until at dusk he was carried away by a stretcher party.

Another officer, rushing forward with his platoon against a strongly defended position, was shot through the right eye and for

---

[1] The automatic rifle used by the Musketeen Battalion was a Swedish model, 18 lbs. in weight, sighted up to 2,000 yards, having an arc of traverse of at least 90°. It was fed by magazines containing twenty-five rounds of " K " ammunition. The rifle was fired from the shoulder, and was supported by two adjustable legs attached by a swivel to the barrel. It could be brought into action as quickly as a rifle, and for this reason was chiefly placed in the front line. Organization of the Battalion was : three Companies, each of three platoons : strength per Company—four officers, fifteen N.C.O.'s and ninety men with thirty automatic rifles.

[2] The casualties of the 62nd (W.R.) Division on the 3rd May were : 116 officers and 2,860 other ranks, killed, wounded and missing.

3RD MAY.   a while rendered unconscious. But on coming to, he collected his men and insisted on going forward and making a further attempt on the enemy's front line.

These are not isolated incidents of bravery, for the records of the number of honours gained by the 62nd Division at Bullecourt demonstrated how well the Division fought that day.

The 62nd had been " Blooded " !

At dusk on the 3rd, the 185th Infantry Brigade was relieved by the 22nd Infantry Brigade (7th Division), only the 2/7th West Yorks. remaining in the line under the command of the General Officer Commanding 7th Division.

4TH MAY.   The remnants of the 2/5th, 2/6th and 2/8th West Yorks. were withdrawn to the caves in Ecoust, to reorganize : on the following day they marched back to Ervillers. The 186th and 187th Brigades remained in the line, the 62nd Divisional front now extending from the Mory—Ecoust—Bullecourt Road (inclusive) to the left of the Vth Corps boundary, Judas Farm—Sensee River, to along the road at T.24.a.9.4.—U.14.c.2.9.

7TH MAY.   On the 7th May, the 7th Division and the Australians carried out another attack on the Hindenburg Line and the south-east corner of Bullecourt, and in spite of determined resistance gained a footing in the village. Hostile counter-attacks failed to dislodge the 7th Division, the guns of the 62nd Divisional Artillery doing great execution on the enemy's troops as they attempted to form up and advance.

At 4 a.m. on the morning of the 8th, the 186th and 187th Brigades were relieved by the 185th Brigade, the latter taking over the whole of the Divisional front line.

12TH MAY.   The final attack on Bullecourt began on the 12th May when the 185th Infantry Brigade assisted the 7th (British) and 5th (Australian) Divisions, by attacking the enemy's strong point at the Crucifix.

The 2/7th Battalion West Yorks. was detailed for this operation, the 185th Trench Mortar Battery and one Section of the 212th Machine-Gun Company co-operating. Two Companies of the Battalion—B and C—attacked the Crucifix at Zero (3-40 a.m.) plus 26 minutes, but for a while no information of the situation of the attacking troops was obtainable. The 91st Brigade (7th Division) had reached the centre of the village, capturing a few Germans, but here very heavy machine-gun fire held up any further advance. About 6-30 a.m., however, an aeroplane report was received at 62nd Divisional Headquarters which stated that men of the 2/7th could be seen well dug in at the Crucifix. But from this 12TH MAY. period onwards, throughout the day, nothing could be ascertained, it being impossible to gain touch with the gallant West Yorkshiremen holding the post at the Crucifix. Possibly one of those isolated fights to a finish which were not uncommon in the War, but of which no authentic records are in existence, took place. For at 8 p.m. another aeroplane reported that the Germans once more held the Crucifix. At 10 o'clock that night patrols which attempted to reach the post were driven back, thus confirming the aeroplane report. Subsequently a few odd men returned through the lines of the 1st South Staffords (7th Division), having lost their way, but of the two officers and thirty-one other ranks who were known to be holding the Crucifix none returned nor was any further information gained concerning their fate. Five killed, thirty-one missing and thirty-two wounded were the casualties suffered by the 2/7th West Yorks. in this affair.

But the capture of Bullecourt was imperative, and at 3-40 a.m. 13TH MAY. on the 13th still another attack by the 7th Division was launched against the village. The 2/7th Battalion Duke of Wellington's Regt. (186th Infantry Brigade) under orders of the General Officer Commanding 185th Brigade, set out to attack the Crucifix, the forming-up operations being carried out under the personal supervision of the Brigade Major. But the enemy interposed a very heavy barrage between the Duke's and their objective and progress was again impossible. So throughout the remainder of the 13th the situation in Bullecourt still remained obscure. Contact patrols reported that there were many posts in the village held by British troops, but pockets of the enemy still existed amongst these posts and vigorous bombing was taking place.

Throughout this period casualties were very heavy, the losses in officers being especially severe : and in some of the Battalions Companies were so weak that they had been amalgamated.

On the 14th, the 186th Infantry Brigade relieved the 185th, taking over the whole of the Divisional front. The latter Brigade moved back to Courcelles and neighbourhood, and the 187th Infantry Brigade to the Reserve area Ervillers—St. Léger—Mory Copse.

Late in the afternoon, the 186th Brigade was ordered to establish 14TH/15TH a strong point during the night 14th/15th at U.27.a.5.9. and patrols MAY. were to be sent out to points " N. and S. of Crucifix in order to clear up the situation, and if possible gain touch with troops in Bullecourt." The new point was established by the 2/5th Duke of Wellington's Regt. which had relieved the 2/7th Battalion. The

E

14TH/15TH MAY. patrols were unable to reach the village, but gained contact with the enemy, who was found to be on the alert.

The Germans, employing two battalions of Garde Fusiliers, launched a heavy counter-attack against the Division on the right of the 62nd Division, but were driven off and by early morning on the 15th the situation was well in hand. The 58th Division had relieved the 7th on the right of the West Riding Division and the 33rd Division had come into line on the left.

16TH MAY. Throughout the 16th, wiring and improvement of the defences engaged the attention of the men, but when darkness fell patrols again crept out to reconnoitre the enemy's position and observe his movements. Seven prisoners belonging to the 228th Reserve Regiment were taken during the night.

17TH MAY. At 2 a.m. on the 17th, the 58th Division on the right of the 62nd Division succeeded in capturing the whole of Bullecourt, and consolidated the ground won.[1]

28TH/29TH MAY. Thereafter, until the 62nd Division was relieved on the night of the 28th/29th May, the Division co-operated with Artillery, machine-gun and rifle fire, in support of operations undertaken by the flanking Divisions, but made no direct attack on the Hindenburg Line. On the morning of the 29th, at 9 a.m. command of the Divisional front passed to the General Officer Commanding 58th Division and later in the day all three Infantry Brigades were quartered in their rest and training areas, the 185th in Gomiecourt, the 186th at Achiet-le-Petit and the 187th in Sapignies and Bihucourt. Divisional Headquarters remained at Achiet-le-Grand.

Very tired and greatly reduced in numbers by the loss of many valuable lives, but still in fine fettle, the 62nd Division set to work to train and re-organize. The first essential was to rest the men after their exhausting efforts. Their first set battle had indeed given them a gruelling, but they had learned many lessons and had emerged from the Battle with a greater understanding of what was required of them: in their own Yorkshire fashion they had taken the measure of the enemy. The task set them was not easy: Bullecourt was a particularly strong section of the Hindenburg Line, the village jutting out and forming a bulge powerfully defended by thick belts

---

[1] The official despatches stated that Bullecourt was finally captured on the 17th May by the 58th and 62nd Divisions. No direct attack by the West Riding Division was made on this date, but the cumulative effect of the efforts of two weeks was without doubt a contributory element in the final capture of the village.

of wire and machine-gun emplacements so placed as to sweep No Man's Land in enfilade.

28TH/29TH MAY.

During May the casualties were very heavy: twenty-four officers were killed, eighty-seven wounded and thirty-two missing, of whom many were afterwards reported killed. The number is an eloquent tribute to the gallantry with which they led their men. In other ranks, the losses were 254 killed, 1,710 wounded and 1,320 missing : a total of 163 officers and 3,284 other ranks.

Of these casualties many were gunners, the Artillery Brigades being heavily shelled during the operations. An instance of this occurred on the night of the 14th, when over two thousand gas shells fell amongst the batteries of the 310th Brigade R.F.A., killing five gunners and wounding twelve more. On the 24th, the camouflage over one of the howitzers of D/312 Howitzer Battery, caught fire, the flames exploding the ammunition collected near the gun. An officer, temporarily in command of the Battery was killed, also ten gunners, including six " Numbers One " of the Battery, and another officer and five more gunners were wounded.

On the 31st May the Vth Corps to which the 62nd (West Riding) Division belonged was transferred from the Fifth to the Third Army (General Sir J. H. Byng).

31ST MAY.

TRENCH WARFARE: THE NOREUIL-LAGNICOURT SECTOR.

Chapter VII.   1917.

TRENCH WARFARE

From 29th June to 19th November, 1917.

"What are the bounds of No Man's Land?
You can see them clearly on either hand.
A mound of rag-bags grey in the sun,
Or a furrow of brown where the earthworks run.
From the eastern hills to the western sea,
Through field or forest, o'er river and lea:
No man may pass them, but aim you well
And Death rides across on the bullet or shell."

James N. Knight-Adkin.

FOR a little over three weeks the Division was out of the front line. Throughout this period training was carried on, particular attention being paid to musketry, for which purpose existing ranges were improved and new ones constructed by the Sappers assisted by large working parties from the three Infantry Brigades. Special ranges upon which to carry out the "Bayonet assault practice" combining the use of rifle, bayonet and bullet were also constructed. In addition large working parties had to be found for work on the light railways about Achiet-le-Grand, the Ecoust defences, roads about Mory, agricultural labour about Ablainzeville, and work on dug-outs in the forward areas. These working parties were a constant drain on the available *personnel* of the Brigades, and each Brigade was therefore detailed to find all working parties weekly, so that the remaining troops could carry out their training satisfactorily. Staff and senior Regimental officers paid periodical visits to the Fifth Army School of Toutencourt, the Musketry School at Warloy, Sniping School at Vadencourt, Tank tactical exercises at Wailly, and to various demonstrations which took place about Auxi-le-Chateau showing final stages of a platoon in the attack.

Between times, games were organized for the troops and "leave"—the first since the Division arrived in France—was given to a certain

See Map No. 5.

number of officers and men. Nevertheless that first period out of the line was anything but a " rest " : hard work and hard training characterized practically every day of it, and gradually it dawned upon all ranks that " rest periods " were a snare and a delusion.

19TH JUNE.   On the 19th June, however, orders were issued for the 62nd Divisional Artillery to relieve the Artillery of the 20th Division in the Noreuil—Lagnicourt sector, the relief to be completed by the night of the 21st/22nd. Later in the day information came to hand that the Division as a whole would relieve the 20th, about the 26th of the month in the same sector. Warning was immediately sent out to the Brigadiers. Subsequently it was decided that the 185th and 186th Infantry Brigades should go into the line, the 187th Brigade to remain in Divisional support. The latter Brigade therefore took over all working parties in order that the 185th and 186th might carry out intensive training prior to going into the front-line trenches. Further orders, in greater detail, stated that the 185th would relieve the 60th Infantry Brigade in the right (Lagnicourt) sub-sector on the night of the 25th/26th : the 186th would relieve the 61st Brigade in the left (Noreuil) sub-sector on the night of the 27th/28th, and the 187th, the 62nd Brigade in the support area (Favreuil) on the 28th June. The Command of the Sector would pass from the General Officer Commanding 20th Division to General
29TH JUNE. Braithwaite at 8 a.m. on the 29th June.

The reliefs duly took place on the dates ordered without incident and at 8 o'clock on the morning of the 29th the Division was again in the front line, with the 7th Division on its left and the 48th Division on its right flank.

A period of Trench warfare was now before the 62nd, for along the whole front between Arras and Amiens no action of outstanding importance took place until the Battle of Cambrai on 20th November. In the intervening five months, however, there happened certain items of interest from a Divisional point of view, which cannot be passed over. For the Division had yet to serve its apprenticeship in trench warfare. Hardly six months had elapsed since the 62nd landed in France and with the exception of that period which covered the operations against Bullecourt (a period of continued efforts to advance) trench warfare, such as had been waged since the first terrible winter of 1914-1915, was practically unknown to these West Riding Territorials. The Flanders Offensive had begun on the 7th June with the Battle of Messines, and the attentions both of the Allies and the enemy were turned to the northern battle-front, comparative peace reigning from Arras southwards. And yet, there 29TH JUNE. was no real peace, for, as Sir Douglas Haig said in one of his dispatches of another phase of the war, but which applied to all periods of trench-warfare, " Artillery and snipers are practically never silent, patrols are out in front of the lines every night, and heavy bombardments by the Artillery of one or both sides take place daily in various parts of the line. Below ground there is continual mining and counter-mining which by the ever-present threat of sudden explosion and the uncertainty as to when and where it will take place, causes perhaps a more constant strain than any other form of warfare. In the air there is seldom a day, however bad the weather, when aircraft are not busy reconnoitring, photographing and observing fire. All this is taking place constantly at every hour, day or night, and in any part of the line. In short....a steady and continuous fight has gone on, day and night, above ground and below it."

The Noreuil—Lagnicourt Sector taken over by the Division at the end of June, 1917, had in the course of three months since the German Retreat to the Hindenburg Line become more or less stabilized. Contrary to Ludendorff's expectations the British troops had established themselves in front of his new line with marvellous rapidity and had taken up a line capable of resisting determined attacks. Trenches had been dug, communications had been established with the back areas, and dumps of all kinds of stores and ammunition were formed in an incredibly short space of time. The splendid devotion of the Sappers and Pioneers deserved far greater notice than it received, though their reward lay chiefly in the gratitude of the infantrymen in the front line and of the gunners who knew full well all that these two splendid arms of the service had accomplished for them. It is true that both infantry and gunners provided considerable working parties, but their labours were largely directed by Sapper and Pioneer officers whose special functions were the construction of defences and communications.

Thus when the Division took over the Noreuil—Lagnicourt 29TH JUNE. Sector and General Braithwaite assumed command on the 29th June, a certain number of trenches and communications had already been dug and were in the course of completion; others had been planned. It must not be forgotten, however, that, compared with the German defences in the Hindenburg Line, the new sector could not accurately be termed formidable, as were the heavily wired trenches across No Man's Land.

Of the Noreuil-Lagnicourt sector, the latter sub-sector was the

29TH JUNE. strongest. Here the defences consisted of an outpost line, wired throughout, and consisting chiefly of posts : a main line of resistance, also wired throughout, consisting of a line of posts connected by spit-locked trenches, carefully sited, and an intermediate line. The spit-locked trenches were subsequently dug out to the full depth.

In the Noreuil sub-sector the lines of defences consisted of a front line, wire throughout, corresponding with the main line of defence in the Lagnicourt sector, and an intermediate line. When the 62nd first went into the line the defence of the intervening space between the front and the intermediate lines was undertaken by machine-guns, distributed in depth, supported by detachments of infantry in short lengths of existing trenches.

From the three spurs running north-east towards Lagnicourt and Noreuil the Divisional forward area afforded excellent observation over the enemy's trenches and back areas.

The enemy's attitude showed little aggressive action. The hostile troops facing the Division belonged to the 1st Garde Reserve Division, which consisted of three infantry regiments. This Division had but recently arrived in the line, having been brought down from Messines, where it had been very roughly handled in the Flanders offensive. Thus, for a few days the line was comparatively quiet, even the enemy's guns selecting only a few points along the front of the West Riding Division, for slow concentrated fire.

1ST JULY. The capture of two prisoners at dawn on the 1st July, belonging to a hostile party of nine Germans who had attempted to raid "No. 9" post provided identifications and valuable information.

About the 3rd or 4th of July, the enemy seems to have realized that a new Division had come into line opposite him, and he therefore set to work to obtain identifications. Both sides were engaged on a similar task. Several unsuccessful attempts on posts along the Divisional front were made, but on each occasion the enemy was driven off and casualties inflicted on him. Meanwhile the 62nd patrols were out each night, carefully reconnoitring the enemy's wire and locating his posts and machine-gun emplacements. Much excellent work was done by these patrol parties and considerable **10TH JULY.** skill and ingenuity displayed. On one occasion (on the 10th) a patrol party consisting of one officer, one N.C.O. and ten men of the 2/7th West Yorks. (185th Infantry Brigade then holding the Lagnicourt sub-sector) crawled forward to the German line with the object of raiding a post. The patrol succeeded in getting to the rear of its objective, but found that it was apparently behind a strong

enemy outpost line of three posts, each strongly held. An attack 10TH JULY.
was therefore impossible and the officer in charge of the party withdrew his men successfully without disclosing his way of approach.

Two days later another German prisoner was captured and information was obtained that the enemy was still uncertain of the identity of the Division facing him.

All along the Divisional front the control of No Man's Land was gradually, but surely, passing from the enemy. The persistence and gallantry with which patrol work was carried out not only reflected great credit upon the Division, but also put the men in fine fettle and gave them confidence. One Battalion, for instance, went into the line on the night of the 21st July, completing the relief at 21ST JULY. 12-10 a.m. Immediately, an officer and ten men went out into No Man's Land on patrol: and on every night until the 29th, when the Battalion was relieved, its patrols were out carrying on their dangerous, but exciting work. And what was done by this Battalion, was done by all Battalions in the line. The moral ascendency gained over the enemy was extremely valuable, for the 62nd had had a hard gruelling during the attack on Bullecourt and had yet to win that extraordinary reputation for never failing to reach its objectives which became its most precious possession before the War ended. In the summer of 1917 it was (so far as France was concerned) a young Division, and experience is only gained in the taking and giving of hard blows. But these Yorkshiremen were fast becoming proficient: these men from the moors and the towns and cities of that great northern county of England were of a breed which could not be discouraged by failure on one occasion. And at the end of July, after a month of active patrol work, a Brigadier of the Division wrote to the Commanding Officer of one of his Battalions expressing his pleasure at " the dash and soldierly qualities displayed by all ranks....your patrols have proved conclusively that the Bosche does not dominate No Man's Land."

During the early days of August a slight re-adjustment of the AUGUST. Divisional Sector took place: the 3rd Division moved into the Lagnicourt sub-sector and the 62nd side-slipped to the left, adding the right sub-sector of the Bullecourt Sector to its front. Thus once more the tumbled ruins of the village came into the possession of the Yorkshiremen.

Throughout the weeks which followed the monotony of trench warfare was broken by occasional raids by, or on, the Division. Artillery shoots by the gunners took place periodically, whilst the

AUGUST.

Trench Mortar Batteries carried out frequent bombardments and, as the C.R.A. said, " knocked the enemy's trenches about handsomely." In these duels many hard knocks were given and taken, for the enemy's retaliation was almost always heavy.

The Divisional Artillery was in the " Valley of Death." The guns were all close together, but somehow they escaped without serious losses, although the enemy regularly plastered the ground in the neighbourhood. The gunners, however, had made their positions secure and had dug themselves well in.

The raids made on the enemy were part of a definite policy for keeping General Headquarters informed of the dispositions of the German divisions. Two of them are of importance, for they admirably demonstrated both the offensive and the defensive spirit of the Division.

1ST SEPT.

On the 1st of September, the 185th Infantry Brigade was holding the Noreuil sub-sector of the line with the 2/7th West Yorks. on the right, the 2/5th in the centre and the 2/8th on the left. The latter Battalion was relieved by the 2/6th Battalion on the night of the 5th.

The 2/6th West Yorks. had been ordered to carry out a raid on the enemy's front line and support trenches between Ostrich Avenue and the Sunken Road (both inclusive) running north-north-east through the British and German lines : the Sunken Road was one of five known as the Star Cross Roads.

11TH SEPT.

The night of the 11th had been selected for the raid and C Company of the 2/6th was to carry out the operations, the objectives of which were " To kill Germans " (as the Brigade Diary has it), take prisoners and any valuable war material, destroying dug-outs and the capture of documents.

The raiding party was sent off to Vaux for training. Meanwhile the officers who were to lead the raiders went out each night across No Man's Land in order to reconnoitre the ground over which the raid was to be made, and to observe the state of the enemy's trenches and wire entanglements upon which the Divisional Artillery had already got to work. But the enemy was very alert and the weather being fine and clear these reconnaissances were attended by the greatest danger. Indeed one of these parties having crossed No Man's Land had practically completed its examination of the enemy's defences when the officer in charge was killed. Another officer who went out to bring in the body also met his death.

Zero hour for the raid was fixed for 11-10 p.m. on the night of the 11th.

11TH SEPT. The raiding party arrived at Pudsey Support Trench about 4 p.m. and at 8 o'clock began to move forward. Three hours later the raiders with the flanking parties were lying out in No Man's Land, and had not been observed by the enemy. At 11 p.m. the field guns and howitzers and the 185th Trench Mortar Battery opened fire, under cover of which the leading wave of the raiding party crept forward to within 50 yards of the hostile trenches. Three minutes after Zero, on the barrage lifting, the raiders jumped to their feet and rushed the enemy's position. Hostile machine-guns had by now opened fire and two men were wounded, but the attack swept forward. The leading wave under Second-Lieut. O. E. Brooksbank, advancing straight on the front trench, came upon the enemy at the junction of the front line with Ostrich Avenue. One German was captured and another who showed fight was killed. Two more were captured outside a dug-out about fifty yards from the trench junction. There were other Germans down inside the dug-out, but as these refused to come up and surrender they were bombed and the dug-out destroyed with " P." bombs. Several more of the enemy were killed in the neighbourhood.

Meanwhile Second-Lieut. J. R. Allett, who was leading the party detailed to raid the support trenches, had passed through and with little difficulty reached his objective. One German who was observed making off in the direction of Riencourt was shot. Not far from the Star Cross Roads another German was wounded whilst endeavouring to escape and was eventually brought in.

The withdrawal began at 11-30 p.m., and shortly after midnight the whole raiding party, having had only one man seriously and two lightly wounded, reached Pudsey Support, bringing with it three unwounded prisoners and one wounded. Twenty of the enemy had been killed, two dug-outs were destroyed and a quantity of documents captured.

Throughout the raid the 2-inch Trench Mortars rendered most valuable assistance and the 3-inch Stokes Mortars, combined with the Artillery and machine-guns, fired a very successful barrage which absolutely prevented the enemy sending forward troops to the assistance of those in the front line who were being raided. The success of the raid was largely due to the very careful reconnaissances carried out by the two subalterns whose names have already been mentioned, and the N.C.O.'s : all ranks behaved with the greatest courage.

11TH SEPT.   Army, Corps and Divisional Commanders wired their congratulations to the Commanding Officer, 2/6th West Yorks., on the result of this very successful little operation : careful organization and training, combined with individual pluck and initiative, had once again demonstrated the offensive qualities of the Division.

12TH SEPT.   Throughout the remainder of the 12th the enemy maintained a passive attitude, and contrary to expectation he did not deluge the Divisional area with torrents of shells of all calibre as a mark of his displeasure. Indeed his artillery retaliation during the raid and subsequent hours was of a feeble nature. On the night of the 12th/13th he was particularly quiet : indeed, a suspicious stillness pervaded the whole front line. If there is such a thing as tangible silence it was present that night. That curious feeling which comes to everyone that something is about to happen was felt in the trenches of the 2/6th West Yorks. And happen it did, for just before dawn

13TH SEPT. on the 13th—at 4 a.m.—hostile field guns, howitzers, trench mortars and machine-guns put down a terrific barrage all along the frontage held by the 2/6th Battalion. The Apex was a special mark and here the shells burst rapidly one after the other, creating havoc where just before order had been : while as far back as Pudsey Support the hostile guns swept the area. For just over an hour this tornado of shells, bullets and bombs fell upon the forward posts and trenches of the West Yorkshiremen, until at 5 a.m. the hostile barrage lifted off the left Company, and off the right front Company fifteen minutes later.

As the enemy's guns lifted, his troops in considerable strength advanced to the attack. Approximately a hundred Germans advanced between the left post of the right front Company and the right post of the left front Company. Every man in the right post (No. 1) had either been killed or was wounded, but none left his position, each man fell where he had fought. " They put up a fine fight," said the report, " and bayonetted one German officer and two men." Some of the enemy's troops penetrated as far as the old Company Headquarters in London Support, where they were met by Second-Lieut. Hodgson and four men. The Germans threw stick grenades at Hodgson and his men, but were soon forced to beat a hastry retreat to their own lines.

Meanwhile other parties of the enemy were attempting to break through opposite Nos. 4 and 5 posts. A German sprang on to the parapet of No. 5, but was shot dead immediately : other Germans were shot in front of the post and in front of No. 4. Only at No. 1

post had the enemy any measure of success and that of a temporary nature. In spite of the very heavy hostile bombardment not a post was abandoned, officers and men clinging to their positions with splendid tenacity and absolute fearlessness.

In this severe test of the defensive qualities of the Division one German officer and three men were killed and two unwounded and one wounded prisoners were taken.[1] The 2/6th West Yorks. lost one officer killed (who, after killing five Germans, lost his own life by the bursting of a hostile trench mortar bomb) and ten other ranks killed and thirty wounded. One N.C.O. and one man who were not in a post were reported missing.

The moral effect of these two raids upon all ranks of the Division was very great and when later congratulations were again received from the Army and Corps Commanders[2] General Braithwaite must have felt that the 62nd had at last passed through the refining fire and had emerged finely tempered steel. Intrepidity in the attack, staunchness and tenacity in the defence—the greatest qualities of a soldier—had come to the Division and never more would it be afraid of itself.

Several more weeks of trench warfare engaged the Division until on 12th October when the General Officer Commanding handed over command of the Noreuil—Bullecourt Sector to the 3rd Division, the Infantry Brigades of the 62nd having been relieved—the 187th on the night of the 9th/10th, the 186th on the 10th/11th and the 185th on the 11th/12th. Only the Gunners and the Trench Mortar Batteries remained in the line, Brigadier-General Anderson (the C.R.A.) taking his guns off to the neighbourhood of Wancourt to cover the 51st (Highland) Division, whilst the T.M.B.'s were temporarily handed over to the 3rd and 16th Divisions.

[1] The enemy's strength was two officers and 120 other ranks, formed of one platoon of the 84th R.I.R., forty Storm troops, and twenty-seven engineers from the 18th Division.
[2] The following message was received from the B. G. G. S. VIth Corps by General Braithwaite, and published in a " Special Order of the Day " : " The Corps Commander desires me to convey to you and through you to Brigadier General Viscount Hampden and the troops of the 185th Infantry Brigade who recently carried out successful raids and patrol work, and also to all ranks who recently repulsed the enemy's raid on the morning of the 12th inst., his high appreciation of their staunch and gallant behaviour.

" The several recent successes of the Division and the repulse of the enemy's Storm troops after a severe bombardment, is a clear proof, if any proof were wanting, of the superiority of our troops. It is above all things important at the present time to maintain our moral ascendency over the enemy, and the more we can harass him now and show him that we are his masters, the easier and more quickly carried out will be his eventual defeat."

12TH OCT. From the Noreuil—Bullecourt Sector the Division marched to a training area round Haplincourt and Barastre. Here followed a fortnight of intensive training of great value. The semi-open nature of the fighting then taking place in the Ypres Salient was adopted as a model, special attention was paid to bringing out the initiative of Company and Platoon Commanders, and to making the platoon the tactical unit in the attack. Battalion attacks against dummy trenches and the forming up of Brigades previous to attack, were constantly practised, and in the time to come the training (all too short though it was) proved very valuable.

30TH OCT. On the 30th October, the Division left Haplincourt and Barastre and marched to the Fosseux area west of Arras (under the XVIIth Corps for Administration and under the IVth Corps for training) in Third Army Reserve.

2ND NOV. A special course of training with Tanks was begun on the 2nd November, for the great Tank Attack at Cambrai had already been planned and decided upon. Each battalion of infantry carried out two days' training with the Company of Tanks with which it was to fight, the steel monsters inspiring the greatest confidence amongst all ranks of the Division.

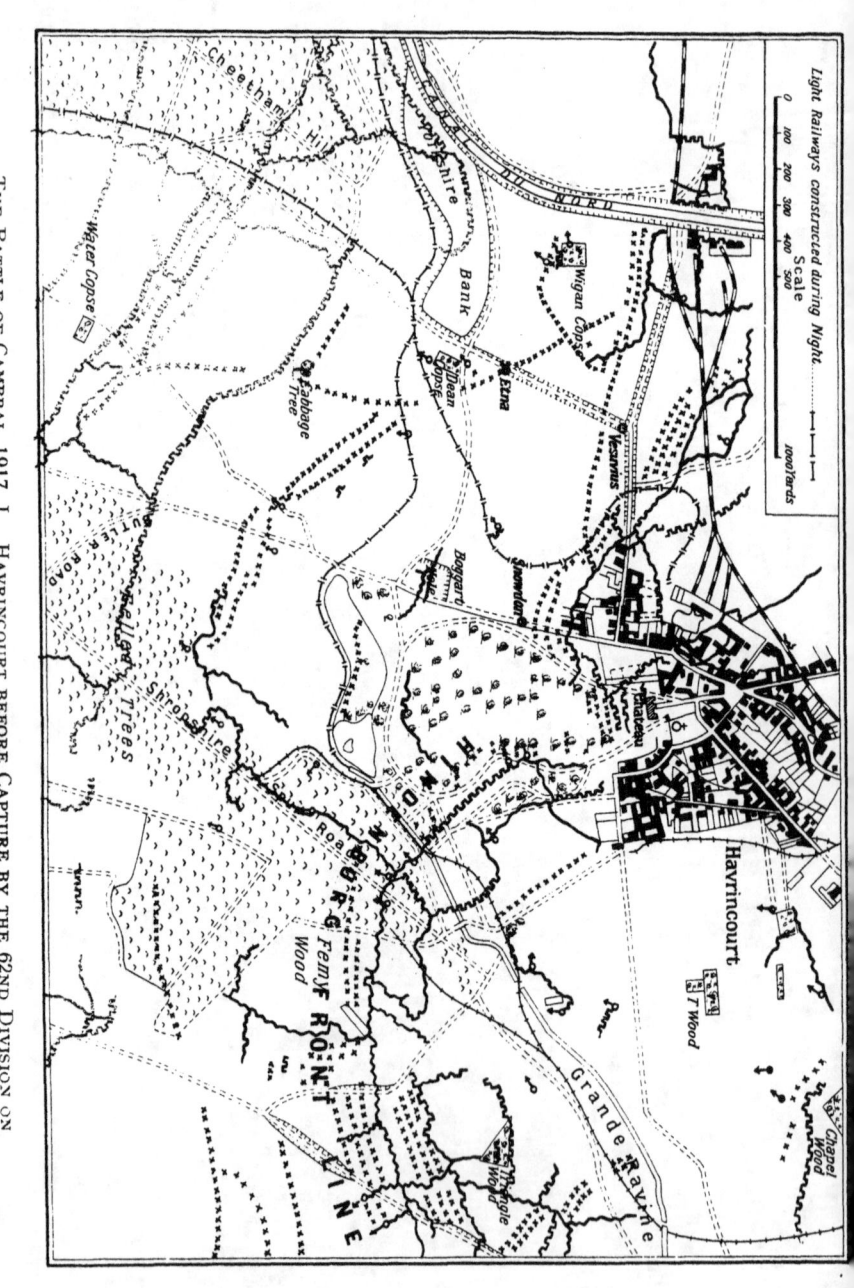

The Battle of Cambrai, 1917. I. Havrincourt before Capture by the 62nd Division on 20th November, 1917.

Chapter VIII.

THE BATTLE OF CAMBRAI, 1917 (I.)

" We were expecting a continuation of the attack in Flanders, and on the French front, when, on the 20th November, we were surprised by a fresh blow at Cambrai."

Ludendorff.

IN order to appreciate the Cambrai Operations of 1917, it is necessary for a brief space to consider the situation created by the Allies' attacks of the spring, summer and autumn of that year.

The new Year found both the Allies and the enemy in a weakened condition; the enemy had been unable to replace his losses in the Somme Battles, which had but recently ended —in November, 1916—whilst the Allies had experienced difficulty in filling their depleted ranks with troops sufficiently trained to take the offensive. And enormous quantities of stores and ammunition had to be collected. By the end of that year the Allies had formulated their plans for 1917, which included a series of attacks on all fronts, " timed to assist each other by depriving the enemy of the power of weakening any one of his fronts in order to reinforce another."

The unrestricted submarine campaign, begun by Germany early in the year, the Russian Revolution followed by the German Retreat to the Hindenburg Line, all threatened to derange the scheme of operations decided upon at Chantilly, at French General Headquarters in November, 1916. For a while the submarine campaign was serious: the Russian Revolution released large German forces for service on the Western Front and the Retirement to the Hindenburg Line had enabled the enemy to shorten his line and thus present a more formidable front. Nevertheless, Sir Douglas Haig launched his offensive on 9th April along the Arras front and on the 16th of the same month the French offensive on the Aisne began. On 7th June the Flanders offensive opened with the

Battle of Messines, and finally the last days of July saw the commencement of the Battles of Ypres, 1917, which continued until early in November.

For nearly five months the Flanders offensive continued and to maintain the defence of the northern part of his line the enemy had been compelled to weaken certain parts of his line to a dangerous extent. Ever on the watch, the Allies could not afford to ignore the opportunities offered by the weakened sectors. Of these the Cambrai front was selected as the most suitable for a surprise operation. The ground over which infantry and Tanks would move forward was, on the whole, favourable and facilities existed for the commencement of the necessary preparations for the attack.

Thus the Battle of Cambrai, 1917, was, in the first place, a surprise operation. To dispense with artillery preparation and depend instead on Tanks to smash down the enemy's wire, a great quantity of which protected his trenches, was an outstanding feature in the plan of attack.[1] Not until the Tanks and infantry had advanced were the guns to assist with counter-battery and barrage fire. Nor for fear of arousing the enemy's suspicions could registration be permitted.

The intention of the Commander-in-Chief was to break through the German defence system from just east of Gonnelieu to the Canal du Nord, opposite Hermies, secure Bourlon and establish a good flank position to the east in the direction of Cambrai; the situation between Bourlon and the River Sensee, and to the north-west, was then to be exploited; the capture of Cambrai was subsidiary to the main operations.

From just east of Gonnelieu to the Canal du Nord opposite Hermies was a distance of approximately 6 miles and along this front the 12th, 20th, 6th, 51st (Highland), 62nd (West Riding) and 36th (Ulster) Divisions (from right to left in the order given) were to carry out the initial attack; the 29th Division was in reserve in Guyencourt; while cavalry would be waiting behind the lines in order to go through and exploit success.

The general scheme of operations from the divisional point of view was issued by 62nd Headquarters on the 12th October, whilst the Division was still training west of Arras.[2]

[1] To General Sir Julian Byng, belongs the credit of this far-reaching innovation.

[2] 62nd Division Instructions No. 2, " Outlines of Scheme for forthcoming operations."

The operations were divided into four phases :—

" (a) 1st Bound of the infantry—including on the IVth Corps front—the capture of the enemy's front line and support systems, and the villages of Havrincourt and Flesquières, the Blue and Brown Lines ;

" (b) 2nd Bound of the infantry—advance to the line Bois des Neuf —Graincourt (inclusive)—Sugar Factory and Trench immediately (about 250 yards) north of the Cambrai-Bapaume Road."

Phases (a) and (b) to be carried out by the assaulting Divisions.

" (c) The cavalry pass through with the following objectives— capture of Cambrai and Bourlon Wood.

" (d) The infantry relieve the cavalry to enable them to push on and exploit the success."

The first element of success—surprise—was to be followed by speed in carrying out the operations in such a manner as to permit the cavalry to go through on the first day.

The IVth Corps had decided to attack on a two-divisional front, each Division having two Brigades in the front line and the third in Divisional Reserve, to pass through the two leading Brigades and capture the further objectives. The 51st (Highland) Division was to attack on the right, the 62nd on the left ; whilst the 36th Division was to roll up the enemy's front line west of the Canal du Nord, as the 62nd Division advanced east of the Canal.

The first objective on the Corps front was the Blue Line, which included Havrincourt and the enemy's trenches to a depth of about 1,500 yards.

The second objective, the Brown Line, included Flesquieres and part of the Hindenburg Support Line, a total depth of about 3,000 yards.

The third objective included Fontaine, Graincourt and the remainder of the Hindenburg Support Line east of the Canal and the capture of Bourlon Wood, in co-operation with the cavalry, who were to break through the gap and attack Bourlon village from the north and east.

On the 62nd Division front, the 185th Infantry Brigade on the right and the 187th Infantry Brigade on the left were to make the attack. To these Brigades were assigned the tasks of capturing the first two objectives, *i.e.*, the Blue and Brown Lines.

The 186th Infantry Brigade[1]—as reserve Brigade—was to pass through the two leading Brigades when the latter had captured the second objective and drive the enemy back, capturing the Hindenburg Support Line up to where it crossed the spur in E 22, and the village of Anneux. After the capture of the village a detachment was to be pushed out to gain possession of the high ground west of Bourlon Wood and join hands with the 1st Cavalry Division which should then be advancing on Bourlon village from the north-east.

Two squadrons of King Edward's Horse were attached to the 62nd Division for the latter operation.

Thirty Tanks[2] were allotted to each assaulting Brigade, of which not less than six in each Brigade were to be retained to accompany the Battalions detailed for the second objective. The surviving Tanks from the first and second objectives were to go forward with the Reserve Brigade on the latter passing through the two leading Brigades.

Besides its own artillery—the 310th and 312th Brigades, R.F.A.—the Division was to have the assistance of three more Brigades of Field Artillery, whilst the 36th Divisional Artillery and a Heavy Army Group were to flank the advance of the Division. Machine-gun and trench mortar batteries and Stokes guns were to join with the artillery in barraging the enemy's positions.

Such was the plan of attack worked out with great labour by

---

[1] " The night before the Battle, Bradford " (Brig.-General, commanding 186th Brigade) " was very anxious to advance early on the 20th and take up a much more forward position. It was the ardour of youth and there was a great deal in it if things went right. But of course the whole plan of the Battle was at the time rather a striking departure from anything which had been done before. For instance there were the Tanks, which were really to act as the barrage, and we did not quite know how they would perform their task. And there was the non-registration of the Artillery to aid in the all important measures of surprise. I did not, therefore, fully concur with Bradford, nor did I like being without some sort of reserve. I felt, however, there was a great deal in what Bradford said, and therefore, I decided that at any rate I would go some of the way with his idea, in fact I decided to ' chance my arm ' and so I gave him instructions to keep moving forward, and directly the leading Brigades had gained their initial success (which we hoped for and anticipated with a certain amount of confidence) that the 186th Brigade should push through. It was taking a bit of a risk, but if it came off it was well worth it. As a matter of fact it did come off and had a tremendous effect on the fortunes of the day alone, because Bradford was a born leader and led his Brigade with conspicuous success."

[2] The number of Tanks to be employed on the whole front from Gonnelieu to Havrincourt was 420.

the Staff of the Division.[1] The day of attack was fixed for the 20th November and Zero hour at 6.20 a.m.

Once the scheme of operations was issued a period of intense activity prevailed. Up to 18th November the 36th (Ulster) Division was holding the Havrincourt sector, but as soon as the general scheme of operations had been decided the Ulstermen were informed of the requirements of the 62nd Division, in extra accommodation and Headquarters. Very thoroughly the 36th Division carried out the additional work imposed upon it. A large amount of extra accommodation in the villages was constructed, "shacks" for three battalions were put up in Havrincourt Wood and several Company Headquarters dug-outs were enlarged to form Battalion Battle Headquarters. The 62nd Divisional R.E. were not available for the work, as they were at work on the road and communications, but too much praise cannot be given to the 36th Division, who so loyally carried out the work of preparing extra accommodation for the assaulting troops of the West Riding Division. For all this work had to be done at night-time in order to conceal from the enemy any outward signs of an impending attack. With the exception of the formation of Brigade dumps for ammunition, bombs, etc., near Brigade Headquarters, of a Divisional ammunition dump at Ruyaulcourt, and the making of tracks through Havrincourt Wood, no other preparations of the area were made. A tremendous amount of work had to be done before the artillery would be ready. With gun positions to find and prepare for twenty batteries, General Anderson, the C.R.A., and his gunners set to work cautiously to select positions for his five brigades, at ranges of from 2,000 to 2,500 yards from the enemy's front line. Along the northern exits of Havrincourt Wood ran a road (Hubert Road) and here the majority of the guns were to be located. The whole country was, however, in full view of the enemy and the task was anything but easy. When the enemy had retired through Havrincourt Wood in April he had cut down the trees in that part of the wood through which ran Hubert Road. Throughout the summer a lot of scrub had grown up in the clearing and, on a certain night, a screen formed of twigs and bushes was

[1] Amongst the official records of the Division are many closely-typed sheets of foolscap dealing with the Battle of Cambrai. Pages and pages of most minute instructions for all units of the Division show how carefully all preparations were made for this important Battle. But it is only possible to give a précis of the most vital orders and to outline briefly the general scheme of operations, which so far as the Division was concerned actually took place between the 20th and 23rd November. On the latter date the Division was relieved and for a few days passed into reserve to refit and reorganize.

erected for a distance of 2 miles along the edge of the wood nearest the enemy. The astonishing thing was that when morning broke the enemy did not notice that the road, hitherto visible, had suddenly disappeared from view. And for nearly a fortnight work was carried out behind this screen of twigs and bushes without the enemy having the slightest suspicion that anything unusual was taking place.[1] The positions were marked, ammunition recesses and telephone pits dug, shelters for the gun detachments constructed, gun platforms prepared, " O.P.'s" and Brigade Headquarters selected, huge dumps for ammunition formed, all without the slightest interruption from the enemy. Each 18-pounder had 700 rounds allotted to it, and each 4·5" Howitzer 450 rounds. As the work proceeded it was carefully camouflaged. It was not very often that the elements favoured the Allies, but fortunately during this period of preparation the weather was cloudy and misty and the enemy's aircraft were unable to detect any change in the area from which the attack was to be launched.

From Fosseux, where the Division was still in training, parties of officers and N.C.O.'s made visits to the trenches and the area over which the assaulting troops were to go forward. These reconnaissances were of the greatest value, for they disclosed the enormous strength of the positions to be assaulted on the 20th.

SEE MAP NO. 6.

Since the beginning of the British offensive in April the enemy had greatly repaired and extended the Hindenburg Line, which consisted of three main systems of resistance.

The first of these three systems constituted part of the Hindenburg Line proper and ran in a general north-westerly direction for a distance of 6 miles from the Canal de l'Escaut at Bancourt to Havrincourt. Thence it turned sharply north skirting the line of the Canal du Nord for a distance of 4 miles to Masnières. In front of the Hindenburg main line strong forward positions had been constructed chiefly at La Vacquerie and in the north-eastern corner of Havrincourt Wood. Behind it lay the second and third systems, known as the Hindenburg Support Line and the Beaurevoir, Masnières and Marquion Lines.

Opposite the 62nd Division, the enemy's defences were especially strong; Havrincourt itself was a maze of trenches (portion of the Hindenburg Main Line) running south-east, west and north-west of

[1] Some idea of the care taken to prevent the enemy obtaining any clue to the impending attack may be gathered from the fact that officers and N.C.O.'s of the 51st (Highland) Division, who had been detailed to attack on the right of the 62nd, when making their reconnaissances wore trousers instead of kilts.

The German Defences

the village. These trenches were protected by broad belts of thick wire entanglements, in places four lines deep. In the front-line trenches and in shell-holes in the midst of the wire entanglements, machine-guns in profusion were established.

From just west of Havrincourt to Moeuvres, the Canal du Nord (the bed of which was dry and in places 100 feet deep) ran through the Main Line of the enemy's defences and provided him with fine shelter from shell-fire. Into the western bank of the Canal he had dug very deep dug-outs, ample protection against the heaviest bombardments.

South of Havrincourt the German main line was protected by an outpost line which ran along the top of Havrincourt Wood[1] through Wigan Copse to a destroyed bridge which once spanned the canal, west of the village.

If the nature of the enemy's defences is considered side by side with the fact that no previous wire-cutting operations or bombardment of the enemy's trenches were permitted before "Zero" day, it will be seen how great was the reliance placed upon the Tanks to crush the thick belts of entanglement and tear a way through which the infantry could pass and complete the work of the steel monsters. The short but intensive training which the infantry of the Division had carried out in conjunction with the Tanks, had given them unbounded confidence in their new comrades.

12TH/13TH NOVEMBER

The gunners were the first to concentrate—the 310th and 312th Brigades arriving in the neighbourhood of Beaulencourt on the night 12th/13th November. The following night, Barastre, where the wagon lines during the attack were to be, was reached. During the advance to the battle area the most elaborate precautions were taken to prevent the enemy obtaining any idea of the impending operations. By day the roads were deserted and bare of life, for the guns with their *personnel* were hidden in the various big woods which are dotted about that part of the country. At night, however, the roads were crowded almost to overflowing with long columns of heavy guns, drawn by caterpillars, transport, etc.[2]

[1] "Wood" was a misnomer, for the Germans had felled all the trees in the northern portion of Havrincourt Wood.

[2] "One of the principal reasons why the enemy was deceived was that all the transport coming North carried lights and we took care that a good deal of transport, most of it empty, should be coming North with lights for the week before the Battle; whereas all the transport going south carried no lights. We were very anxious that the enemy should think we were thinning our line and there is no doubt that he did think so."

Lieut.-General Sir W. Braithwaite.

12TH/13TH NOVEMBER.

A maze of light railway had been put down in Havrincourt Wood, and was constantly in use during the dark hours.

On the night of the 17th/18th, the 312th Brigade, R.F.A.[1] manned its gun positions, and on the following night the 310th, 77th, 73rd, 93rd and 153rd Brigades did likewise.

Meanwhile the infantry had left Fosseux, and marching also by night in order to conceal their movements, reached the concentration area west of Havrincourt, on the night of 16th/17th November. On the following night the two leading Brigades (185th on the right and 187th on the left) took over their battle fronts with the exception of the outpost line which the 36th Division continued to hold so as to avoid any chance of the enemy gaining identification of the relief. The wisdom of this procedure became almost immediately apparent, for during the night the enemy raided one of the posts and captured two men belonging to the Ulster Division; thus, the only identification he obtained was "normal."

Intense excitement prevailed throughout the 18th and 19th; for the enemy still gave no signs that he had any knowledge of the coming operations. But apparently he had discerned nothing abnormal, and not a stone was left unturned to deceive him. Even "D.A.D.O.S." played an important part in the deception, for in his diary is the following entry:—"Received instructions to select site at Barastre, to leave all except urgent stores at Fosseux, to take only one tent and issue stores during darkness."

19TH/20TH NOVEMBER.

But at last "Y/Z night" (19th/20th) arrived and when darkness fell all ranks of the Division made ready for the great assault at 6.20 a.m. on the following morning.

Along tracks, through Havrincourt Wood, which had been previously prepared and taped, the 185th and 187th Brigades moved up to their assembly positions.

From the advanced "Tankodrome" in the south-west corner of the Wood, the Tanks following the white tapes laid for their directions nosed their ungainly way forward to their lying-up places, roughly 1,000 yards from the enemy's outpost line; they were in position by midnight.

On the back of each Tank was a huge fascine resting on a giant pair of arms. An ingenious contrivance provided means by which the fascine could be dropped into an unusually deep trench across which the Tank could pursue its way, without having to dip its nose

---

[1] Lieut.-Colonel Lough, commanding 312th Brigade, R.F.A., left on the 17th and was succeeded on the 19th by Lieut.-Colonel A. G. Eden.

into the trench with the possibility of getting stuck. The wire-cutting Tanks were in the front line.

19TH/20TH NOVEMBER.

At 1 a.m. it really looked as if the enemy had discovered everything, for his guns suddenly opened a heavy bombardment and continued pouring shells upon the front line and Oxford Valley until 6 a.m.

" The night of the 19th," said the C.R.A., " was a very anxious time, and will long be remembered by all who took part in the battle. It was impossible to tell whether the enemy had any suspicions of what was in store for him. He might even know all about it, and this was the more possible, as he had made a raid two nights before the battle and had captured one or two of our men. There was a chance that he might have wormed some information out of them, for an uneducated man may often give away valuable information quite innocently, out of pure ignorance or indiscretion. If he did know, the enemy might have wrecked the attack before it began, by bombarding the long line of guns, which had the most definite orders on no account to fire a round till 6.20 a.m., when the attack was to be launched. As it happened the Boche showed great uneasiness and fired very heavily during the night, though fortunately not on any vital places. We listened to the firing in great suspense, and watched the flashes of the shells bursting apparently very near our line of guns, but one could get no information of attack, for no telephones were allowed until the moment of attack, lest indiscreet things might be said and tapped by the enemy's listening apparatus. At 5.45 a.m. there was a particularly furious burst of firing which died down at a few minutes before six and was succeeded by a dead silence, during which one could fancy one heard the anxious beating of fifty thousand hearts. Did the Boche know? Had he some infernal surprise for us?"

Zero hour drew nearer and still the enemy gave no sign of unusual activity.

Along the front of the Division the two leading infantry brigades were drawn up in their assembly positions from left to right, as follows:

187th Infantry Brigade.		185th Infantry Brigade.	
Brigadier-General R. O'B. Taylor.		Brigadier-General Viscount Hampden.	
2/5th K.O.Y.L.I. (Lt.-Col. B. J. Barton)	2/4th K.O.Y.L.I. (Lt.-Col. R. E. Power)	2/6th W. Yorks. (Lt.-Col. C. H. Hoare)	2/8th W. Yorks. (Leeds Rifles). (Lt.-Col. A. H. James)
2/4th York & Lancs. R. (Lt.-Col. A. E. Maitland)	2/5th York. & Lancs. R. (Lt.-Col. L. H. P. Hart)	2/5th W. Yorks. (Lt.-Col. R. H. Waddy)	2/7th W. Yorks. (Lt.-Col. C. K. James)

19TH/20TH NOVEMBER.

The 186th Infantry Brigade (Brigadier-General R. B. Bradford, V.C.[1]) was disposed in artillery formation facing N.E. in Havrincourt Wood : 2/6th (Major R. Coombe) and 2/4th (Lieut.-Col. H. F. P. Nash) Duke of Wellington's Regiment, and 185th T.M.B. in depth S.E. of the Shropshire Spur Road, and the 2/5th (Lieut.-Col. T. D. Best) and 2/7th (Lieut.-Col. F. S. Thackeray)[2] Duke of Wellington's Regiment in depth N.W. of the same road : the Brigade was to advance through the 185th and 187th Brigades after they had captured the first and second objectives.

The 36th (Ulster) Division was on the left of the 62nd and the 51st (Highland) Division on the right.

The enemy's troops in the Havrincourt sector consisted of the 84th Infantry Regiment of the 54th Division and the 384th Landwehr Infantry Regiment of the 20th Landwehr Division. The former held Havrincourt and the line south of the railway to the Canal du Nord ; the latter north of the railway line of Canal to the Slag Heap inclusive. Each Regiment[3] had two Battalions in the front and support lines and one Battalion in Reserve, *i.e.*, at Noyelles and Containg respectively. Each Battalion disposed two Companies in the front and outpost line and two Companies in support. The 107th Division, which had been brought from Russia, and had arrived on 18th/19th November was east of Cambrai.

Thus at 6 a.m. on the morning of the 20th November, 1917, the attacking troops were ready to fall upon their unsuspecting enemies : and the Tanks were on their trial.

" We were expecting a continuation of the attack in Flanders, and on the French Front when, on the 20th November, we were surprised by a fresh blow at Cambrai."[4]

[1] Brigadier-General R. B. Bradford, V.C., M.C., took over command of the 186th Infantry Brigade from Brigadier-General F. F. Hill, C.B., C.M.G., D.S.O., on 10th November. This gallant young officer was but twenty-five years of age when he became a Brigadier.

[2] Lt.-Col. F. S. Thackeray assumed command of the 2/7th Battalion Duke of Wellington's Regiment on 6th November, *vice* Lt.-Col. F. G. Chamberlin.

[3] A German Regiment consisted of three Battalions.

[4] Ludendorff.

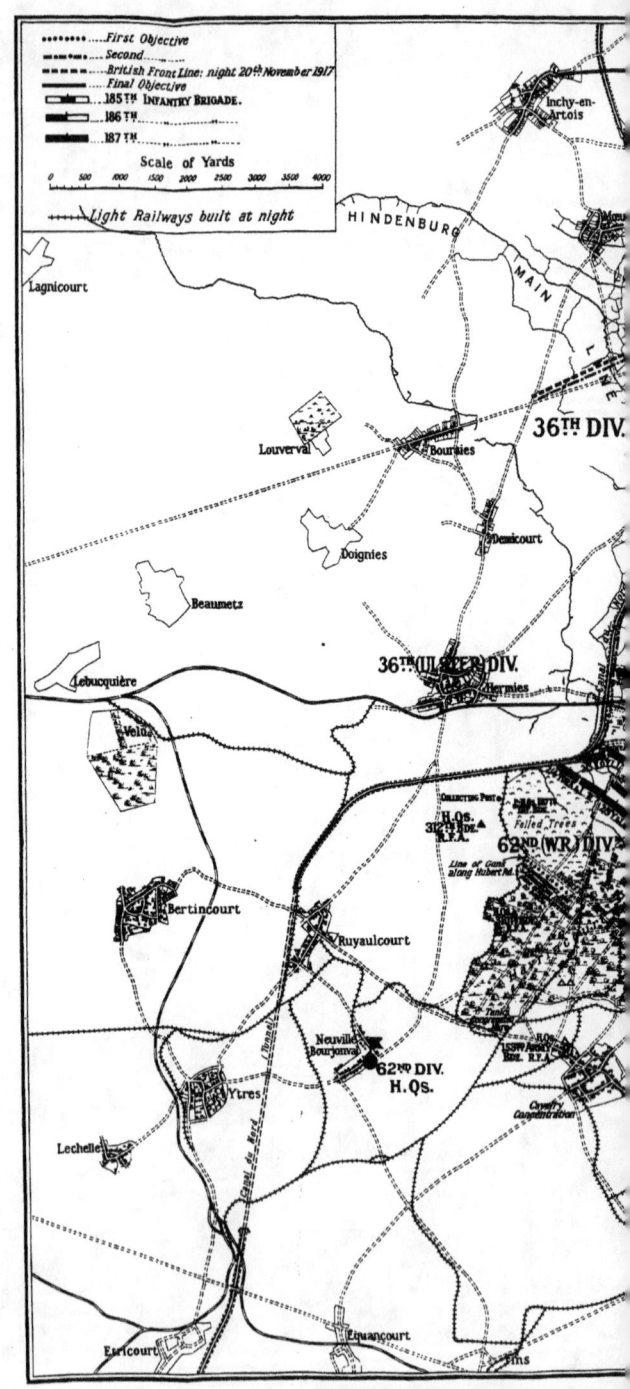

THE BATTLE OF CAMBRAI, 1917, II. THE CAPTU[RE...]
62ND DIVISION ON 20[...]

of Havrincourt and Graincourt by the
November, 1917.

Chapter IX.

1917.

THE BATTLE OF CAMBRAI (II.)

"We stood in a little group outside the hut which served for our Headquarters and fixed our eyes on the long grey line of the road along the edge of which the guns lay waiting."

Brigadier-General A. T. Anderson.

AT 6-18 a.m. there was 'not a sound.'" Only in the valley the Tanks were emitting volumes of smoke, like impatient chargers straining to go forward. Two more minutes and then the quiet stillness of the morning was rent by a sudden tremendous roar; the grey sky grew red as the guns poured destruction and death upon the enemy's forward trenches. The barrage was timed to keep well in front of the Tanks, to ensure that the latter were not delayed in their advance. The field guns used a proportion of smoke shell, whilst a regular smoke barrage fell on the eastern exits of Havrincourt Village and on the Flesquières Ridge. Several strong points between the enemy's front and outpost lines were engaged by the Heavy and Medium Trench Mortars, and the latter continued firing until the Tanks approached the points. The M.G. Companies also fired a barrage in front of the assaulting troops.

20TH Nov.

SEE MAP No. 7.

The four Battalions of infantry in the front line had been ordered to allow the Tanks approximately 100 yards for each five minutes.

As the barrage fell the Tanks nosed their way forward, the wire-crushers leading. Three minutes later, one was reported going round the Tip and the enemy's shells began to fall in Trescault Valley, but at present his retaliation was only slight. At 6-25 six Tanks were observed going down behind Femy Scrub.

C Company of the 2/7th West Yorks., which had been detailed to capture the enemy's outpost line in order that the 2/8th West Yorks. might pass through to the first objective, pressed forward in rear of the tanks and quickly overcame the opposition

[1] The action is described from right to left.

20TH Nov. of the enemy's advanced troops. Here 100 prisoners and four machine-guns were taken, the " Company " after " mopping up " the area, forming itself into platoons. The four Companies of the 2/8th Battalion passed through immediately and half-an-hour after " Zero " had reached the main Hindenburg Line. The Tanks had done their work well! The enemy, completely cowed, offered but little resistance; the wire in front of his lines had been torn and twisted and broken and his troops had, for the most part, temporarily lost their powers of defence, and although a few of them were shot down or bayoneted or bombed in their dug-outs, having refused to come out, eighty surrendered and six more machine-guns and a trench mortar were captured by the Battalion. According to the scheme of operations A Company took over this sector, while the three remaining Companies, headed by C, followed the Tanks to the next objective.

The leading Company found Triangle Wood occupied, and as the enemy showed fight and the left flanking Battalion of the 51st Division had not yet arrived, an outflanking movement was necessary. A machine-gun which was causing a great deal of trouble was rushed from both flanks and captured, and twenty-nine prisoners were also taken. D and B Companies now advanced on to the final Battalion Objective—the Blue Line.

On the right B came under fire from the direction of Ribecourt and suffered some forty casualties. D on the left had lost all its officers before reaching " T " Wood. But the senior sergeant at once took command and led the Company towards the final objective. On reaching " T " Wood another hostile machine gun was unpleasantly active, but the crew was bombed and scattered, two of the gunners being bayoneted. On passing " T " Wood two platoons of the Company were temporarily held up by fire from a concrete emplacement to the left of a small copse. In the vicinity twenty of the enemy were killed and three officers and sixty other ranks captured. Considerable opposition was next met with in Chapel Trench, the enemy being encountered in large numbers. Many were killed and 110 more prisoners taken. At 1.0 p.m., under orders from 185th Brigade Headquarters, the Battalion assembled in Chapel Trench and consolidated the position, C Company forming a defensive flank on the railway embankment 400 yards N.E. of the Trench.

Meanwhile the attack of the 2/6th West Yorks. had not gone with that clockwork regularity which had attended the advance of the 2/8th Battalion. One Company of the 2/5th West Yorks. assisted by six Tanks, had been detailed to overcome the enemy's outpost line before the 2/6th passed through to the first objective. Two of the Tanks, however, which should have moved, one up The Glade and the other down Trescault Valley road, did not arrive. In consequence one platoon of the 2/5th Battalion did not attack the point on the right of the 2/6th and, although the remaining Companies of the latter Battalion were able to advance towards the Main Hindenburg Line with little difficulty, C Company on the right became involved in heavy fighting with the enemy's strong point. However, with the assistance of the Stokes mortars, which did excellent work, the latter was eventually captured, though not before all but one platoon commander of C Company had become casualties, as well as many other ranks.

20TH Nov.

"A" Company of the 2/6th, admirably led by Capt. H. Moorhouse, had pushed through the Hindenburg Main Line unassisted by Tanks and had established itself along the line of the road running N.N.W. from the Grand Ravine to the S.E. corner of Havrincourt, thence northwards along the outskirts of the village. From this point, however, the Company could not advance, heavy machinegun and rifle fire being encountered from the village, until B had come up on its left. But by 9-30 a.m. B, reinforced by D Company, and with the assistance of a Tank, entered the village. Havrincourt Park and the Chateau were still sheltering numbers of the enemy, who kept the Hindenburg Main Line, from which they had been driven, continually harassed by machine-gun fire. The Brigade Major and the Brigade Intelligence Officer of the 185th Infantry Brigade organized a party to clear up the situation, which resulted in the capture of another 100 prisoners, the village being finally cleared by 10-15 a.m.

The 2/6th West Yorks. were now on the Blue Line—the first objective—having on their right flank the 2/8th Battalion.

In the meantime the two leading Battalions of the 187th Infantry Brigade (2/4th K.O.Y.L.I. on the right and the 2/5th K.O.Y.L.I. on the left) had similarly swept forward in line with the advance of the 185th Brigade.

At "Zero" the Tanks which had been detailed for the 2/4th K.O.Y.L.I. were not in position in front of the infantry. General Taylor, to provide for all possible contingencies, had issued orders that, Tanks or no Tanks, the Battalions were to advance on their objectives at Zero hour and so, without waiting for their arrival, the

20TH Nov. Battalion went forward as the barrage fell on the enemy's trenches. The Tanks, however, followed and soon caught up the advancing infantry. One Tank developing engine trouble dropped out, but the 2/4th K.O.Y.L.I. pressed on, over-running the enemy's outpost line, the garrison of which apparently had small stomach for a fight, as little resistance was encountered. Heavy machine-gun fire, however, came from the right flank, the Lake and Havrincourt Park concealing nests of machine-guns. Boggart Hole offered trouble, but the Tanks literally fell on it and a trench mortar and two machine-guns were captured. Snowden was then dealt with. One of the Tanks belonging to the left Battalion (2/5th K.O.Y.L.I.) had been detailed to deal with Etna, a crater, and an enemy strong point. But the Tank did not arrive, so the left platoon of the 2/4th K.O.Y.L.I., with two platoons of the 2/5th set out to capture this stronghold unaided. Working forward through the remains of Dean Copse the Yorkshiremen rushed on Etna and another machine-gun and seventeen prisoners were added to the list of captures.

Meanwhile enemy machine-guns firing from Chateau Wood on the right continued to cause casualties. The right Company of the second wave of the 2/4th entered the Wood and after stiff fighting took seventy prisoners and two machine-guns. Vesuvius, another crater turned by the enemy into a formidable strong point, was next attacked. The flanking platoons of both the 2/4th and 2/5th K.O.Y.L.I. rushed this point, taking two machine-guns, a trench mortar and fourteen more prisoners. The two front Companies of the 2/4th were by now in the German front line, the two rear Companies therefore passed through them and attacked the left half of the village of Havrincourt.[1] From the roofs and top windows of the houses, snipers fired down on the advancing troops, but the latter dashed into the buildings and soon this annoyance ceased. A hostile machine-gunner with more bravery than discretion had mounted his gun in the square in the centre of the village ; he was quickly dealt with and the Companies pressed on to their objective, reaching the Blue Line at 9-0 a.m. In all the 2/4th K.O.Y.L.I. had captured some 200 prisoners, ten machine-guns and three trench mortars. The 2/5th K.O.Y.L.I. had been ordered to advance at Zero plus 15 minutes. But the Tanks which were to accompany (or rather precede) the Battalion had not arrived, and the two front Companies set out without them. The Tanks, however, followed

---

[1] It should be remembered that the left flanking Battalion of the 185th Brigade was also attacking the right half of the village simultaneously.

The Slag Heap near Havrincourt on 20th November, 1917:
British Troops moving up and German Prisoners being sent back under Escort.

Face p. 82.

on behind, and here also they were able to reach the German front
line behind the infantry.

20TH Nov.

After passing Wigan Copse, the first German trench in the Sunken road was found to be strongly held. Nothing daunted, Captain Lynn (on the left), who, with Lieut. James, on the previous night, had reconnoitred the German wire,[1] in spite of the non-arrival of the Tanks, led his Company through the wire into the trench. Grim work followed. Lynn himself accounted for four Germans, whilst his subaltern (James) was instrumental in killing no less than eighteen of the enemy. None of the enemy escaped from the trench, all being either killed, wounded or taken prisoner. The two rear Companies of the 2/5th K.O.Y.L.I. now passed through, and though considerable opposition was experienced from various posts and trenches, the Blue Line was reached by 8-15 a.m. with little further loss. Besides killing a very large number of the enemy, this Battalion had also taken 200 prisoners, eight machine-guns and four trench mortars.

Thus the whole of the Blue Line along the front of the Division was completely captured—the Battalions holding it, being from right to left—2/8th West Yorks., 2/6th West Yorks., 2/4th K.O.Y.L.I. and 2/5th K.O.Y.L.I.[2]

The advance to the Brown Line was the next phase in the operations, for which the 2/7th and 2/5th West Yorks. (185th Infantry Brigade) and the 2/5th York and Lancaster and 2/4th Battalion (the Hallamshires) of the same Regiment (187th Infantry Brigade) had been detailed.

At 7-5 a.m. the 2/7th and 2/5th West Yorkshiremen (less one Company each, which had been detailed to deal with the enemy's posts on the flanks of the 2/8th and 2/6th West Yorks.), moved off from their assembly places in Trescault Trench. They passed through the Hindenburg Main Line, which had been captured in the first stride, and assembled on the road below " T " Wood. From

---

[1] They did this on their own initiative in case anything happened to the Tanks. Not only did they reconnoitre their route, but they cut portions of the wire and actually left tapes to guide them the next morning. This very gallant action showed great enterprise and a very real appreciation of what might be the situation, and indeed what actually proved to be the case, for their forethought was of inestimable value on the morning of the attack.

[2] There are discrepancies in the times given in the official reports as to the hour of occupying the whole of the Blue Line; 8-20 a.m. is the earliest time given.

20TH NOV. this position the advance to the Brown Line was begun. The 2/7th West Yorks. reached the forming-up place without much difficulty, but the 2/5th Battalion appears to have been held up on the way by machine-gun fire from the direction of Havrincourt, which at that time (it was between 7-30 and 8-0 a.m.) had not been fully captured.

Eventually, however, both Battalions, preceded by Tanks, detailed for the second objective, left their assembly positions at (so the Battalion Diary of the 2/7th West Yorks. states) Zero plus 145 minutes, *i.e.*, 8-45 a.m. "A" Company, the leading Company of the 2/7th, passing through the Blue Line, captured and cleared the area north of the Railway; B and D Companies following behind and passing through A, next assaulted the Hindenburg Support Line, which was speedily captured.[1] C Company (which had already had one tussle with the enemy, having captured his outpost line in front of the 2/8th West Yorks.), now passed through B and D Companies and established a post in the Brown Line at K.17, a central. Some 200 prisoners and machine-guns were captured in this operation.

On the left of the 2/7th, the 2/5th West Yorks. had, as stated, encountered opposition from enemy machine-guns. First, the unpleasant "zip-zip" of machine-guns came from Femy Scrub; they were silenced by rifle grenades. Next, a gun in the northern end of "T" Wood caused trouble, but this was rushed with the bayonet, a Tank joining in the fight. A hostile machine-gun mounted in a house in Havrincourt now held up the advance, but here again a Tank took a hand, firing into the house with its 6-pounder; another Tank crushed out of action a gun with its team, which had been firing from the trench north of the Blue Line. Finally an enemy machine-gun, firing from the northern edge of Havrincourt village (and which had been missed by the Tanks) was first brought under the concentrated fire of four Lewis guns and then rushed by a party of riflemen. When these several obstacles had been cleared up the 2/5th advanced on the Brown Line, which was captured with little opposition and seventy prisoners taken. "The advance of this Battalion" said the official narrative, "was very well carried out" ......also it should be noted that, owing to the unavoidable delay of the 2/6th West Yorks. in and about Havrincourt, it fell to the lot of the 2/5th West Yorks. to capture part of the first objective (Blue Line), as well as the second objective (Brown Line).

[1] The portion allotted to the Battalion, of course.

The two rear Battalions of the 187th Infantry Brigade, 2/5th York and Lancaster Regiment on the right and the 2/4th York and Lancaster Regiment (Hallamshires) on the left, moved forward from their forming up trenches at 7-0 a.m. The 2/5th York and Lancaster had a very difficult manœuvre to perform; it had to advance on the western side of Havrincourt Village, skirt round the north-west end of it and then advance north again.

The two Battalions were timed to start from the Blue Line at 8-35 a.m., but by this time Havrincourt had not been cleared of the enemy. The 2/5th York and Lancaster, therefore, soon came under machine-gun fire and casualties were appreciable. But nothing could daunt the spirits of these men; the Battalion swept on and by 10-0 a.m. had captured the whole of its objective, together with 300 prisoners, five machine-guns and three trench mortars.

The Hallamshires (2/4th York and Lancaster) met with but little opposition, excepting from isolated riflemen who were speedily dealt with, and by 10-20 a.m. they also were consolidating their position on the Brown Line, having captured in their advance about 450 prisoners, six machine-guns and five trench mortars. There was, however, a large amount of " mopping up " to do, for once the enemy's trenches were entered the men did not wait for the assistance of the Tanks, but rushed ahead and in many instances, so impetuous were they that they almost ran into their own barrage. " The whole attack " states the official narrative, " was carried out with astonishing dash and all ranks behaved splendidly. The Tanks rendered valuable assistance in wire cutting and in dealing with strong points."

While the capture and consolidation of the Blue and Brown Lines was proceeding the 186th Infantry Brigade had already left its assembly position to pass through and complete the capture of the Divisional objectives. From the condition of his troops it was evident that the enemy was very badly shaken; this had been anticipated and the original orders of the 186th Infantry Brigade, to pass through as soon as the Brown Line was captured, were varied. In the revised scheme of operations[1] it was decided to dispense with the plan of keeping a Brigade in reserve, once the leading Brigades had gained an initial success, and to push the 186th Infantry Brigade forward as soon as reports were received from the leading Brigades that they had made a satisfactory start.

[1] *Vide* previous footnote *re* Brig.-General Bradford.

20TH Nov. "In fact it was realized that this was no time for half-measures."[2]

The 186th Infantry Brigade, therefore, was to keep moving gradually forward so that when the Brown Line was captured, it would be ready to advance in line with the 51st Division to the capture of the third objective. Two Brigades of artillery and the 201st Machine-Gun Company were attached to the Brigade to cover the advance. In addition all the surviving Tanks from the operations of the 185th and 187th Infantry Brigades were to assist the 186th Brigade.

The four Battalions of the Duke of Wellington's Regiment, forming the Brigade, spent a comfortable night in billets in Bertrancourt, and at 5-20 a.m. on the 20th moved forward to their assembly positions in Havrincourt Wood. At 8 a.m. the Brigade was assembled ready to move forward on receipt of orders. All four Battalions were disposed in artillery formation facing north-east. The 2/6th and 2/4th Duke of Wellington's and 186th Trench Mortar Battery were in depth south-east of the Shropshire Spur road, and the 2/5th and 2/7th Duke of Wellington's Regiment were in depth north-west of the same road. The 213th Machine-Gun Company was already in action supporting the attack of the leading Brigades by barrage fire from near Butlers Cross.

At 9 a.m. Brigadier-General Bradford, V.C., moved his Brigade forward. Battalions were, however, warned that pockets of Germans were still holding out and might be met with during the advance. The 2/6th Duke of Wellington's, followed by the 2/4th and 2/7th Battalions (in that order) moved off along the Shropshire Spur road and by " T " Wood ; the 2/5th Battalion moved *via* Oxford Road and to the west of Havrincourt Village. All Battalions moved at first by Companies in columns of fours, deploying subsequently into artillery formation.

The 2/6th Battalion after leaving " T " Wood came under shell fire from Flesquières, which had not been captured by the 51st Division. But in spite of this all four Companies continued the advance across country to their forming-up positions in the Brown Line (from the Hindenburg Support Line to the Canal near Lock No. 7). At 11 a.m. the Battalions attacked the enemy. One Company (A), was employed in clearing the ground between the Hindenburg Support Line and the Canal, both being inclusive. The remaining three Companies, B, C and D, advanced astride the Hindenburg Support Line, each Company

[2] Divisional Narrative.

advancing on the "leap-frog" principle, being allotted an objective about 600 yards in depth. Heavy machine-gun fire from a point in the Hindenburg Support Line, about 500 yards north of the Brown Line, held up the attack for a while, but on the arrival first of the 2/7th Battalion on the right of the 2/6th, and a little later the 2/5th in the area of Hughes Switch and Support Trenches, the 2/6th pressed on and bore down all resistance. By 2 p.m. the whole of the objectives of the 2/6th Battalion were captured, together with two officers and 165 other ranks, one battery of 5·9 in. Howitzers, one battery of 77 mm. guns and eleven machine-guns.

On the left of the 2/6th Duke of Wellington's the 2/5th Battalion marched down the Oxford Road and crossing the old Blue Line approached the Chateau Wood and Havrincourt Village. On nearing the grounds and road near the Chateau the Battalion came under heavy machine-gun and rifle fire from an enemy strong point which had not been "mopped up." The gallant Commanding Officer (Lieut-Colonel T. A. D. Best) was killed and three other officers and a considerable number of men became casualties. The enemy's strong point was, however, located by Captain Goodall's Company (D) which, dashing forward, speedily put the Germans out of action, capturing one officer and fifty-eight other ranks. This Company also rescued a Corps Intelligence Officer and a wounded sergeant of the K.O.Y.L.I., previously taken by the enemy. The Battalion then reorganized and continued the advance, D Company still leading, towards its forming-up line, *i.e.*, north of 2/6th Battalion. But again opposition was encountered. Heavy machine-gun and rifle fire met the Battalion from the direction of K.4 d.1.5. where an enemy strong point evidently existed. A subaltern took forward a platoon to deal with this point and very soon came upon a miniature battle in full progress. A Tank had "ditched" in a particularly deep part of the Hindenburg Support Line, near the enemy's strong point. The Tank was being bombed fiercely by the enemy who, however, was unable to leave his strong point, as the Tank commander and his crew were defending the Tank from the outside. The platoon then worked round the point, rushed it and killed five Germans and captured three more; the rest of the garrison ran off towards Graincourt, but being caught by Lewis-gun fire before reaching the village, again suffered casualties.

Once more the Battalion reorganized, this time on its actual forming-up line, for the attack northwards, *i.e.*, the Sunken Road

20TH Nov: in K.4 c. At this point the Brigadier arrived "to see how we were getting on," recorded a private diary.

Preceded by Tanks, D Company of the 2/5th then attacked Kangaroo Alley, which was captured without much opposition and consolidated. The remaining Companies, A, B and C, then passed through D Company and advanced towards their objective, the enemy's trenches north of and running parallel with the Cambrai —Bapaume Road. B Company had a stiff fight with an enemy strong point, but it fell eventually and two more machine-guns, two officers and forty-nine other ranks were captured. C Company captured a strong point near Lock 6, taking two officers and sixty-four other ranks. The remainder of the garrison with true Teutonic arrogance refused to leave their dug-outs; a " P " bomb was therefore thrown into it and the dug-out with its occupants was destroyed.

At dusk the 2/5th was disposed as follows : B Company on the right flank with a defensive flank down the Hindenburg Support Line, A Company in the centre and C on the left in touch with the 36th Division on the Canal Bank, D Company occupied Kangaroo Alley in support. No less than 350 prisoners, fifteen machine-guns and one trench mortar had been captured during the day, the casualties being three officers killed, one wounded, ten other ranks killed, fifty-five wounded and four missing.

Meanwhile the 2/4th and 2/7th Duke of Wellington's had advanced through the Blue and Brown Lines and had continued the successes already gained by the 2/6th and 2/5th Battalions.

The 2/4th passed the northern exits of Chapel Wood at 10 a.m., halting on the line of the railway just north of the Blue Line. Here the Battalion was delayed for half-an-hour, as the 51st Division on the right flank was held up by heavy fire from the Hindenburg Support Line just north of Flesquières. The two right Companies of the 2/4th were unable to pass the Hindenburg Support Line, but the two left Companies, screened from Flesquières by the conformation of the ground, continued to advance in touch with and slightly in rear of the 2/7th Battalion, which had pressed on past the 2/4th after the latter had halted on the line of the railway. The two left Companies, therefore, continued to press forward and only halted on nearing the village of Graincourt, to await the arrival of the remainder of the Battalion.

The two right Companies finally side-stepped into the valley (up which the two left Companies had advanced) and followed the two leading Companies towards Graincourt.

At Graincourt after the Village had been Captured: Machine Gunners cleaning and filling the Cooling Chamber of their Gun with Water.

Led by a Tank, C and D Companies (the " two left Companies ") 20TH Nov. of the 2/4th, attacked Graincourt and, though opposition was met with in the village, it was captured, with many prisoners and several guns. B Company then moved forward to attack the factory, the second objective allotted to the Battalion. It was now dark (about 5 p.m.) and as the leading platoons reached the Bapaume—Cambrai Road, a large body of marching men was heard approaching; they were obviously enemy troops. Rifle and Lewis-gun fire was, therefore, directed on the roadway with the result that fifty Germans were killed, thirty wounded and thirty captured. The Factory fell into the hands of B Company, which at once established posts in the north and north-east. Throughout the advance of C, D and B Companies, A Company of the 2/4th was kept in reserve.

Although on setting out for its assembly positions in Havrincourt Wood, it was the rear Battalion of the 186th Infantry Brigade, the 2/7th Battalion, Duke of Wellington's Regiment, as already related, passed the 2/4th Battalion when the latter was west of Flesquières. The Battalion moved directly north, but came upon the 2/6th Battalion held up in K.10 and for a while the 2/7th halted. But delays were dangerous and General Bradford, who had in the meantime arrived on the scene, ordered the 2/7th to pass through the 2/6th. This was done and all four Companies pushed on quickly in artillery formation, A and B Companies leading and C and D Companies (all four Companies in the order as given) following. Three abandoned 77 mm. guns were found in K.10 b. and as the leading Companies passed on they came under fire from two more in K.4. These guns were attacked, and with the assistance of a Tank were captured, together with one officer and fifteen other ranks. A and B now pushed on to their final objectives. B Company with its left flank on the Bapaume—Cambrai Road and A Company astride the Hindenburg Support Line, S.W. of the Factory. C and D Companies had passed on over the Bapaume—Cambrai Road, and after being delayed for some time owing to a shortage of bombs, eventually won through, capturing the Hindenburg Support Line up to the northern divisional boundary, *i.e.*, between the 36th and 62nd Divisions.

This portion of the enemy's line was a mass of dug-outs and the clearing operations took a considerable time and were not completed until about 10 p.m. At that time C Company was on the right in touch with the right flank of the 2/5th Battalion. D came

20TH Nov. next, with its right flank resting on the Bapaume—Cambrai Road, and its left in touch with the right of C Company in E.22 d.

Touch between Battalions and Companies was maintained all along the front line by means of patrols.

About noon two squadrons of King Edward's Horse had reached Havrincourt and moved forward with the intention of advancing between Flesquières and Graincourt, on Anneux. But having safeguarded the right flank of the 62nd Division, as it advanced the cavalry could do nothing until Graincourt was captured, all attempts to advance being met by a withering machine-gun fire. On the capture of Graincourt, however, the cavalry supported by one Company of the 2/6th Duke of Wellington's, was sent forward to capture Anneux, but they were held up and were withdrawn to Graincourt for the night.

Thus when night had fallen on the 20th November, all three Infantry Brigades had won through to their allotted objectives and had achieved what, at that period, must be regarded as a remarkable performance,[1] having advanced 4½ miles from their original front,[2] over-running two powerful German systems of defence and gaining possession of two villages.[3] Everywhere the attack had gone splendidly, the Tanks were a great success and the period of combined training early in November had produced just that degree of co-operation between infantry and Tanks essential to success.

During the day when the right flank of his Division, from the Hindenburg Support Line to Graincourt, was exposed (owing to the 51st Division being held up in front of Flesquières) General Braithwaite had taken grave risks; but they were fully justified. He who risks nothing gains nothing! Undoubtedly the success of the 62nd Division was due to careful preparation, bold leading and the method of attack; the "attack in depth" had been followed and had once more proved its value. The attack as ordered had gone like clockwork and at the close of the first day of the battle General Braithwaite and his Staff had reason to be proud of their achievement in conducting operations which had resulted in such brilliant

---

[1] "This attack of the 62nd West Riding Division constitutes a brilliant achievement in which the troops concerned completed an advance of 4½ miles from their original front, over-running two German systems of defence and gaining possession of three villages."—*Official Despatches*.

[2] The advance made by the Division on 20th November was not only the record up to that time, but it remained the record advance in battle up to the end of the war.

[3] Anneux was captured, not on 20th, but on the 21st November.

success. The surprise of the enemy was complete and although he would, of course, hurry up reinforcements (such indeed were actually due to arrive by the morning of the 21st) he had nevertheless received a hard knock. " We were expecting a continuation of the attack in Flanders and on the French front," said Ludendorff, " when on the 20th November we were surprised by a fresh blow at Cambrai."

Throughout the day there were many instances of the benefit which had been derived from the period of training spent near Arras. It will be remembered that initiative in the attack had been one of the lessons to be learned, in a necessarily long programme of instruction, but none was more necessary or more thoroughly imbibed or bore better fruit. One instance is sufficient : D Company of the 2/8th West Yorks. had followed immediately behind B Company of the same Battalion at " Zero " hour. On B gaining its first objective, D passed through, going towards the second objective. Almost immediately the Company commander was wounded and handed over his Company to a subaltern. A little later the subaltern also was wounded and handed over command of the Company to a sergeant who throughout the day led the men with gallantry, displaying fine leadership. The men " carried on " just as splendidly under this N.C.O. as under their own company commander,[1] and by the end of the day had captured over 110 prisoners and many machine-guns.

Hitherto only the actions of the infantrymen, as they swept on, first through the jungle of tossed and broken barbed wire, and later across the well-defended Hindenburg Support Line, have been described, but, however bravely the men in the front line fought, they could not have made such splendid progress had they not been supported by machine-guns, trench mortars and light and heavy artillery. There was no preliminary bombardment before " Zero," nor had any of the guns registered on the enemy's positions, nevertheless the barrage was perfect and was admirably timed so as to keep clear of the Tanks as the latter preceded the infantry.[2]

[1] Two days later this same N.C.O. again commanded the Company, his officer being wounded.

[2] The following amusing story is told by Sir Walter Braithwaite :—
" After the battle I asked a private in 187th Brigade, what he thought of the barrage and he replied :
" ' It was perfect : just in the right place. *I could have stroked it as it rolled along in front of me* ! '
" I think the idea (continued the General) of a private soldier in the middle of the battle walking along behind the barrage, *stroking it*, is too good to be lost."

20TH Nov.   The first artillery advance was made about 10-30 a.m., the LXXVIIth Brigade sending forward a battery to the north-east of Havrincourt Wood to support the 185th Infantry Brigade. It was one of the first battles in which the Field Artillery really advanced as the battle progressed. The spectacle of the gunners trotting into action south-west of Graincourt, just as if they were on Salisbury Plain, was one of the most inspiring sights of the first day of the operations. In their advance the gunners found abandoned German guns with lots of ammunition, so they saved their own, and served the German guns with German ammunition on the retreating enemy. Eight guns were captured by an advanced reconnoitring party from B/310 Battery.

The Machine-gun Companies of both the 185th and 187th Brigades were at the disposal of their Brigades, two sections for each Company accompanying the Battalions. The other two sections were at first employed against the enemy's outpost line and the Chateau in Havrincourt grounds and in covering the British Line. Later they assisted in consolidating the Brown Line. The Machine-gun Company of the 186th Infantry Brigade with the Divisional Machine-gun Company formed a barrage in front of the assaulting troops, both Companies on completion of the barrage limbering up and joining the 186th Brigade in its move forward, the Divisional Machine-gun Company being temporarily attached.

And just as the guns had assisted the infantry, so the Sappers played well their part in preparing the way for the artillery to advance. All three Field Companies that day had a strenuous time. One Company (461st) details the work on which it was employed thus : "At Zero plus 2 hours 50 minutes the Field Company was moved forward ; the work, which was carried out under desultory shelling and sniping, consisted of clearing barricades of sandbags, wire, trees felled across the road, etc. Also making deviations of sleepers round the large craters and crossings over the trenches, filling shell holes in roads with bricks and chalk floats. A passage through to Havrincourt was cleared by Zero plus 4½ hours, suitable for field guns and first line transport, a distance approximately of 3,520 yards."

Road space (or the want of it) was always the trouble in any advance. " The chief difficulty in the clearance of wounded was due to the rapidity of the advance. By a comparatively early hour our troops were in Havrincourt Village and soon beyond it. The Centre Road, running from Place d'Hubert, was full of advancing guns and ammunition limbers, and on the outskirts of the village both this road and the Havrincourt-Trescault roads were stopped by huge craters (Etna and Vesuvius); these craters effectively prevented motor ambulances getting forward. The clearance of wounded, however, proceeded satisfactorily, though it entailed strenuous work on the part of the bearers."[1]

The medical arrangements included the establishment of Advanced Dressing Stations on the northern borders of Havrincourt Wood, a Dressing Station for walking wounded close to Mill Farm on the Metz-Ruyaulcourt Road, and a Main Dressing Station at Ruyaulcourt. The Casualty Clearing Station was at Ytres.

The following message was received at Divisional Headquarters during the evening of 20th: "Army Commander sends special congratulations to all ranks of the 62nd Division on their very fine achievement to-day."

Not only the 62nd Division in the Havrincourt sector, but every other Division along the front of attack had gained ground splendidly. On the left flank of General Braithwaite's Division, the Ulstermen (36th Division) had advanced in line with the flanking Brigade of the 62nd; on the right flank, Flesquières proved to be too well defended for the 51st Division to capture and all that the gallant Scotsmen could do was to hold on to the Hindenburg Support Line just south of the village. Early in the battle many of the Tanks attached to the 51st Division had been knocked out of action, one German battery in particular scoring six direct hits in succession on as many Tanks. A story was told of a brave German artillery officer who served a field gun himself, all his men having been killed, obtaining many direct hits on Tanks until he too was killed at his gun.

The 6th Division, on the right of the 51st, carried Ribecourt only after stiff fighting; the 20th captured La Vacquière and had stormed the powerful defences on the Welsh Ridge. The 12th Division on the right of the 20th Division, moving along Bonavis Ridge, had a grim struggle with the enemy for the possession of Lateau Wood, which sheltered a number of German batteries. The Wood fell eventually to the gallant troops of the 12th Division and the enemy's guns also. The 29th Division, which at Zero hour was at Guyencourt, had moved up into the battle and having entered Masnières and captured Marcoing, secured the bridges of the Canal de l'Escaut at both villages.

[1] A.D.M.S., 62nd Division.

20TH Nov.   At the end of the day three German systems of defence had been broken to a depth of 4½ miles on a wide front, some 5,000 prisoners had been taken with many guns, machine-guns, trench mortars, etc. But for the check at Flesquières and the wrecking of a bridge at Masnières, which held up the advance of the troops, still greater results might have been obtained. But the want of cavalry in large numbers to exploit the success gained was everywhere along the whole battle front imperative.

The Tanks had proved their worth and justified the claims made for them by their inventors ; they alone had made it possible to dispense with artillery preparation, and so conceal the intentions of the British Army from the enemy right up to the moment of attack.   In fact—Tanks have, once more, made possible surprise, that greatest of all instruments of victory !

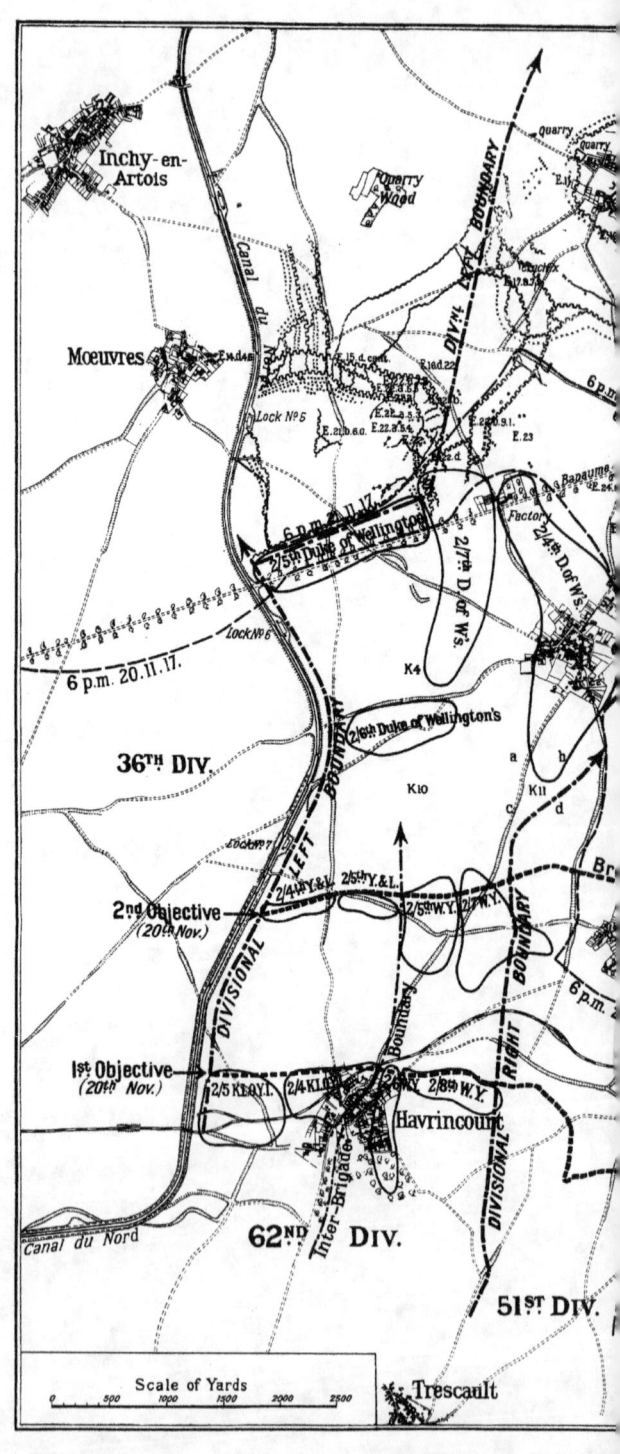

THE BATTLE OF CAMBRAI, 1917, III.

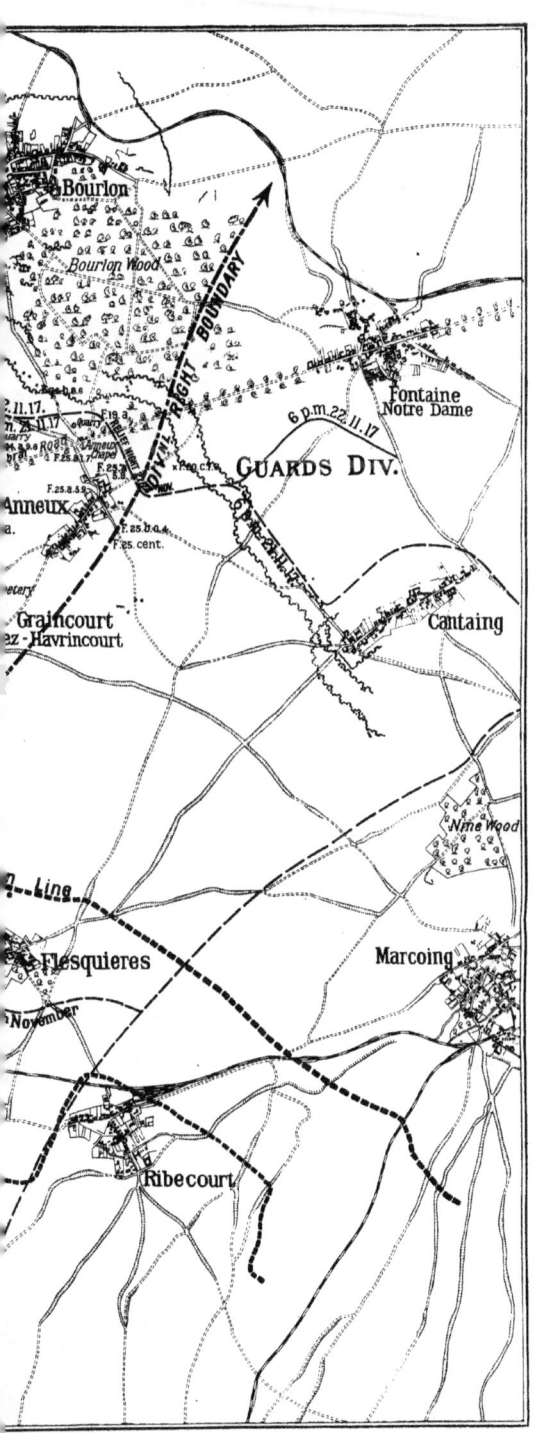

Taking of Anneux.

Chapter X. 1917.

THE BATTLE OF CAMBRAI (III.)
THE TAKING OF ANNEUX.

"At 7 p.m., 20th November, orders were received from the Corps that the advance would be continued the following day. The 51st Division was to attack Flesquières at dawn and, subsequently, advance to the Nine-Wood—Graincourt Road and to Fontaine. The 36th Division was to attack on the left of the 62nd Division: the dividing line between Divisions being the Road at E 15 d.4.6 (a road running direct east from the village of Mœuvres to Bourlon Wood): 62nd Division was to advance to capture the high ground west of Bourlon Wood and Bourlon Village."—*Divisional Narrative.*

GENERAL Bradford's Brigade (186th) was detailed to carry out the attack on Bourlon Wood and Village. For this purpose all the surviving Tanks and a regiment of cavalry (which had been attached to the Division) were allotted to the Brigade. And Zero hour had been fixed for 10 a.m. on the 21st.

SEE MAP No. 8.

The night of the 20th/21st passed quietly, though considerable preparation went on in the Divisional area. Two Brigades of the 36th Division had moved across the Canal into Havrincourt and the trenches west of the village: the 185th and 187th Infantry Brigades, to make room for the Ulstermen, having been ordered to clear all their troops from south of the Blue Line to north of it.

20TH/21ST NOVEMBER.

The guns had been ordered forward and should have moved up during the night, but the ground was sodden and heavy and deep in mud, the constant traffic having broken the roads very badly. Moreover in the thick darkness, in the midst of an intricate system of newly-captured trenches, to move forward across the scarred battle-field pitted with great shell-holes and huge craters, littered with all the awful

20TH/21ST NOVEMBER.

impedimenta and terrible remains of a bloody struggle, it was impossible for the gunners to take up new positions without the assistance of a little daylight, be it only the dimness of dawn.

The guns, therefore, remained in the positions they had occupied at nightfall on the 20th—the Vth Brigade R.F.A. and 310th Brigade R.F.A. in action east of Havrincourt : LXXVIth Brigade R.F.A. in action in K.32.d. (between Water Copse and Cabbage Tree) : 312th Brigade R.F.A. in its original positions. All four Brigades were, however, ordered to move forward as early as possible on the 21st after firing the barrage.

It was not until 10 p.m. that Divisional Headquarters were able to issue orders for the attack, and not until 2 a.m. that 186th Brigade Headquarters could inform all units of the Brigade of the impending attack and the objectives of the four Infantry Battalions.

The 2/4th Battalion Duke of Wellington's Regt. was to capture Anneux and the enemy's trench running from F.20.c.1.3. to the road at E.24.b.8.6. : the 2/7th Battalion Duke of Wellington's Regt. was to secure the enemy's trench line from E.24.b.8.6. to the Crucifix at E.17.a.7.9. : 2/5th Battalion Duke of Wellington's Regt., a line from the Crucifix along the road to E.15.d.4.6. The 2/6th Battalion Duke of Wellington's Regt. was ordered to pass through the 2/7th Battalion and clear the hostile trenches running along the N.W. and S.W. sides of Bourlon and as soon as that had been accomplished, push patrols forward through Bourlon to the S.E. outskirts of the village where posts were to be established. A warning was issued to the 2/6th—" The Village must be thoroughly mopped up." How often in the past had successful attacks been turned to failure through neglecting to clear the enemy's dug-outs and underground shelters of lurking foes with their deadly machine-guns, only waiting until their opponents had passed over them, that they might turn their guns on the backs of the advancing troops with results which may better be imagined than explained.

Tanks were again to co-operate, but it was not known how many would be available, for casualties had been heavy on the 20th and many others had become " bogged " when endeavouring to negotiate the intricacies of the Hindenburg Line. Orders issued by 186th Infantry Brigade Headquarters were therefore in this strain : " It is hoped that Tanks will act as follows at Zero." Then followed details of the co-operation hoped for, which briefly may be stated : six were to advance through Anneux at a slow rate, up to the enemy's trench east of the village ; they were then to turn to the left and advance along the objective given to the 2/4th Duke's. Four Tanks were to advance from the Cemetery just north of Graincourt, on to the objective laid down for the 2/7th Duke's. Four more were to move along the trench which had been detailed as the objective of the 2/5th Duke's, and finally, four Tanks were to move on Bourlon. 20TH/21ST NOVEMBER.

Anneux and the enemy's trenches east of the village were to be shelled by the Artillery from Zero to Zero-plus 50 : barrages were to be placed on Mœuvres and Tadpole Copse.

In addition to the two Squadrons of King Edward's Horse already in Graincourt, a regiment of Cavalry was also attached to the Division.

And what was happening on the other (the enemy's) side of the wire? The attack had been a surprise and the Hindenburg Line, so Ludendorff stated, was but lightly held, though prisoners of two divisions were taken by the 62nd Division. Be that as it may, immediately on receipt of the unpleasant intimation that some thousands of yards of his front had been broken into, and that deeply, Ludendorff ordered several German divisions which were more or less rested and located in rear of the Crown Prince's Army, to be railed to the neighbourhood of Cambrai and south of it. He also requested Prince Rupprecht of Bavaria to move forces north, up to Cambrai. On the morning of the 20th, the 107th Division had just arrived on the Cambrai front, where the blow had fallen, but the 21st was the earliest date upon which fresh reinforcements could reach Cambrai and it would be the 23rd before sufficient forces could arrive to hold up the attack and by then anything might have happened !

At 2-45 a.m. on the morning of 21st November, patrols of the 51st Division reported that they had advanced to the Brown Line, along the Divisional front. At dawn, therefore, two Battalions of Highlanders pushed forward and, passing through Flesquières Trench and the village, established themselves on the Brown Line ; during the night the enemy had retired. At 6-15 a.m. two more Battalions of Highlanders passed through Flesquières and also established themselves on the Brown Line without opposition. And about 10 a.m., when the 62nd launched its attack, the 51st Division, on the right flank, was ready to go forward also. 21ST Nov.

"Zero" hour for the Division had been fixed for 10 a.m., but the six Tanks which had been detailed to assist the 2/4th Duke of Wellington's experienced difficulty in traversing Graincourt and, in consequence, the attack did not begin until twenty minutes after the

21ST Nov. hour. Long before "Zero," however, the two squadrons of King Edward's Horse had reconnoitred the ground between Graincourt and Anneux and, just east of the former village, had captured some men belonging to the 52nd Brandenburgers. From these men information was obtained that Bourlon Wood was held by 52nd and 224th Brandenburgers; these troops belonged to the 107th Division, which had left Russia on the 13th, detraining east of Cambrai on 18th.

At 10 a.m. the guns opened fire and poured shell on to Bourlon Village and the north-western slopes of the spur running west from Bourlon; a smoke barrage was also put down on Tadpole Copse, *i.e.*, west of Mœuvres.

Preceded by six Tanks, two directed on either side of the village and two on the centre, C Company of the 2/4th Duke of Wellington's, on a three-platoon frontage, advanced at about 10-20 a.m. on Anneux; A Company was echeloned on the outer, or right flanks of C, which was thought to be "in the air." Resistance was first encountered south of the village, where the enemy in considerable strength still held to his trenches and opened a heavy machine-gun fire on the men of the West Ridings. As the two Companies of the 2/4th drew near the trenches, however, the enemy's defence partly collapsed. Some of the enemy surrendered speedily, but others, showing a better spirit, fought on grimly until utterly wiped out. The two Tanks on each side of Anneux passed on to the enemy's trenches east of the Village, whence heavy machine-gun fire was now coming. The two Tanks detailed to go through Anneux, however, followed closely by infantrymen, entered the village and were soon engaged in clearing the enemy from the houses, at the windows of which many Germans had stationed themselves in order to snipe the troops as they passed through. Here also grim fighting took place. The Lewis gunners, on this occasion, fired their guns as the German infantry had fired their rifles at Mons in 1914, from the hips. This method effectively cleared the enemy from the windows of the houses and the centre platoon of C Company pushed on to the further end of the village. Far more difficult was the advance of the left platoon, attacking across the open towards Anneux Chapel. Heavy machine-gun fire from the Chapel Cross Roads held up the advance of this platoon and it was obliged to come to a standstill. The whole of C Company had, by now, pushed through and established positions on the northern edge of the village. Here the Company reorganized preparatory to an advance to the final objective. But the enemy's machine-guns were too well placed and the opposition far too strong—enfilade fire from numerous enemy posts on the reverse slopes of a spur running north-east—sweeping the front and holding up any advance in the vicinity of the Chapel. "A" Company, advancing well outside the south-eastern edge of the village, after considerable clearing of enemy posts, reached the line of the road about F.25.b.0.4. The two company commanders now agreed that any further advance was impossible, they therefore decided to entrench and place a series of posts round the north and north-eastern edge of the village, A Company from about F.25.b.0.4. to the Cross Roads F.25.a.5.9., C Company from F.25.a.5.9. to F.25.a.1.7. During the afternoon both Companies were subjected to heavy gun fire, but their posts escaped direct hits and with the assistance of five Vickers guns, held the village.

Meanwhile B and D Companies of the 2/4th Duke of Wellington's had advanced on and had captured Anneux Chapel.

At 10 a.m. B Company, which on the night 20th/21st had held the Sugar Factory, moved off astride the Cambrai—Bapaume Road towards Anneux Chapel, and at once came under heavy rifle and machine-gun fire. In E.24.b., at the Cross Roads, there were one or two buildings and from these the enemy swept the road and both sides of it so that B Company, advancing along what was practically an open valley, without any cover whatsoever, suffered many casualties. The Company, however, steadily gained ground and when at about E.24.c.2.3. 2nd Lieut. Castle, by skilfully manœuvring his platoon and by section covering fire, rushed the buildings with two more sections and killed or captured all the enemy's troops holding them. He then signalled to the remaining platoons of the Company to advance. More machine-gun and rifle fire from the direction of the Quarry (north of the Cross Roads) threatened to hold up the advance, but the enemy's positions here also were rushed and the Quarry bombed with smoke bombs. Pressing on, the Company reached the Sunken Road in E.24 b. Here, however, strong opposition was met with both from a series of small posts in front of the road and from the road itself. But again, led by the same Subaltern (2nd Lieut. Castle), and assisted by a Tank, the Company, by section rushes, reached the road, where a number of the enemy, estimated at 200 men, were found. Lieut. Castle managed to detach about forty of them, who at once surrendered. But the others showed fight. Every available Lewis gun was therefore turned on and the remaining Germans either shot down or forced to surrender. In the Sunken

21ST NOV. Road the Company reorganized and then set out towards the final objective, the enemy line of trenches. This was reached and further progress was made towards the edge of the Wood, compelling the enemy's riflemen to retreat still further into the latter.

Consolidation was now begun, but the line was deemed untenable, as it could be enfiladed by machine-gun and rifle fire from the Wood. The Company, under orders from Battalion Headquarters, withdrew again to the Sunken Road in E.24.b., where, after the position had been consolidated and the Company reorganized, preparations were made for passing the night.

Shortly afterwards, as darkness set in, touch was gained on the left with the 2/7th Battalion in the Sunken Road in E.24.a.

Meanwhile D Company, the support Company to B, had left the northern edge of Graincourt at 10 a.m. and advanced towards the Cambrai-Bapaume Road, *via* the Sunken Road in E.30 a. In the latter, however, the Company was caught by heavy machine-gun fire from Anneux Chapel and, for a while, forced to take shelter along the road. Eventually, the men reached the main Cambrai Road about the cross roads, where again, owing to the storm of bullets which swept the road, it was necessary to line the deep ditches on either side of the roadway. By the early afternoon the remnants of D Company—in all about forty men—seem to have progressed as far as the Sunken Road in E.24.b. From this position an attack on Anneux Chapel and the farm buildings around it was planned. From the Sunken Road sections were organized to deal with the buildings. Assisted by a Tank, the Chapel and the buildings were rushed and cleared of the enemy, about thirty prisoners being taken from the cellars. Enemy dug-outs in and adjacent to the Quarry in F.19.a.1.2. were also cleared of the enemy.

By the evening the remnants of both B and D Companies— they had both suffered very heavy casualties throughout the day— were established in the Sunken Road about E.24.b., with posts by the Quarry and in and around Anneux Chapel. About 300 prisoners and thirteen machine-guns had been captured by the Battalion during the day.

Towards dusk two squadrons of King Edward's Horse (dismounted) went forward to the line of the road between Anneux Chapel and Village, thus filling in the gap between A and C and B and D Companies of the 2/4th Duke of Wellington's.

At 10 a.m. the 2/7th Battalion, Duke of Wellington's, on the left of 2/4th, moved forward from the forming-up line in the Sunken

Road running N.W. and S.E. through the Sugar Factory. "A" Company was on the right, D Company in the centre and C on the left; B Company was in support. Although the Tanks did not arrive up to time rapid progress was made, but just before reaching the Sunken Road running through E.24 a, and b., the Battalion came under heavy machine-gun fire from the same trench which had caused trouble to the 2/4th Battalion. The 2/7th, however, managed to get forward to the road about E.24.c.9.8., capturing, on the way, two 5·9 howitzers. Further progress could not be maintained and, although assisted by the Tanks, no material advance was made beyond this point.

The advance of the 2/7th had been so rapid that the 2/5th Battalion (on the left of the 2/7th), which had to make an oblique attack on the road from the Crucifix to E.15.d.central, could not keep up and a dangerous gap was formed between the two Battalions. Two Companies of the 2/6th were therefore asked for and these, advancing immediately, filled the gap and so prolonged the line.

Owing to the non-arrival of the Tanks detailed to assist the 2/5th Duke of Wellington's Regt., the Battalion was unable to make a frontal attack on the objective allotted to it (from Crucifix along line of Road to E.15.d.4.6.), as the enemy's uncut wire was too formidable. A bombing attack was therefore begun along the Hindenburg Support Line as far as E.22.a.5.3.[1]

The attack was made by three Companies of the Battalion—B, A and C—the remaining company D being held in reserve[2]. Severe opposition met the attack of the 2/5th, an enemy strong point at E.22.a.5.5., holding up the advance. A platoon of A Company, under Lieut. Ridgway, rushed the point and captured it, taking forty prisoners, but unfortunately the platoon commander was killed.

The three Companies had by now reached the following positions: A Company was in the Sunken Road at E.16.d.2.2., B Company was in the Hindenburg Support Line at E.22.a.7.8., C Company was also in the Hindenburg Line and had placed a block at E.22.a.5.4.

Strong enemy reinforcements were now pouring down the trenches from the direction of Mœuvres and further progress was impossible. But about 3-30 p.m. the Adjutant found a Tank which

[1] Just before D Company "went over," the M.O. (Capt. Robertson) came round with some boxes of cigars found in an enemy dug-out and these were handed round to the men in the Company; so they went "over the top" smoking cigars. It was a laughable sight.

[2] Major F. Brook arrived at 7 a.m. on 21st November and had taken over command of the Battalion.

21ST Nov. had lost direction and easily persuaded its commander to assist the 2/5th in getting forward. Entering the Tank, the Adjutant personally directed it towards the point where the Battalion was held up. All four Companies then attacked with the Tank and captured the enemy's trench system as far as E.21.b.5.7. and E.21.b.6.0. As the Tank moved forward ahead of the 2/5th, it stumbled on a Battalion of enemy troops being formed up for a counter-attack. The steel monster dashed at this Battalion and dispersed it. The position was then consolidated—C Company being on the left, A Company left centre, B Company right centre and D Company right. At 5 p.m. the enemy, having in the meantime re-assembled, counter-attacked, but was driven off by Lewis-gun and rifle fire.

Two Companies of the 2/6th Battalion Duke of Wellington's, which had been ordered to remain in Brigade Reserve, had about midday gone forward to fill the gap between the 2/7th and 2/5th Battalions. The original objective of the 2/6th was the trench W. of Bourlon in E.12.E.11 and E.6. But the attack had not succeeded sufficiently to allow the 2/6th to make a push forward to their objective and the Battalion was employed in filling the gap between the 2/7th and 2/5th Battalions. The two Companies, which had been sent forward at midday, were later reinforced by the remaining two Companies and at dawn the Battalion occupied the line of the Sunken Road in E.23.b., E.17.d. to E.17.c.8.3; thence along the trench to E.22.b.9.1. The 2/6th was now in touch on both flanks with the 2/7th and 2/5th Battalions.

From the above it will be gathered that the 186th Infantry Brigade had been unable to reach its final objective, although in places an advance to a depth of 2,000 yards had taken place.

What had happened? The Tanks, which had started fresh and filled up with supplies on the morning of 20th, found it increasingly difficult to refill as the line advanced. No one was to blame; the Tank was on its trial and had fulfilled all its inventor had claimed for it. But there were still difficulties to overcome and refilling was one of them.

Until this battle it was not fully realized that the strain on the crews, shut up all day inside the Tanks and subjected to physical exhaustion, was so great that, for a two-days battle fresh Tanks must be kept in reserve for the second day, or, the Tanks must be withdrawn to a rallying point where the crews could rest and the Tanks be refilled and refitted.

The difficulty of getting forward the large supplies of petrol, oil, 21st Nov. grease, etc., required for the Tanks was immense; everything had to be sent up in limbers, as no carrier Tanks then existed—and miles of slippery muddy ground (for rain had been falling since the early afternoon) cut up by heavy shell-fire intersected with trenches, separated the petrol supplies from the Tanks. Over such ground and along the few tracks crowded with numberless vehicles, the limbers toiled all night to reach and replenish the Tanks.

As regards the infantrymen, they were much exhausted. Since the early morning of the 20th November they had been on the move; the splendid advance of 7,000 yards had not been made without great effort and physical labour. The fighting had been heavy, the marching heavy and the "going" heavy. There is a limit to human endurance.

Finally, the enemy's resistance was gradually increasing; his reinforcements had already been successful in preventing the cavalry from breaking through, which was its special function and from which so much had been hoped.

At dusk on the 21st the dispositions of the 186th Infantry Brigade were 2/4th Duke of Wellington's, from approximately F.25 central, round the north-eastern outskirts of Anneux, Anneux Chapel, the Quarry in F.19.a and the eastern portions of the Sunken Road in F. 24.b. The 2/7th Duke of Wellington's continued the line from the left of 2/4th Battalion, along the Sunken Road in E.24.b and a to E.33.b. At the latter point the right flank of the 2/6th Battalion joined up with the left of the 2/7th; thence the line ran westwards to E.17.c.8.3, along the trench to about E.22.c.9.1. The 2/5th Battalion occupied the Hindenburg Support Line in E.22.d.b. and a, and as far west as E.21.b.5.8.

In two days (20th and 21st) the 186th Infantry Brigade had captured eight officers and 1,130 other ranks, thirty-four field guns (including 4·2, 5·9 and 8″ Howitzers), thirty-eight machine-guns and one trench mortar.

Meanwhile the 185th and 187th Infantry Brigades, throughout the 21st November, had not been involved in the attack. The former Brigade had moved gradually forward and by 1 p.m. Brigade Headquarters were established in Graincourt and all four Battalions of the Brigade in K.4 and K.10. The Brigade had been detailed to relieve the 186th Brigade in the line during the night 21st/22nd.

The 187th Infantry Brigade had moved forward about midday to K.11, south of Graincourt, where the 2/5th Y. and L. were

21ST Nov. disposed in K.11.b, 2/4th Y. and L. in K.11.a, the 2/5th K.O.Y.L.I. in K.11.d, and the 2/4th K.O.Y.L.I. in K.11.c.

When darkness had fallen on 21st the 185th Infantry Brigade moved up and relieved the 186th Infantry Brigade in the front line. The 2/7th West Yorks. took over Anneux and the positions round it, including the Quarry and the Chapel from the 2/4th Duke of Wellington's and placed three Companies in the outpost line and one in Reserve; the 2/8th West Yorks. relieved the 2/7th Duke of Wellington's and the two Companies of the 2/6th Duke of Wellington's, who were holding the Sunken Road, south-west of Bourlon Wood. One Company of the 2/5th West Yorks. (C) relieved the two left Companies of the 2/6th Duke of Wellington's Regt. in E.17.c and d—E.23.a, and there formed a defensive flank for the 2/8th West Yorks., to whom this Company was attached. This relief was completed about 2 a.m. on the 22nd. D Company of the 2/5th West Yorks. was also attached later to the 2/8th West Yorks.; A Company was moved to the junction of the Hindenburg Support Line and the Bapaume-Cambrai Road, under orders of the 2/6th West Yorks.; B Company was in reserve. The 2/6th West Yorks relieved the 2/5th Duke of Wellington's, but there was evidently some confusion as to the exact position taken over and it was not until early dawn that the Officer Commanding the Battalion, after a personal reconnaissance, found the position of his troops.

On the right of the 62nd, the 51st Division, after hard fighting had captured Fontanie-Notre-Dame (at 5 p.m.) and had maintained touch with the right of the 62nd Division. On the left of the Division the Ulstermen (36th Division) had advanced north of the Bapaume-Cambrai Road and had reached the outskirts of Mœuvres, where strong opposition was encountered. Two Brigades of the Division had crossed the Canal du Nord and had attacked on the left of the 62nd.

The Battle had lasted two days, and on the evening of the second day the position along the whole front was, in Sir Douglas Haig's own words:—" From our old front line east of Gonnelieu the right flank of our new position lay along the eastern slopes of the Bonavis Ridge; passing east of Lateau Wood and striking the Masnières-Beaurevoir line, north of the Canal de l'Escaut at a point about half-way between Crèvecœur and Masnières. From this point our line ran roughly north-west past and including Masnières, Noyelles and Cantaing to Fontaine, also inclusive. There it bent back to the south for a short distance, making a sharp salient round the latter

village and ran in a generally westerly direction along the southern 21st Nov.
edge of Bourlon Wood and across the southern face of the Spur to the
west of the Wood to the Canal du Nord, south-east of the village of
Mœuvres. From Mœuvres the line linked up once more with our
old front at a point about midway between Boursies and Pronville."

The time had, however, now arrived when a momentous decision was necessary, either to go on or to attempt to hold what had been gained. In spite of the splendid advance of the flanks of the attack on 20th, it was obvious that the results aimed at had not been, and could not now be, obtained. The element of surprise had passed and the enemy's reinforcements were not only being rushed up with all speed, but had begun to arrive; some of them had in fact taken part in the operations of the 21st. From the enemy's records it is clear that both the 20th Landwehr and the 54th Divisions, who were holding the line on the left of the attack, were relieved during the 21st; the former had lost 2,773 officers and men and the latter, 2,789. On the 21st November fresh enemy troops, belonging to the 52nd Infantry Regt. of the 107th Division, the 175th Infantry Regt. of the 36th Reserve Division, the 77th Infantry Regt. of the 20th Division and the 358th and 362rd Infantry Regts. of the 214th Division were taken prisoner in the vicinity of Anneux and S.W. of Bourlon Wood.

The positions already captured were completely dominated by the Bourlon Ridge and either the latter must be occupied or the British Line withdrawn to the Flesquières Ridge. That was the option that confronted Sir Douglas Haig on the evening of the 21st November. The British Commander-in-Chief decided to go on! But before any further advance could be made, the worn and weary troops who had borne the brunt of the heavy fighting of 20th and 21st must be relieved and rested. There was no other course! The delay was a bitter pill to swallow, but it could not be avoided. And all the while the enemy's resistance was growing more powerful and his forces rapidly increasing. Good news from Italy, where the Italians, between the Brenta and Piave, had repulsed the Austrians, suddenly placed two more divisions, previously earmarked for Italy, at Sir Douglas Haig's disposal. With these divisions the prospect of succeeding seemed favourable.

So the 22nd November " was spent in organizing the captured 22nd Nov.
ground, in carrying out certain reliefs and in giving the troops the
rest they greatly needed."

The 62nd had received instructions that it was to be relieved by

22ND Nov.

the 40th Division on the night 22nd/23rd November, but before the Division went out of the line, another attempt to capture the high ground west of Bourlon Wood was to be made.

At dawn the enemy delivered a heavy counter-attack against the 2/6th and 2/8th West Yorks., located in E.22 and E.23, and by 9 a.m. the former Battalion had been driven back to the Bapaume-Cambrai Road. Here the Battalion reorganized and, assisted by one Company of the 2/5th West Yorks., drove the enemy back and regained its original trenches. The 2/8th West Yorks. had also given ground under very heavy pressure, but with the assistance of the 2/4th York and Lancs. Regt. (187th Infantry Brigade) this Battalion also again attacked the enemy and re-established its line.

By 10 a.m. the position was once more satisfactory.

But soon after midday the 51st Division was forced out of Fontaine and fell back south-west of the village; this was a severe blow to the plans formed by the 62nd for the attack on Bourlon. The loss of Fontaine, combined with the disorganization spread by the enemy's counter attack at dawn, caused the temporary abandonment of the attack on Bourlon.

No incident of tactical importance took place during the remainder of the day and when darkness had fallen the relief of the 62nd Division by the 40th Division began, and was continued throughout the night until the early hours of 23rd November. The 185th Infantry Brigade marched back to Havrincourt and, on the 23rd, moved further back still to the Lechelle area.

23RD Nov.

The 187th Infantry Brigade, on relief by units of 40th Division, was withdrawn to the Hindenburg Support. Only one Battalion—the Hallamshires—had been engaged throughout the day, but this unit fought hard, having been placed at the disposal of the 185th Infantry Brigade and put into the line when the latter was hard pressed. The 2/4th and 2/5th Battalions, York and Lancs. Regt. did not arrive in the Hindenburg Support Line until about 8-30 a.m. on the 23rd. Later on in the day the 2/4th K.O.Y.L.I. moved to Neuville, 2/5th K.O.Y.L.I. and the 187th Y.M.B. to Ruyaulcourt and the two Battalions of the York and Lancs. Regt. to shelters in the south-western corner of Havrincourt Wood; the 208th M.G. Company, however, remained in the forward area.

The 186th Infantry Brigade, which on relief by the 185th Infantry Brigade had been withdrawn to K.4, K.11 and K.16, moved back during the night of 22nd/23rd to shacks in Havrincourt Wood.

"Marched through the night," said a private diarist, "having to go very slowly on account of the traffic, going forward through Havrincourt, Trescault into Havrincourt Wood, arriving there just before dawn, having been seven hours on the journey. Rested there and had breakfast and then marched back through Ruyaulcourt to Bertrancourt." By 2 p.m. the 186th Infantry Brigade was complete in billets in the latter village. The Divisional Artillery remained in the line to support the 40th Division.

Thus, so far as the 62nd was concerned, ended the first phase of the Battle of Cambrai.[1] The second phase was the Capture of Bourlon Wood. The third, the (inevitable) German counter-attack.

Apart from the Divisional Narrative of the operations from 20th to 23rd November, which is evidently the story of the first phase of the Battle from an infantry point of view, there is no collective account of the actions of the Divisional Artillery or Engineers or any other unit of the Divisional troops.

The Divisional Artillery, throughout the three days of battle, had splendidly supported the infantry in the front line, though having to move forward to do so under extraordinary difficulties. Only the 310th Brigade, R.F.A., moved on the 20th, the guns advancing just after noon, battery by battery, to east of Havrincourt to cover the line gained by the 186th Infantry Brigade in the vicinity of Graincourt. Early on the 21st the 312th Brigade, R.F.A., set off to forward positions south-west of Graincourt. Here guns of the 310th and 312th Brigades, with the 77th Brigade, R.F.A., and the 5th Brigade, R.H.A., north-east of Havrincourt, came into action. On the 21st the 310th Brigade, R.F.A., and the 5th Brigade, R.H.A., barraged Bourlon Wood and Village.

The Divisional Ammunition Column which, when the Battle opened on 20th, had a dump near Clayton Cross in the north-west corner of Havrincourt Wood, had, by the 22nd, formed its forward dump at Havrincourt. Owing to the state of the ground the D.A.C. had a most strenuous time and most of the carrying was done by means of pack animals, which were invaluable.

The Field Companies, Royal Engineers, had been ordered to pay special attention to the clearing of the tracks, the filling in of shell holes and the making of deviations round craters. The battered and wrecked roads were to be made good, special wire-cutting parties

---

[1] During the first phase of the operations from 20th to 23rd November, the infantry of the 62nd Division lost twenty-one officers and 224 other ranks killed; fifty-two officers and 1,194 other ranks wounded, two officers and 195 other ranks missing—a total of seventy-five officers and 1,613 other ranks.

23RD Nov. formed, while each man was ordered to carry two sandbags. In all these things the Sappers did their part well. The Signal Company responsible for communications throughout the operations recorded that poles and wires held well, but unpoled wires were constantly broken by shell fire. Communications by means of runners and wireless were adequate and pigeons were also used with marked success.

The 212th M.G. Company, one section of which was attached to each of the four West Yorkshire Battalions of the 185th Infantry Brigade, seems to have had a very strenuous time, for it started with a very large excess of ammunition and, going forward with the Brigade, kept its guns in action throughout most of the period it was in the line. The 213th M.G. Company attached to the 186th Infantry Brigade, came into action with excellent effect in its attack on Anneux on 21st, but on the capture of the village and relief of the Brigade the Company remained in reserve.

On the 20th twenty-seven Germans and several machine-guns were captured by the 201st M.G. Company attached to the 187th Infantry Brigade. Two sections of the Company had been placed at the disposal of the 2/4th Duke of Wellington's, to support the outpost line of the latter in front of Graincourt. "These guns," records the Company's narrative, which is excellent, "found themselves 200 yards in advance of the infantry and Lewis gunners. During the night one was rushed by a small party of Germans, who were wiped out by the fire of the gun and by rifle fire of the spare numbers." Another section—A—supported the attack of the 186th Brigade on Anneux on 21st, and entered the village.

Back in reserve the Division set to work to "clean up" and refit. To use a slang term, then in vogue in France, the "tail of the Division was right up"; it had achieved a record advance and to all ranks had come unbounded (and legitimate) confidence; the days of apprenticeship had passed for ever. Henceforth, until the end of the war, the high reputation which the 62nd Division had won had to be maintained.

24TH Nov. On the 24th of the month General Braithwaite issued a Special Order of the Day to his troops :—

"The Divisional Commander has the honour to announce that both the Commander-in-Chief and the Army Commander have expressed their high appreciation of the achievements of the 62nd Division in the Battle. The Divisional Commander had the most implicit confidence that the Division would acquit itself with honour.

To have advanced 7,000 yards on the first day, taken all objectives, held them against counter-attack and handed over all gains intact to the relieving division, is a feat of arms of which any division may be justly proud. The number of prisoners taken by the Division is not far short of 2,000. Thirty-seven guns have been captured, which include two 8-inch howitzers, one complete 4·2″ battery, one complete battery of 5·9″ and the remainder, guns of various calibres, many of which were brought into action against the enemy. The number of machine-guns, granater-werfer, etc., etc., which have fallen into our possession, is so considerable that it has not been possible yet to make an accurate tally of them. The advance of the Artillery to Graincourt and the accuracy of the barrage is worthy of best traditions of the Royal Regiment. To Y Battalion, the Tanks, all ranks of the Division express their admiration of the skill, bravery and the splendid self-sacrifice which made success possible. The discipline, valour and steadiness of all ranks has been beyond praise. It is with great and legitimate pride that I have the honour to sign my name as Commander of the 62nd West Riding Division."

" WALTER BRAITHWAITE,
Major-General."

There yet remains one incident worthy to be related. As the Division was marching back to the rest area, General Braithwaite stood by the side of the road watching his troops go by. As each unit passed, not one, but many men, seeing their General, cried out to him, " This wipes out Bullecourt, sir."

The Battle of Cambrai, 1917, IV. The Capture of Bourlon Wood.

Chapter XI.

1917.

THE BATTLE OF CAMBRAI (IV.)
THE CAPTURE OF BOURLON WOOD

THE story of the second phase of the Battle of Cambrai, *i.e.*, the capture of Bourlon Wood—is one of hard fighting of a ding-dong nature, which ended in the ultimate triumph of British valour. It was essentially a British action, seeing that English, Irish, Scottish and Welsh troops took part in it and fought side by side, against a foe of proved fighting skill, for Ludendorff's reserves had arrived and had been flung into the line to stem the tide which threatened to sweep on even to Cambrai itself. Fontaine-Notre-Dame, Bourlon Wood, and a portion of Bourlon Village, were all won and lost, changing hands time after time until, at last on 28th November, only the latter remained in German hands.

SEE MAP No. 9.

The official despatches stated that on 23rd November the 51st Division again attacked Fontaine-Notre-Dame, but was unable to force an entry into the village. On the same morning the 40th Division attacked Bourlon Wood and, after four-and-a-half hours' hard fighting captured it;[1] while the 36th and 56th Divisions made progress in the neighbourhood of Mœuvres and Tadpole Copse respectively. During the morning of the 24th the enemy, having been reinforced, regained the north-east corner of Bourlon Wood, but by noon the line had been re-established. At evening a further heavy attack upon the Wood was beaten off. Progress had also been made west of Mœuvres, but the enemy's resistance had become very strong. Late at night on 24th (at 11 p.m.) orders were issued from Corps Headquarters that the 62nd was to relieve the 40th Division on the following night, and, about midnight, a warning order was issued to all units of the Division.

23RD NOV.

24TH Nov.

[1] The village was entered, but not captured.

25TH Nov.   At 10 o'clock on the morning of 25th November, detailed orders for the relief were issued from 62nd Divisional Headquarters. The 186th Infantry Brigade was to go into the line on the right, the 187th Infantry Brigade taking over the left sub-sector; the 185th Infantry Brigade was to be in Divisional Reserve west of Graincourt. The front line of the 40th Division was then approximately as follows :—F.14.a.5.3 — F.7.d.3.4 — F.7.c.1.4 — E.17.b.5.5 — E.17.d.0.0. — E.23.c.0.9.

Between 1 and 2 p.m. the 186th Infantry Brigade moved forward *via* Hermies and the crossing over the Canal du Nord, just north of Lock No. 7 to Graincourt. The 2/7th Duke of Wellington's had been ordered to relieve the 2nd Scots Guards[1] (Guards Division) in the right sub-sector of the line and the 2/6th Duke of Wellington's Regt., elements of the 119th Infantry Brigade (40th Division) holding the left sub-sector ; the 2/4th Duke of Wellington's were to relieve the 4th Grenadier Guards at the Quarry (F.19a) and vicinity, whilst the 2/5th Duke of Wellington's were to take up positions in area E.24b. All four Battalions, as they left Graincourt and marched off towards Bourlon Wood, came under shell fire.

The 2/7th on going into the line found that the position held by the Scots Guards consisted of unconnected posts close up to the top of the Ridge, which was the highest feature in Bourlon Wood. The Battalion placed three Companies in the front line, one platoon in the strong point at F.13.b.5.5 and two platoons near Battalion Headquarters, which were in The Chalet. The highest part of the ridge was in No Man's Land.

Dusk had fallen when the 2/6th Battalion relieved the elements of the 119th Infantry Brigade in the left sub-sector and work in the line was at once begun.

The 2/4th Battalion, on arriving at the Quarry, found that the 4th Grenadiers had received orders that they were *not* to be relieved ; in consequence, until the situation was cleared up, the West Ridings had to wait about in the open and, although in artillery formation and seemingly protected by the darkness, hostile shell fire caused some forty casualties. About two hours later, however, the relief began. The 2/5th had no difficulty in taking up its position, as supporting Battalion, in the Sunken Road, north-west of Anneux, though one officer and four other ranks were wounded in

---

[1] Two Battalions had been attached to the 40th Division, owing to the weakened state of the latter.

Bourlon Wood in November, 1917.

moving forward. Of the 213th M.G. Company two guns were attached to each of the 2/6th and 2/7th Battalions, while six guns relieved E.17.b.5.5—E.17.d.0.0 to E.23.c.0.9.[1]

The 2nd Guards Brigade was on the right of the 186th Infantry Brigade. The relief was completed by about 10 p.m.

It was not, however, until about 3 a.m. on the morning of the 26th November, that the 187th Infantry Brigade completed the relief of the 21st Infantry Brigade (40th Division), on the left of the 186th Brigade. The 2/4th York and Lancs. Regt. was on the right, joining up with the 2/6th Duke of Wellington's (186th Infantry Brigade); two companies of the 2/5th K.O.Y.L.I. came next, then a Battalion of dismounted Cavalry, and the 2/4th K.O.Y.L.I. held the left sub-sector of the Brigade front, in touch on its left with the 36th Division. The two remaining Companies of the 2/5th K.O.Y.L.I. were in support about the Factory on the Bapaume-Cambrai Road and the 2/5th York and Lancs. Regt., with another cavalry Battalion, were in the reserve trenches south of the Factory. The 208th M.G. Company had eight guns in position just north of the Factory and seven in Brigade Reserve in the Sunken Road, between Graincourt and the Factory.

The line taken over by the 62nd from the 40th Division, on the night 25th/26th, ran as follows:—From F.14.a.5.3—F.7.d.3.4—F.7.c.1.4 through Bourlon Wood, thence through Marquion Trench.

Sniping and desultory machine-gun fire, with intermittent shelling, which at times became almost intense, characterized the night of the 25th/26th.

On the morning of the 26th a Corps Conference[2] was held at 62nd Divisional Advanced Headquarters to decide operations. At the Conference it was decided to renew the attack at dawn on the 27th November; the 62nd and Guards Divisions, with Tanks, were to attack Bourlon Wood and Bourlon Village, and Fontaine-Notre-Dame respectively.

[1] The 62nd Divisional Artillery had remained in the line, and during the 23rd, 24th and 25th November, when the 40th Division launched several attacks on Bourlon Wood and Village, effectively supported the Division in its gallant efforts. On being relieved the G.O.C., 40th Division, expressed his thanks to the G.O.C., 62nd, "for the excellent and untiring support which the 62nd Divisional Artillery gave to the Infantry" under his command on those days.

[2] This Conference was held in a small hut in the grounds of Havrincourt Chateau and was of an historic nature. There were present: Sir Douglas Haig, Sir Julian Byng, Sir Charles Woolcombe (Commanding IVth Corps), General Braithwaite and many Divisional Generals and their Staffs. It was at this meeting that the decision to carry on the battle was come to.

26TH Nov

Zero hour was to be 6-20 a.m.

The 62nd was to attack Bourlon Wood and Village on a two-brigade frontage; the 186th Infantry Brigade on the right and 187th Infantry Brigade on the left; two Battalions of the 185th Infantry Brigade were to be placed at the disposal of the two attacking Brigades, *i.e.*, one to each. The 185th Infantry Brigade (less two Battalions) and the 2nd Cavalry (dismounted) Brigade, which had been placed at the disposal of the Division, were in Reserve. Twenty Tanks were available; sixteen were to be allotted to the 187th Infantry Brigade for the capture of Bourlon Village and four to the 186th Infantry Brigade.

Five Brigades of Field Artillery were to support the attack (1) by a rolling barrage; (2) by a smoke barrage to protect the left flank; the "Heavies" were to bombard Quarry Wood; several machine guns of the 186th Infantry Brigade were on the left flank of the Brigade, the remaining guns being in reserve in the trenches at the southern exits of the Wood. Two Stokes guns were also attached to the 2/7th Duke of Wellington's Regt.

A preliminary bombardment of Bourlon Village on the 26th had to be abandoned, for troops of the 14th Highland Light Infantry and 13th E. Surrey Regt. (40th Division), who had attacked the village on 24th, were still missing, and it was thought they might still be holding out amidst the tumbled houses and buildings.[1] This lack of bombardment seriously affected the attack of the 187th and 186th Brigades.

By the time the Conference at 62nd Divisional Headquarters broke up, mid-day had passed and but little daylight was left in which to make final preparations; the scheme, therefore, had to be explained verbally by staff officers.

The plan of operations necessitated certain changes in the Divisional area; the 186th Infantry Brigade handed over portions of its front to both the Guards Division and the 187th Infantry Brigade, whilst the latter handed over a part of its line (from the left flank

---

[1] During the late evening of November 26th, an officer of the 120th Brigade (40th Division) arrived at Headquarters, 185th Infantry Brigade, and reported that the Headquarters of the 13th East Surrey Regt. and the 14th H.L.I., with about 200 men were still in some buildings in the south-east corner of Bourlon Village, which they had fortified. These Battalions had taken part in the attack on Bourlon Village on November 24th, had got cut off from their Brigade and had defended themselves in the south-east end of the village for two days. Steps were immediately taken to get into touch with these troops, and during the night they were extracted from the village and brought back to Havrincourt."—[*Narrative by 62nd Divisional Headquarters.*]

BOURLON WOOD: THE CHALET.

Face p. 114.

up to E.17.b.5.5) to the 99th Infantry Brigade of the 2nd Division, which had just relieved the 36th Division.

On these readjustments taking place the 186th and 187th Infantry Brigades were disposed for battle as follows :—

The 2/5th Battalion Duke of Wellington's had relieved the 2/7th Battalion in the right sub-sector (186th Infantry Brigade Sector), the latter Battalion moving into support behind the left front Battalion (2/6th) of the Brigade; the 2/4th Battalion was in reserve concentrated behind the 2/5th Battalion. The 2/7th West Yorks. (185th Infantry Brigade), which had been allotted to the 186th Brigade lay behind the 2/7th Duke of Wellington's.

The objectives allotted to the Battalions of the 186th Infantry Brigade were :—2/5th Duke of Wellington's, the line of the railway which cut the north-western corner of Bourlon Wood; 2/6th Duke of Wellington's, Bourlon Village Road from F.7.b.2.3 to F.7.a.0.9, including all buildings on the northern edge of the road; 2/7th Battalion to follow the 2/6th Battalion at 400 yards distance and then pass through the Battalion to the line of the railway beyond, within the Brigade area.

Of the 187th Infantry Brigade, the 2/4th York and Lancs. Regt. held the now-shortened front of the Brigade. The attack by this Brigade was to be made with the 2/5th York and Lancs. Regt. on the right and the 2/5th K.O.Y.L.I. on the left, the 2/4th K.O.Y.L.I. were in support behind the right flank of the Brigade. The objective allotted to the 2/5th York and Lancs. Regt. was the trench north of Bourlon Village from the railway to where the road cut the trenches; the 2/5th K.O.Y.L.I. was to capture the trench from the left of the 2/5th York and Lancs. Regt. to a point on the road between the two Quarries north-west of the village. One Company of 2/4th K.O.Y.L.I. was (if possible) to extend the left of the 2/5th K.O.Y.L.I. to F.11.d.7.7, while the O.C. 2/4th York and Lancs. Regt. was to push forward his right to join up with the left of the one Company of 2/4th K.O.Y.L.I.; the three remaining Companies of the 2/4th K.O.Y.L.I. were to support the attacking Battalions and clear Bourlon Village. The 2/5th West Yorks. (185th Infantry Brigade) were at the south-west corner of the Wood, at the disposal of the G.O.C., 187th Infantry Brigade.

By 2 a.m. on the morning of the 27th the Tanks, detailed to assist the Division, were concentrated on the Bapaume—Cambrai Road, and here they were met by officers from each Brigade and conducted to their assembly positions. The four allotted to the

27TH Nov. 186th Infantry Brigade formed up on the road in Bourlon Wood on the right flank of the 2/6th Duke of Wellington's. Of those allotted to the 187th Infantry Brigade, twelve were on a line running west and east in front of the two attacking Battalions and four were along the Sunken Road, west of the 2/5th K.O.Y.L.I. At 5-30 a.m. all Battalions had reported "ready" in their assembly positions.

The artillery opened fire at 6-20 a.m., and the Tanks and infantry advanced. Immediately, the enemy put down a very heavy barrage over the whole of Bourlon Wood and on the roads and the buildings along the Bapaume—Cambrai Road, east of the Sugar Factory and on Anneux Chapel. It was, at this hour, quite dark and the maintenance of direction was a matter of great difficulty. The line held by the 186th Infantry Brigade was immediately in rear of the crest of the hill which ran through the centre of Bourlon Wood. The centre of the Wood formed a shallow basin, the edges of which followed approximately the 100 contour. The north-eastern portion of the Wood was filled with undergrowth of great density, it being impossible to see for more than 20 or 30 yards in any direction and very difficult to move through. On the left of the 186th Brigade the Wood was more open, and the northern slopes commanded the railway and eastern exits of the village. The 2/5th Duke of Wellington's Regt. (186th Brigade) especially, experienced a considerable obstacle in trying to force its way through the dense undergrowth, which clogged the advance. A nest of hostile machine-guns in an enemy point east of the Battalion held up the right and centre Companies (A and B) ere they had gone 50 yards, but the left and support Companies (C and D) pressed on, overcoming whatever resistance was met with, fetching up on the southern and eastern outskirts of the village and the star cross roads in the Wood, respectively. From these positions no further advance could be made until early afternoon, when the 2/5th reorganized and forced its way right through the Wood, holding the northern edge for a distance of 500 yards. It was in this position when it was relieved by the dismounted Cavalry during the night. On the right of the Battalion the Guards had also been held up and had withdrawn to their jumping-off positions.

The 2/6th Duke of Wellington's also lost direction and moved in a north-westerly direction. Strong opposition was met with from hostile machine-gun fire, but eventually, though losing heavily, the

THE TILE FACTORY: BOURLON VILLAGE.

Battalion reached Bourlon Village at about E.12.b.9.o.¹ Four officers killed, four wounded, twenty-eight other ranks killed and 137 wounded and four missing, were the casualties of the 2/6th Battalion on this day.

The 2/7th Duke of Wellington's, who had followed 400 yards in rear of the 2/6th, pushed through the latter Battalion and advanced straight on its objective, occupying buildings along the side of the road. The area and the buildings on the southern side of the road were occupied by A (left) and C (right) Companies; D Company was on the right of C and B Company had formed a defensive flank running north-east and south-west, as touch had not been obtained on the left with troops of the 187th Infantry Brigade. Neither had touch been obtained with the 2/5th Battalion on the right.

The attack of the 2/7th Duke of Wellington's (through the 2/6th Battalion) was supported by three Companies of the 2/7th West Yorks. Regt. On the first-named Battalion gaining its objective along the Bourlon Village Road, the West Yorkshiremen moved forward, extending their right flank along the road eastwards. These three Companies had advanced up the road which ran due north and was the dividing line between the right and left attacks of the 186th Infantry Brigade. They reached their objective at Zero plus 90. "Here they found themselves under heavy machine-gun fire, which made a further advance impossible." The fourth Company of the Battalion remained in support.

The 2/4th Duke of Wellington's also remained in support of the 2/5th Battalion, i.e., the right of the Brigade.

Meanwhile, the 187th Infantry Brigade, which had at first made fine progress, had been driven back.

At Zero, the two attacking Battalions (the 2/5th York and Lancs. Regt. on the right and the 2/5th K.O.Y.L.I. on the left) moved off punctually at 6-20 a.m., in spite of the heavy hostile barrage which caused many casualties. Preceded by the Tanks, the two Battalions pushed on, and had succeeded in getting about half-way through the village, when they found themselves confronted

¹ The Battalion Diary stated that: "The Battalion attacked and took Bourlon, but further progress was not made as the Battalion was not supported either on the left or right flanks. The village was held until 5 p.m., when the Battalion retired and took up a position in Bourlon Wood on the crest. The position commanded the village and a good field of fire was obtained."

27TH Nov. by street barricades. The barriers prevented further progress of the Tanks. Stiff fighting now ensued, heavy machine-gun fire sweeping the streets, and many more casualties were suffered, especially in officers who, with great gallantry, made every endeavour to push their way forward.[1] Eventually both the attacking Battalions were forced back to the original Brigade front.

The 2/4th K.O.Y.L.I., who had supported the attack, also succeeded in penetrating the village, but they likewise were pushed back to trenches south of Bourlon; their casualties were heavy— five officers and 110 other ranks killed, wounded and missing.

Owing to the failure of the attack on the village, the 2/4th Battalion York and Lancs. Regt. was not called upon to advance from its original position.

Thus although the right Brigade of the Division had made a slight advance, little or nothing had been achieved on the left. The troops were tired and worn out, having been brought up from the rest area before they had properly recovered from the exhausting attacks between 20th and 22nd November.

But one thing was essential, the maintenance of the high ground in and west of Bourlon Wood, which had been won only at enormous cost. This ridge was the highest feature for a considerable distance, and commanded the surrounding country for some miles. It was, therefore, imperative to hold it. To do this, the 2/5th Battalion West Yorks. (185th Brigade) was ordered up to support the 2/4th York and Lancs. Regt. and, eventually, two Companies of the former, with remnants of the 2/5th K.O.Y.L.I., reinforced the 2/4th York and Lancaster Regiment. One Company of the 2/5th K.O.Y.L.I. was still holding on to the trench running north-west through the Brigade front. At about 2 p.m. the 2/8th Battalion West Yorks. was advanced to the ridge west of Bourlon Wood, and here it was disposed in depth.

Throughout the remainder of the day, until about 4·30 p.m., the situation remained unchanged. But at that hour, a strong counter-attack, accompanied by heavy shelling of the positions occupied by the 186th Infantry Brigade along the Bourlon Village

---

[1] Casualties of the 2/5th K.O.Y.L.I. were: Officers—three killed, five wounded, two wounded (at duty) and one wounded and missing; other ranks—twenty-two killed, 146 wounded, wounded and missing four, missing nineteen.

The casualties of the 2/5th Y. and L. were: Officers—one killed, three wounded, two wounded and missing, one missing; other ranks—seventeen killed, 172 wounded, six wounded and missing, one missing.

Road, forced the gallant troops, who had gained and held this position 27TH Nov. all day long, back to the centre of the Wood, to a line a short distance in advance of the original line held in the morning. The line on the right, however, remained unchanged.

In the evening the 185th Infantry Brigade relieved the 187th Infantry Brigade, while two Battalions of the 2nd Dismounted Cavalry Division relieved the units of the 186th Infantry Brigade in the front line.

The relief of the 186th Infantry Brigade was completed without incident by 11 p.m., the four Battalions of the Duke of Wellington's Regt. and the 2/7th West Yorks. (185th Brigade) being drawn back into Bourlon Wood; the 187th Infantry Brigade, on relief, had been withdrawn to the Hindenburg Support Line, west of Flesquières.

On the right of the 62nd, during the day, the Guards Division had temporarily gained possession of Fontaine-Notre-Dame, but had later to relinquish their hold on it. On the left of the Division heavy attacks against Tadpole Copse were repulsed.

"During the day of November 28th," said the Divisional Narrative, "there was no change of any importance, but both our own and the enemy's artillery were active."

At night on 28th/29th, the 47th (London) Division relieved the 62nd, the relief being carried out successfully, though the enemy was at the time shelling Bourlon Wood with large quantities of gas shells. The 186th Infantry Brigade marched back to positions just east of the Canal du Nord and south of Lock No. 6; the 185th Infantry Brigade to Beaumetz, and the 187th Infantry Brigade to the Lebucquière area, to a tented camp, which was reached about 10-30 p.m. 28TH/29TH NOVEMBER.

During the afternoon of the 29th all three Infantry Brigades were established in reserve areas—the 185th at Beaumetz, 186th at Bertincourt, and the 187th at Lebucquière.[1] 29TH Nov.

Thus ended the operations of the 62nd Division in the Battle of Cambrai, 1917; for although during the final phase—the German counter-attack on 30th November—the 186th Infantry Brigade was placed under the orders of the 2nd Division and moved up in reserve 30TH Nov.

---

[1] The losses of the 62nd Division during the second phase of the Battle of Cambrai, 25th—28th, were: Officers—fifteen killed, sixty-two wounded, two missing; other ranks—199 killed, 1,089 wounded, 277 missing. Total—officers seventy-nine; other ranks 1,569. The totals for both phases were officers 154; other ranks 3,178.

I

30TH Nov.   late in the afternoon to east of the Canal du Nord,[1] the Brigade was not called upon to take an active part in the fighting. The 2nd and 47th Divisions, although attacked again and again, succeeded in beating off all attacks.

The 62nd Division, and especially 186th Infantry Brigade, were always mindful of the fine way in which the 2nd Division treated the Brigade. When the latter moved up and arrived at the rendezvous they found an excellent example of staff work, for although the 2nd Division was even then fighting hard on the Bapaume—Cambrai Road, to their surprise the troops of the 186th Brigade found every detail prepared for them, even down to their rations, which the Divisional Staff thought (as the 186th Brigade had been ordered up in a hurry) it might have been difficult to obtain. It chanced, however, that the Brigade *had* brought rations, but the brotherly forethought of the 2nd Division was very greatly appreciated.

In the first phase (20th-21st November) rested troops attacked on a well-rehearsed plan and made an immediate and record advance ; in the second phase, tired and battle-worn troops, brought up from the rest area, fought well, but they were pitted against fresh enemy forces just flung into the field, and had they done no more than maintain their positions, they would have done well ; they did more, they made an appreciable advance and broke up the attacks of some of the enemy's best troops.[2]

Between the attacks of 20th-21st and 23rd-28th November, the opportunity of using cavalry could not be taken advantage of, only two squadrons of King Edward's Horse were allotted to the 62nd Division ; two Brigades might have achieved the desired object.

On the morning of 3rd December, orders were received for

---

[1] It was near 186th Infantry Brigade Headquarters, which were in a dug-out in K.4.d.4.5, that Brigadier-General R. B. Bradford, V.C., M.C., was killed, on 30th November, by a shell, Lieut.-Col. H. E. Nash (O.C., 2/4th Duke of Wellington's Regt.) taking temporary command of the Brigade. Lieutenant-General Sir W. Braithwaite writes this of the late Brigadier-General Bradford :— " He was a very exceptional man, though only a boy, and might have risen, in fact would have risen, to any height in his profession. His power of command was quite extraordinary. He certainly knew every officer in his Brigade, although he had only commanded it for quite a short time, and I honestly believe he knew every non-commissioned officer, and a great many of the privates. He had extraordinary personality, and that personality, linked with his undoubted military genius, made him a very extraordinary character, and a very valuable commander of men. His services during the battle can hardly be too highly appraised."

[2] In particular a German Guards Division.

the 62nd Division to move next day, by train, to the Arras—Bailleul- 3RD DEC.
mont—Blaireville areas. The 185th and 186th Infantry Brigades,
which had been employed in improving the reserve lines, were
withdrawn to the Lubucquière area.

The following day (on the 4th) the Division entrained at
Fremicourt and moved to its new area.

Only the Divisional Artillery stayed behind in the line, supporting the 47th (London) Division during the heavy attacks launched by the enemy against the Bourlon Salient.

The guns were withdrawn about the middle of December and,
on the 29th, reached the rest area behind Arras.[1]

---

[1] The G.O.C., R.A., of the 47th Division, addressed the following letter, dated 11th December, to the G.O.C., 62nd Divisional Artillery: "To-morrow I shall be parting with your Brigades and D.A.C. and I take the opportunity of thanking you most heartily for all the work they have done since you handed them over to me. Our infantry have been greatly pleased with the support your gallant fellows have given them, not only on November 30th, but ever since, and I am only sorry that they have had to put up with so much discomfort, but the conditions have made it impossible to do much for them. Colonel Sherlock has been a tower of strength." 29TH DEC.
Signed: E. N. Whitley, Brig.-General, R.A..

Chapter XII.

1917.

FROM THE BATTLE OF CAMBRAI, 1917, TO THE GREAT GERMAN OFFENSIVE— 21st MARCH, 1918.

BACK in the rest area, west of Arras, the Division began a month of reorganization, refitting and training. Many valuable lessons were learned during the Cambrai operations, but the one which transcended all others was the effectiveness of the "attack in depth." Had a fresh division been available to push through the 62nd on the first day of the Battle (20th November), instead of troops who were only able to take over the fighting from their wearied comrades, much more might have been accomplished. Constant support from behind to give impetus to the attack was shown to be an absolute necessity. The formation adopted by the Division had been excellent; the careful training in the use of rifles, which the infantry had received during the period out of the line immediately before the Battle, was of the greatest value and the men went into action fully confident in their prowess as marksmen; the work of the Lewis gunners and machine-gunners and their training in holding up hostile counter-attacks had borne good fruit. Other items, such as the value of pack animals, the unsuitability of light trench mortars for open warfare, and the manner in which both tanks and infantry worked together in close liaison, were only a few of the many lessons learned during the Battle.

Apart from the training programme a somewhat restless month was passed by the Division. On the 6th it moved from the XVIIth to the XIIIth Corps area, on transfer to the latter. Two days later it was transferred from the XIIIth Corps to the Ist Corps; on the 17th the Division was transferred back again to the XIIIth Corps at Monchy-Breton. From the 20th to the 31st December the Division was in Corps Reserve, but on the latter date, Divisional Headquarters having received warning, all units were informed of the impending relief of the 56th (London) Division, by the 62nd, in the right sector of the XIIIth Corps front, *i.e.*, from 500 yards south of Gavrelle to 500 yards north-west of Oppy.

1918.
5TH JAN.

On the 5th January, 1918, the relief began, the 187th Brigade taking over the right and the 185th Brigade the left sub-sector; the 187th Brigade was to hold the former alternately with the 186th Brigade. It was not, however, until 9th January that the relief of the 56th Division was finally completed and the G.O.C. 62nd assumed command of the sector.

No action of importance took place along the Divisional front during January, but in the meantime a drastic decision had been arrived at by General Headquarters, which created great soreness amongst practically every division in France and Flanders, *i.e.*, the reduction of the number of Battalions in Infantry Brigades from twelve to nine.[1]

24TH JAN.

This decision necessitated not only the disbandment of many Battalions which had won great honour in many a hard fought battle, but also the transfer of Battalions from one division to another, and the amalgamation of many others. This unpopular decision was first mentioned in the Divisional Diary on 24th January:—
" The number of Battalions in British divisions of the Expeditionary Force is to be reduced to nine per division. The 62nd Division is to receive Headquarters and the remainder of three Battalions from 49th (W.R.) Division, *i.e.*, 1/8th West Yorks. Regt., 1/5th Duke of Wellington's Regt. and 1/5th King's Own Yorkshire Light Infantry. These will be amalgamated with their sister Battalions in 62nd Division. The amalgamated Battalions will be known as 8th West Yorks., 5th West Riding Regt. and 5th K.O.Y.L.I. The following Battalions will be disbanded :—2/6th West Yorks. Regt., 2/6th West Riding Regt., and one Battalion York and Lancs. Regt. One Battalion, 50th Division, will be transferred complete to 62nd Division. This Battalion will either (1) be transferred as a Pioneer Battalion, in which case the 2/5th York and Lancs. Regt. will be disbanded, or (2) one Battalion, 50th Division, is transferred to make the third Battalion of the 187th Infantry Brigade, in which case 2/4th York and Lancs. Regt. will be disbanded and 2/5th York and Lancs. Regt. will be converted into a Pioneer Battalion."

29TH JAN.

On the 29th January, notification was received at Divisional Headquarters that the 2/5th York and Lancs. Regt. was to be disbanded and a Pioneer Battalion sent to the 62nd from 50th Division.

The nucleus of Battalions from 49th to be amalgamated with

---

[1] The falling off in the drafts sent out from home had not enabled Sir Douglas Haig to maintain the strength of his divisions; he had perforce to break up three Battalions in each division and distribute the officers and men amongst those divisions which sorely needed reinforcements.

Battalions of the 62nd, arrived in the Divisional area on 30th. On 30TH JAN. the following day the 1/8th and 2/8th West Yorks. Battalions were amalgamated, henceforth to be known as the 8th West Yorks.; the 1/5th and 2/5th West Ridings (Duke of Wellington's Regt.) became the 5th West Riding Regt. and 1/5th and 2/5th K.O.Y.L.I., the 5th K.O.Y.L.I. The transfer of troops of the 2/6th West Yorks. Regt. and 2/6th West Riding Regt. to other units in and outside the Division also took place.[1]

Early in February the 62nd Division was relieved by the 56th Division and, between 8th and 11th, moved into the XIIIth Corps Reserve area, with Divisional Headquarters at Villers Chatel.

On the 12th the Pioneer Battalion allotted to the Division 12TH FEB. arrived:—" 9th Battalion D.L.I. (T.F.) from the 50th Division was transferred to the Division as a Pioneer Battalion. They arrived in buses from the Ypres Salient, organized in four Companies. This Battalion has a fine fighting record, commencing with the 2nd Battle of Ypres. They were at one time commanded by Brigadier-General Bradford, V.C., who lost his life in the Cambrai Battle, commanding a brigade of the Division. 9th D.L.I. was reorganized on a three-company basis; the reorganization was completed on 27-2-18."[2] The Durhams were at this time commanded by Lieut.-Col. Crouch, who had come out with the Battalion as its Sergeant Major.

[1] " Q " Diary, 62nd Division.

[2] Of the 2/6th West Yorks., nine officers and 300 other ranks were transferred to the 2/7th Battalion; seven officers and 150 other ranks to the 2/5th Battalion; the remainder of the Battalion to the 6th West Yorks. (49th Division) and Corps Reinforcement Companies; of the 2/5th Battalion York and Lancs. Regt., eight officers and 202 other ranks were transferred to the 1/4th Battalion (49th Division), nine officers and 238 other ranks to the 1/5th Battalion York and Lancs. Regt. (49th Division), and thirteen officers and 221 other ranks to 2/4th York and Lancs. Regt. (62nd Division). The 2/6th Battalion Duke of Wellington's Regt. was split up amongst other Battalions of the 186th Infantry Brigade. On the 31st January, Lieut.-Col. J. Walker arrived with the nucleus of the 1/5th Battalion Duke of Wellington's and assumed command of the new 5th Battalion Duke of Wellington's Regt.

On the 1st February, 1918, the Order of Battle of the three Infantry Brigades was as follows:—

185th Infantry Brigade—8th Battalion West Yorks. Regiment.
                              2/5th   ,,   ,,   ,,   ,,
                              2/7th   ,,   ,,   ,,   ,,
186th Infantry Brigade—5th Duke of Wellington's Regiment.
                              2/4th   ,,   ,,   ,,
                              2/7th   ,,   ,,   ,,
187th Infantry Brigade—5th Battalion K.O.Y.L.I.
                              2/4th   ,,   ,,
                              2/4th York and Lancaster Regiment.

12TH FEB.

During February also the formation of the 62nd Machine Gun Battalion from the 201st, 208th, 212th and 213th Machine-Gun Companies, was ordered.[1] Between the 28th February and the 3rd March the Division moved back into the line, taking over the left

1ST MARCH sector of the XIIIth Corps front. On the 1st March the 187th Infantry Brigade relieved the 4th Guards Brigade (Guards Division) in the right (Arleux) sector; the 187th Infantry Brigade relieved the 92nd Infantry Brigade in the Acheville sector (left) on the night 3rd/4th March, while the 185th Infantry Brigade relieved the 93rd Infantry Brigade (31st Division) in the Ecoivres area on 4th March as Reserve Brigade to the Division. Of the Divisional Artillery, the 310th Brigade R.F.A. was on the right and the 312th Brigade R.F.A. on the left, the batteries were mostly in or about Willerval and Farbus, with R.A. Headquarters at Roclincourt.

For nearly three weeks after the relief trench warfare occupied the Division, patrol work, raids, bursts of machine-gun fire on selected positions, wiring and the repair and maintenance of trenches —such was the almost daily round of the Brigades in the front line, whilst the Brigade in reserve " carried on " with a training programme which included such items as bombing, musketry, etc., in short, it was a busy though uneventful period.

A few days before the German offensive opened the 2/7th Battalion Duke of Wellington's Regt. made a successful raid on the enemy's trenches, about midway between Acheville and Arleux. The object of the raid was to find out, if possible, what was happening behind the enemy's front line. The raiding party consisted of Lieut. H. L. Hopper, Second-Lieut. J. Buckley, ten N.C.O.'s and sixty other ranks; six sappers were also detailed by the C.R.E. to complete the cutting of gaps in the enemy's wire by means of Banga-

17TH MARCH lore Torpedoes. Zero hour was to be 11 p.m. on 17th.

The enemy's wire had partly been cut by 6-inch T.M.'s when, at Zero minus ten minutes, a dummy barrage was put down on the enemy's trenches south-east of Arleux, which successfully drew attention from the real point to be raided. At 11 p.m. the Divisional Artillery opened fire on the real front to be raided and formed a

---

[1] The official date of the formation of the 62nd M.G. Company seems to have been 9th March, 1918, on which date the Battalion was constituted as follows :—Commanding Officer, Lieut.-Col. G. N. Harrison, D.S.O., Border Regiment, 2nd in command Major A. O. Gordon, M.C., M.G.C. The Battalion was organized into four companies : A (late 201st M.G. Company), B (late 208th M.G. Company), C (late 212th M.G. Company), and D (late 213th M.G. Company). Each Company was divided into Nos. 1, 2, 3 and 4 Sections.

box barrage round it. The raiding party then went forward and by 11-25 p.m. had returned to its own lines, with five German prisoners of the 469th Infantry Regt. (240th Division), having killed several more of the enemy's troops. The 2/7th Duke of Wellington's had three men wounded, one of whom afterwards died. The success of the raid was largely due to the excellent barrage put down by the Divisional Artillery. "The raiders wish me to say," said the G.O.C. 186th Infantry Brigade to the C.R.A., "that the barrage was perfect. Would you please accept for yourself and your batteries, thanks for the large part you contributed towards the success of the show? To show the accuracy of the shooting, the Bangalore Torpedoes were inserted in the wire while the barrage was still on the front line. This, and the absence of casualties from short shooting, and the fact that the garrison of the trench was discovered prostrate on the floor of the trench, I think speaks for itself."

Chapter XIII.

THE GREATEST GERMAN EFFORT: THE OFFENSIVE OF 21st MARCH, 1918

> "If the blow succeeded the strategic result might indeed be enormous, as we should separate the bulk of the English Army from the French and crowd it up with its back to the sea."
>
> Ludendorff.

DURING the months which intervened between the Battle of Cambrai, 1917, and the great German offensive of March, 1918, a change had come over the respective positions of the Allies and the Germans along the Western Front. For the former it was a change very much for the worse. Since the close of the Cambrai operations, transition had set in and had continued, until the power of the offensive had gradually passed from the Allies to the enemy. Superiority in numbers, with which the Allies had begun their offensive of 1917, had not availed to defeat the enemy and, when November of that year dawned, Ludendorff had already begun the transfer of divisions from Russia to France and Flanders. For some months he had drawn drafts of fresh troops from the Eastern Front, but it was not until late in that year that he began the wholesale transfer of men and material from east to west. The coming of these troops was well known to Sir Douglas Haig and Marshal Petain, who, in January, 1918, were convinced thereby and by other signs, that somewhere in the near future (the spring was accurately gauged), the enemy would launch a great attack, which would try the resources of the Allies to the very utmost. It was also apparent that not until the enemy *was* superior in numbers would the attack take place.

When, therefore, the year 1918 dawned the relative forces of the Allies and the enemy were briefly as follows :—The British Army was relatively weaker than it was in January of the previous year; drafts for Sir Douglas Haig's divisions, to man the depleted ranks after the operations of 1917, had become totally inadequate and their quality also had deteriorated; the Government at home was responsible for this shortage. It was responsible also, that early in the year Sir Douglas Haig had to take over an additional 28 miles of front from the French. The British Front then extended some 130 miles and, comparatively, less troops were available to hold it than were available in 1916 to hold a front of 80 miles. It was, therefore, obvious that in the early months of 1918 the British Armies were not in a favourable situation. Moreover, the strongest enemy forces were massed opposite Sir Douglas Haig's divisions. The reason of this was that every yard of ground which British troops defended was precious—for it was the way to the Channel Ports.

The decline in the strength of the French Army had been one of the principal arguments used when Sir Douglas Haig was induced to take over extra frontage, so that it was obvious here also that weakness instead of strength prevailed.

Finally, the American Armies could not arrive in sufficient numbers to help stem the tide should a great and violent attack take place in the Spring, as was anticipated.

As to the enemy, one sentence of Ludendorff's is sufficient to give a clue to the condition of the German Armies : " Numerically we had never been so strong in comparison with our enemies."

Such then was the comparative strength of the opposing forces in the west when 1918 dawned. By the end of January, the French had been relieved as far south as Barisis, south of the River Oise, and Sir Douglas Haig had added to his responsibilities—already sufficiently grave.

All along the Western Front a defensive policy was adopted, everywhere behind the front lines Labour Battalions, large working parties of infantry, in fact every man who could be so employed, were set to work on the defence systems, on the roads and communications and in the building of normal and narrow gauge railways. There is no doubt whatsoever, that the enormous amount of work to be done robbed the men of a great deal of time which should have been devoted to military training; this was especially so with newly-arrived recruits.

Towards the middle of February it became known that in three-and-a-half months the enemy had transferred twenty-eight divisions from the Eastern to the Western Front, and six divisions from Italy; large increases in his artillery had also taken place. Aeroplane reconnaissances over the enemy's lines showed a great increase in the number of ammunition dumps and communications, and they showed what was still more significant—a very marked increase opposite the Fronts held by the Third and Fifth British Armies, from the Sensee southwards.

The days of February passed feverishly and, when March arrived, conjecture had given way to certainty, and by all the signs of modern warfare the attack was to be launched against the Third and Fifth British Armies, from the Sensee to the junction of the British and French Fronts, just south of Barisis; the date alone puzzled the Allies.

The earliest mention of the expected attack, contained in the diaries of the 62nd Division, is on the 12th March: "Letter received from XIIIth Corps 13c/XX/G.A., saying that from information received an attack by the enemy, in the neighbourhood of Arras, might be expected at an early date, possibly on 13th March. From 6 p.m. the Division is to maintain a state of immediate readiness and Reserve machine-gun emplacements are to be manned. The Division will 'stand to' at 5 a.m."[1] But nothing happened, and a programme of harassing fire by the Divisional and Corps Heavy Artillery, arranged for and carried out on the night 12th/13th drew only half an hour's bombardment from the enemy's guns in retaliation. Harassing fire was also carried out on the night 13th/14th and 14th/15th March, but still nothing happened. 12TH/13TH MAR.

On the 19th March, Sir Douglas Haig was informed by his Intelligence Department that, judging by the advanced state of the enemy's preparations and other signs, the attack would be launched either on the 20th or 21st. The enemy's heaviest attack would probably fall between the Sensee River and the Bapaume—Cambrai Road. 19TH MAR.

The German plan of attack is here given in Ludendorff's own words: "It was decided to strike between Croisilles, south-east of Arras, and Mœuvres and, omitting the Cambrai re-entrant,[2] between Villers-Guislain and the Oise, south of St. Quentin. It was to be supported on the left by a subsidiary attack from La Fère. The preliminary work and the conduct of the attack made it necessary to interpolate two Army Headquarters and new Line of Communication Inspectorates. The Seventeenth Army, formerly the Fourteenth in Italy, under General Otto von Below...... was put in between the Sixth and Second opposite Arras, and the Eighteenth, formerly

---

[1] G.S. Diary, 62nd Division, March, 1918.
[2] Known to the British as the Flesquières Salient.

19TH MAR. Woyrsch's Group Headquarters, now commanded by General von Hutier......between the Second and Seventh Armies, opposite St. Quentin and La Fère. The boundary between the Seventeenth and Sixth was about half-way between Lens and Arras, that between the Seventeenth and Second approximately at Mœuvres. The boundary between the Second and Eighteenth Armies was formed roughly by the Ormignon brook, that between the Eighteenth and the Seventh was just south of La Fère.

"The Seventeenth Army, therefore, had to make the attack on the line Croisilles—Mœuvres, the Second and Eighteenth that between Villers-Guislain and La Fère. In this operation the Seventeenth and the Second were to take the weight off each other in turn, and with their inner wings cut off the enemy holding the Cambrai re-entrant, afterwards pushing through between Croisilles and Péronne. This advance was to be protected on the south flank by the Eighteenth Army, in continuation with the extreme left wing of the Second. The strength and equipment of these Armies were adapted to their tasks."

The front of attack originally selected by "O.H.L." (German General Headquarters) was just over 30 miles in length, and to each 1,100 yards of front from twenty to thirty batteries of artillery, without trench mortars, had been allotted.[1]

As early in January and February the superiority of the enemy over the whole Allied forces in the West was from twenty-five to thirty Divisions, in March his superiority was even greater. His Seventeenth Army numbered twenty-eight Divisions, his Second Army twenty-two Divisions, and his Eighteenth Army twenty-six Divisions.

Against these forces Sir Douglas Haig disposed :—Third Army —ten Divisions in line and seven Divisions in reserve; Fifth Army —eleven Divisions in line and three Cavalry and three Infantry Divisions in reserve; in all thirty-four Divisions, of which twenty-one were in the front line.[2]

The British troops were disposed in depth; three defensive

---

[1] The attack of 21st March was launched on a front of about 54 miles and, by 28th, had stretched to a front of 63 miles.

[2] As follows, from right to left in the order given :—Fifth Army from just west of La Fère to Gonnelieu—58th, 18th, 14th, 36th, 30th, 61st, 24th, 66th, 16th, 21st and 9th Divisions. Third Army from just north of Gonnelieu to the northern bank of the Scarpe—47th, 63rd, 17th, 51st, 6th, 59th, 34th, 3rd, 15th and 4th Divisions.

The right flanking division of the First Army (on the left of the Third Army) was the 56th (London) Division just north of Gavrelle and Oppy.

belts, sited at considerable distances from one another, had been, or 19TH MAR. were in the process of construction. The most advanced line of all was in the nature of a lightly-held outpost screen, covering the main positions.

Thus was the stage set for the greatest German offensive throughout the whole war and upon which enormous store had been set by the Kaiser's General Staff: " The Army was assembled," reported Ludendorff to the Emperor, " and well placed to undertake the biggest task in its history ! "

No one will ever forget that morning—the 21st March, 1918. For some days previously the enemy had drenched the British lines with gas, and thousands of casualties had been suffered from the noxious fumes; one division alone lost 3,000 men, who had to be sent down suffering from gas poisoning.

All through the night 20th/21st the three defence systems on the British side were manned; the troops waiting for the German offensive to begin. Then, shortly before 5 a.m. on the 21st, such 21ST MAR. a roar of artillery as had never been heard before rent the peaceful early hours of the morning. Gas and high explosive shells fell in enormous quantities along the whole front of the Fifth and Third Armies, from the Oise to the Scarpe. Away behind the front lines, as far back as St. Pol, the roads and railways were plastered with shells from high velocity guns. Between the River Scarpe and Lens, from the La Bassée Canal to the River Lys, thence to the Ypres— Comines Canal, the British Line was drenched with gas and pounded with " H.E."; the French Front also north-east and east of Rheims was heavily shelled and finally Dunkirk was shelled from the sea.

A thick white fog hung over the whole battlefield, hiding the S.O.S. signals which went up from the outpost lines, as out of the mist loomed wave upon wave of the enemy's troops. In many places they were upon the British trenches ere ever the defenders had a chance of snatching up their rifles and emptying them into the living masses as they arrived line upon line.

At this period—early morning on the 21st March, 1918—the 62nd Division still held the Right Sector, Left Divisional Front of the XIIIth Corps (First Army), *i.e.*, the Arleux—Acheville Sector. The 186th Infantry Brigade occupied the left sub-sector (Acheville) and the 185th Infantry Brigade the right (Arleux); the 187th Infantry Brigade was in Divisional Reserve in the Bray—Ecoivres area. From 5·15 a.m. to 8 a.m. the front line trenches of the Division were heavily bombarded by hostile trench mortars, whilst the battery

21ST MAR.   positions were badly shelled during the same hours. About noon, news was received at Divisional Headquarters that the enemy offensive had started opposite the Third Army. But throughout the day no attack was launched against the 62nd, nor indeed was there any change in the line of the First Army, north of the Scarpe, or in the line held by the 15th and 4th Divisions, the left flanking Divisions of the Third Army. The enemy had pushed the line from La Fère to Gonnelieu back for a distance of from 1 to 3 miles; the Flesquières Salient had not been attacked and the line there was held intact from Gonnelieu to Boursies; from Boursies, however, to just north of Croisilles there was another dent in the British line of from 1 to 3 miles. Such was the position at the end of the first day of the great German offensive. There is no doubt that, from the enemy's point of view, it was disappointing, for nowhere along the British front had that wholesale retirement taken place which Ludendorff confidently expected *would* take place as the result of the attacks of the Seventeenth, Second and Eighteenth German Armies.

In all sectors of the line, not attacked by the enemy, the greatest uncertainty prevailed as to what was happening along the front of the Third and Fifth Armies. The wildest rumours were current and extravagant exaggeration floated up and down the line, only to be put right, officially, a little later. It was a day of nerves. Orders issued for the relief of the 62nd by the 31st Division were later cancelled and final instructions stated that the Division would be relieved on the night 23rd/24th March by the 3rd Canadian Division.

22ND MAR.   When morning dawned on the 22nd news had begun to filter through of the retirement of the Third and Fifth Armies, under
23RD MAR.   pressure from overwhelming enemy forces. On the 23rd it was reported that he had retaken Ecoust, Noreuil and the Mort Homme heights (evacuated during the retreat to the Hindenburg Line in March, 1917), and that the XVIIth Corps (Third Army) on the right of the XIIIth Corps (First Army) had withdrawn from the important heights of Monchy. At mid-day still further news was received that the Fifth Army was retiring on Peronne and the Third Army was being pressed back still further by sheer weight of numbers.

The relief of the 62nd by the 3rd Canadian Division was carried out on the 23rd was ordered; the 185th Infantry Brigade was relieved in daylight and all units marched back into camps in the vicinity of Roclincourt; the 2/7th West Yorks. to Stewart's Camp, the 8th West Yorks. to Springvale Camp and the 2/5th West Yorks. to Ecurie Wood Camp. The 186th Infantry Brigade, on relief, marched back to the area Lancaster Camp—Bois des Arleux, with Brigade 23RD MAR. Headquarters at Mont St. Eloy; the 5th Duke of Wellington's Regt. billetted that night in Lancaster Camp, the 2/4th and 2/7th Battalion Duke of Wellington's Regt. in Mont St. Eloy.

The 187th Infantry Brigade, which had been in Divisional Reserve at Ecoivre, moved during the afternoon of 23rd to Arras, where it came under the orders of the XVIIth Corps. All units and Brigade Headquarters billeted in the town.

The relief of the Division was completed by midnight, 23rd March. Orders received at 9-30 on the morning of the 23rd stated that the Division, as it came out of the line, was to be transferred Brigade by Brigade to the XVIIth Corps of the Third Army.

At 9 a.m. on the 24th the 185th Infantry Brigade marched from 24TH MAR. Roclincourt to Arras and Agny, and the 186th Infantry Brigade marched from Bois des Arleux to " Y " huts Agnes les Doisans; Divisional Headquarters were at Warlus. The 187th Infantry Brigade was placed at the disposal of the 15th Division, Third Army, and the three Battalions of the Brigade marched out of Arras, southeast to some old trenches under the lee of Telegraph Hill. D Company of the 62nd Battalion M.G.C. and the 187th T.M.B. also moved forward with the support Battalion.

The C.R.E., with his Field Companies and the 9th D.L.I. marched, on 24th, to the Caves at Ronville. From the latter place the Sappers and Pioneers set out for Telegraph Hill, where, assisted by working parties of infantry, they dug a trench.

No units of the 187th Brigade were, however, called upon by the 15th Division, for the left flank of the Third Army (XVIIth Corps), after the retirement to west of Monchy and St. Martin, held firm until the 26th.

But further south, events were moving rapidly for Byng's line, which at nightfall on the 23rd March, ran northwards from half-way between Saillisel and Manancourt, west of Bus, just east of Bertincourt, thence immediately west of Beugny, east of Mory, west of St. Leger, east again from Boyelle and through St. Martin to the Scarpe at Fampoux and Roeux, had been forced back by the night of 24th to a line which ran almost direct north from Hardecourt-aux-Bois to Boyelles. The Flesquières Salient had not fallen as rapidly as the enemy had anticipated it would fall, but when that part of the line was also evacuated the retirement was very rapid, the enemy making violent efforts to penetrate between the inner flanks of the Third and Fifth Armies.

K

24TH MAR.

The British reserves were now being flung in to stem the tide and Divisions from the northern flank of the attack, which had stood firm, were despatched hurriedly south to assist in holding up and finally bringing to a standstill the ambitious offensive launched by the enemy.

25TH MAR.

Thus it came about that the entry of the 62nd Division into the actual scene of battle was like that of many other Divisions, both hurried and somewhat confused. For shortly after mid-night on the 25th March, Divisional Headquarters received the following wire from Third Army Headquarters : " 62nd Division less one Brigade[1] will move at once to Ayette, where they will come under order of the IVth Corps, A A A 62nd will send a staff officer to IVth Corps Headquarters, Mailly Maillet, on receipt of this order."

A staff officer was despatched in haste to IVth Corps Headquarters at Mailly Maillet, and in the meantime all Brigades were warned by telephone ; at 2-20 a.m. orders were despatched to all units. At 3 a.m. the Division set out along the various roads converging on Ayette.

" The head of the Column," records the 185th Infantry Brigade Diary, " moved off about 3 a.m."

Before leaving Arras all surplus stores and kits were dumped in the town ; it was as well, for as the troops moved southwards the roads became ever more congested—guns and transport, despatch riders, staff cars and supply lorries and ambulances encumbered the highway and progress was tedious and slow. Through the dark hours of the night the 185th and 186th Infantry Brigades trudged on towards Ayette, hoping to go into the line east of that place, but they were doomed to disappointment for, on reaching the village, the staff officer who had been sent to IVth Corps Headquarters brought orders that the Division was to push on immediately to Bucquoy. Before reaching Ayette numbers of French peasants, who had returned to their farms during the Summer of 1917, were encountered about Adinfer ; they had packed up and were once more fleeing westwards before the oncoming enemy.

Divisional Headquarters had left Warlus at 6-30 a.m. and reached Ayette at 7-30 a.m. On finding that the 62nd had been ordered to Bucquoy, the staff issued orders to that effect to representatives of units who had been sent to meet Divisional Headquarters on arrival in Ayette. Divisional Headquarters then set out forthwith for Bucquoy, arriving at about 8-30 a.m. Here, General Braithwaite

---

[1] 187th Infantry Brigade still at the disposal of XVIIth Corps.

went forward immediately to the Headquarters of the 40th and 42nd 25TH MAR. Divisions, just west of Bucquoy, to learn the tactical situation. So far as could be judged the position was approximately as follows : the 41st and 25th Divisions were on the line Biefvillers and Sapignies ; the 19th Division La Barque—Avesnes-les-Bapaume ; the 51st Division in Logeast Wood. The G.O.C., 62nd Division, learned also that throughout the night 24th/25th constant fighting had taken place in the northern portions of the battle front about Sapignies and Behagnies, but all the enemy's efforts to break through had been unsuccessful ; he had been driven back with great loss. Shortly after, another very heavy attack on the Divisions east of the Arras —Bapaume Road, between Favreuil and Ervillers, was repulsed and the enemy driven out of Sapignies, which he had penetrated.

Meanwhile the tired troops of the 185th and 186th Infantry Brigades were trudging along the road from Ayette to Bucquoy. The vanguard of the 185th Brigade began to arrive in Bucquoy about 10 a.m. The roads were in a terrible state of congestion (being blocked by all sorts of transport) and it was almost impossible to get along. In consequence, the Brigade was not concentrated in Bucquoy until about noon. The Corps had ordered the men to have a meal and get rested, but the Division was instructed to hold itself in readiness to move at short notice. As usually happens in such instances, orders arrived before the men had fed, and they had to march off without their dinners, to take up a position between Logeast Wood and Achiet-le-Petit, the 8th West Yorks. on the right, the 2/5th West Yorks. on the left and the 2/7th West Yorks. in support. These positions were taken up by 2 p.m. and the troops began immediately to consolidate the line.

The 186th Infantry Brigade arrived at Ayette about 10 a.m. and passed on through the village to Bucquoy. The latter place was reached about 2 p.m.

" If one had any doubts about the seriousness of the situation," said a C.O. of one of the Battalions of the 186th Infantry Brigade, " they were settled here ; the whole area was a mass of guns of all types, limbers, ambulances, ammunition and transport and, moving at the rear, limping and worn-out men, many of them wounded, of the 41st, 19th, 25th, 42nd and 51st Divisions, seeking their units, too tired from heavy fighting and lack of sleep to have any idea of what was happening in front—no news, no orders, *and yet no panic.*"

This Brigade (186th) was more fortunate than the 185th for, before taking up a defensive position, the troops were fed : "An

25TH MAR. hour's rest and a good meal and then the Division moved up the crowded roads and as soon as we cleared Bucquoy our bands halted and played us into action."[1] It was not until 4-30 that the advance was made towards Achiet-le-Petit. " Packs were dumped, ammunition issued and off the columns moved in artillery formation to their various positions, the men laughing and joking like schoolboys." The Brigade had been ordered to guard the railway running in a south-easterly direction, east of the village; the 5th Duke of Wellington's was on the right, the 2/7th Duke of Wellington's on the left and the 2/4th Duke of Wellington's in reserve. The 5th "Dukes" met with little shelling and no opposition, and finding the remains of an old divisional camp, with unlimited blankets and unexpected comforts, waited for the expected attack with much cheerfulness.

Thus about 5 p.m. on the 25th both the 186th and 185th Infantry Brigades of the Division (right and left respectively) were in line guarding the village of Achiet-le-Petit; the 42nd Division was on the left, but the right flank was " in the air." For on the 186th and 185th Infantry Brigade taking up their positions in front of Achiet-le-Petit the situation in front of them was somewhat obscure. Heavy attacks in the morning had forced the 19th Division to fall back on the 51st Division, who held the Logeast Wood line. This forced the 41st Division to swing its right flank back in order to form a junction with the left of the 19th Division. Just after noon the 2nd Division, which at daybreak was on the right flank of the 19th Division and south of Le Barque, had given way and had been pressed back to a line south of Pys; the left flank of the 63rd Division, on the right of the 2nd Division, had also retired, thus the right flanks of the 51st and 19th Divisions, who were still holding the line Butte de Warlencourt—Logeast Wood were " in the air." Along the whole front of the IVth Corps the enemy was now making heavy attacks, and between Bapaume and Ervillers it was calculated that he had thrown at least 10,000 men into his front line. Constant pressure, and the dangerous right flank, still uncovered, compelled the British line to swing back, pivoting on Ervillers. On the right flank and south, the enemy was advancing on Courcelette. From Sapignies to Ervillers the 42nd Division had staunchly maintained its line, but had also to swing back its right to conform to the movements of the 41st Division. About 1-30 p.m. the enemy again violently attacked towards Bihucourt, but was held up by the 25th

[1] They stepped along cheerily to the tune of "Colonel Bogey."

and 42nd Divisions. Between 3 and 4 p.m. the 2nd Division 25TH MAR. reported the withdrawal of their troops to the west bank of the Ancre, which still further widened the gap between the inner flanks of the IVth and Vth Corps.

It was at this stage that the 62nd Division came into line in front of Achiet-le-Petit. " Divisions," said the official report, " had now got intermingled owing to pressure of the enemy and to passing through each other during the withdrawal." Orders were, therefore, issued by IVth Corps Headquarters to hold the line on a two-division front—62nd right and 42nd left, and during the early evening the Divisions which had been fighting all day in front of Achiet-le-Petit gradually withdrew behind the line held by the 62nd and 42nd Divisions, now the IVth Corps front line.

The four front line Battalions of the Division, as they took up their allotted positions, set to work to consolidate and make themselves as secure as possible, though it was obvious that it would not be long before they were in contact with the enemy. At 7 p.m. General Braithwaite took over command of the right sector, front line IVth Corps, with his Headquarters at Bucquoy.

About 6 p.m. a wire from the 187th Infantry Brigade had reached Divisional Headquarters, in which it was stated that the Brigade had received orders to rejoin the Division and was already on the march.

Of the Divisional Artillery (not relieved by the Canadian Artillery until after the infantry relief had been carried out) the advanced parties began to arrive in Bucquoy about noon; they then moved northwards to Ayette, in order to turn the two Brigades away from Bucquoy (where they would have been of little use) to take up positions near Monchy-au-Bois. It was late before the 310th and 312th Brigades brought the guns into action in positions of observation near Essarts and Hannescamps.

The three Field Companies, R.E., having reached Bucquoy, were sent to Gommecourt, and there the Sappers went into bivouacs and trenches.

The Divisional Pioneers (9th D.L.I.) arrived in Bucquoy late in the afternoon, having been held up along the congested road between that place and Ayette. They were immediately set to work to dig a trench in front of, and east of, Bucquoy, which was not finished until 10 p.m. A little later the Pioneers were ordered up to fill the gap between Puisieux and the right flank of the 186th Infantry Brigade, which was now very exposed.

The recently constituted 62nd Battalion Machine Gun Company

25TH MAR. had gone into the front line with the 186th and 185th Infantry Brigades. "The machine-guns of all three Companies holding strong and carefully selected positions from which good fields of fire, sweeping the valley and spurs, were obtained......The situation was now most obscure, the positions of our own troops and those of the enemy being inaccurately known. The position we held was a strong one, but the flanks were "in the air "[1] as far as could be ascertained. Little hostile shelling had been met with so far, a few 4·2s and 5·9s had, however, disturbed the apparent peace. All night long sounds of transport moving in Bucquoy could be heard. By midnight the (machine) gun teams had...... dug themselves in and were as safe and comfortable as a very cold and clear night would permit. The men and officers had no coats[2] and were very tired after a long and trying march. The men's spirits were good and they were confident of their ability to hold on in their present position.[3]

It was well after midnight before the 187th Infantry Brigade began to arrive in Bucquoy, where the Brigade had been ordered to concentrate, after sending forward one Battalion to occupy the trench, east of the village, dug by the Pioneers.

At 11 p.m. the Corps Commander rang up and found that the 62nd Divisional Headquarters had left for Gommecourt. At the latter place instructions reached General Braithwaite that, owing to the right of the IVth Corps being exposed and the withdrawal of the VIth Corps on the left, it would be necessary to withdraw to the line Puisieux—Bucquoy—Ablainzevelle, the movement to take place either under cover of darkness or in daylight, whichever the G.O.C. 62nd Division preferred. There was, however, little doubt as to which course was advisable, and the G.S.O.1 (Lieut-Colonel C. R. Newman) hurried out at once to give instructions to the Brigadiers to withdraw their troops to the above line before dawn. But owing to the state of the roads and the block of traffic, it was impossible to convey these orders to the Brigadiers until between 2 and 3 a.m. and, in consequence, several of the forward Companies did not begin their withdrawal until dawn had broken.

[1] Only the right flank, the left was in touch with 42nd Division.

[2] As the 186th and 185th Infantry Brigades with Machine-gun Companies of the 62nd Battalion M.G.C. moved to positions east of Achiet-le-Petit packs, etc., were dumped on the ground east of Bucquoy; the troops went into action practically only in the things they stood up in.

[3] Battalion Diary, 62nd Battalion M.G.C.

All along the front during the night of 25th/26th there had 25TH MAR.
been comparative quietude, but certain units had had brushes with
the enemy.

About 11 p.m. the 5th Duke of Wellington's (the extreme right
flank of the Divisional front line) noticed large fires, evidently
lighted by the Germans to denote the flanks of attack. Shortly
after, the Battalion outposts came into conflict with a hostile outpost
and fighting ensued. Several prisoners were taken and other
Germans killed. " The prisoners were well clothed and well fed,
and most optimistic—quite certain that the war was now over *and
that they had won.*" Unfortunately for the enemy there happened
to be someone even more optimistic than he was—the Yorkshireman !

On receipt of orders the 186th and 185th Infantry Brigades
began to retire on the Bucquoy—Puiseux line, but dawn was already
breaking, and before the movement could be effected it was broad
daylight and the enemy, in large numbers, were already pressing
close on the heels of the retiring troops. The 186th Infantry Brigade
had been ordered to withdraw to the high ground between Bucquoy
and Puiseux; the 185th to continue the line on the left of the 186th
Brigade; the 187th Brigade to be in reserve.

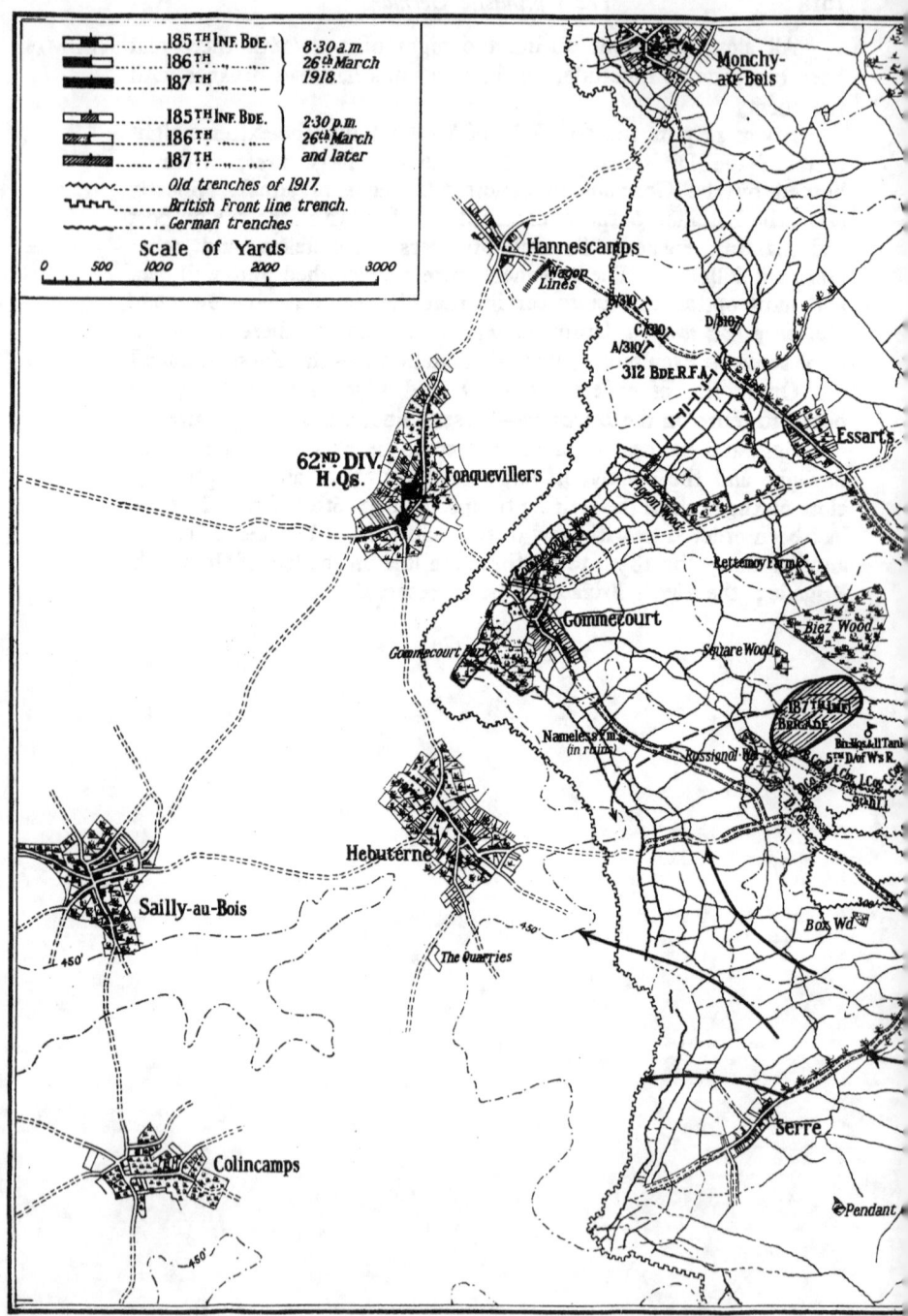

THE DEFENCE OF BUCQUO

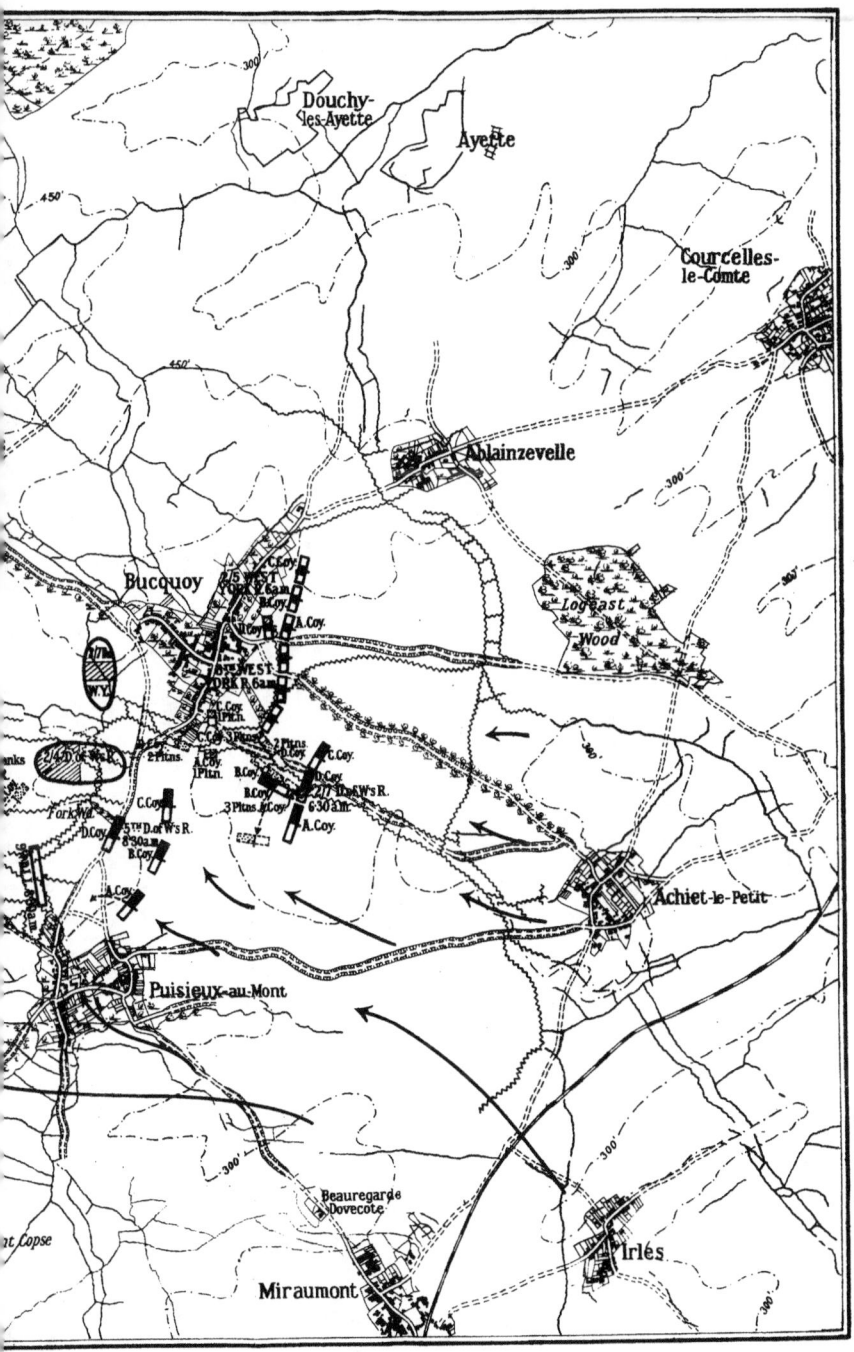

Chapter XIV.

1918.

THE DEFENCE OF BUCQUOY

"In blood and sweat, with slaughter spent,
They thought us beaten as we went;
Then suddenly we turned and smote
The shout of triumph in their throat."
                    Charles G. D. Roberts.

IN many ways the 26th March, 1918, was a momentous and critical day. On this date the enemy further south, in the vicinity of Nesle, made energetic efforts to drive a wedge, and sever connection, between the British and French Armies.

26TH MAR.

SEE MAP No. 10.

North of the Somme the battle was entering upon its final stages, and the retirement to the Ancre, though followed by obviously tired enemy troops, was still hazardous. Between Hamel and Puisieux the position was still obscure; the gap between the IVth and Vth Corps had been exploited by the enemy and, but for the supreme gallantry of the troops, his penetration might have resulted in disaster. As it was, confusion and disorganization (but not panic be it remembered) were everywhere evident and the fighting resembled isolated actions rather than a well-ordered battle front; the enormous superiority in numbers of the enemy's troops had produced this effect.

It was on this day that the Governments of France and Great Britain decided to place the supreme control of the operations of the French and British forces in France and Belgium in the hands of General Foch, who assumed command; this decision was made imperative by the immediate danger of the separation of the French and British Armies.

On this day also the 62nd Division may be said to have entered properly into action, the Division defending Bucquoy with splendid gallantry.

Under cover of the 2/7th West Yorks. (Lieut.-Col. C. K. James), who remained on outpost duty, the 2/5th (Lieut.-Col. A. R.

26TH MAR. Waddy) and 8th West Yorks. (Lieut.-Col. A. H. James), withdrew from Achiet-le-Petit. The 2/5th Battalion left the Logeast Wood line about 5 a.m. and, passing through the 2/7th moved back practically unhindered to positions east of Bucquoy, between the northernmost of the two roads running west from Achiet-le-Petit and the light railway about L.28 central. The Battalion disposed three Companies—A, B and C (in the order given from right to left) in the front line, with D Company in close support on the right. "A" Company threw out two Lewis gun posts and was assisted by a machine-gun post pushed out in front of its right flank. The 62nd Battalion M.G.C. also had two guns with the 2/5th West Yorks.; these were placed in B Company's line, one facing northwards and flanking the wire and the other facing down the valley towards Achiet-le-Petit. These guns were later put out of action, but they were replaced by two guns belonging to the 42nd Division, a machine-gun officer of the latter, with four guns, having retired with the 2/5th West Yorks. as they moved back from the Logeast Wood line. The front of the Battalion was strongly wired.

The 8th West Yorks., who had also retired through the 2/7th Battalion, had taken up a position just east of Bucquoy, between the two roads leading from Achiet-le-Petit to Bucquoy, in touch on the left with the 2/5th Battalion. A section of the 62nd Battalion M.G.C. was also attached to the 8th West Yorks. The 2/7th West Yorks. retired to positions north of Bucquoy.

The withdrawal of the 186th Infantry Brigade (Brig.-General J. G. Burnett), owing to the late receipt of orders, had to be carried out partly in daylight; the 2/7th Duke of Wellington's (Lieut.-Col. F. S. Thackeray) moved back without interference and took up a position about 500 or 600 yards in front, but on the right flank of the 185th Infantry Brigade (Brig.-General Viscount Hampden). But the retirement of the 5th Duke of Wellington's Regt. (Lieut.-Col. J. Walker) was observed by the enemy, who followed closely in large numbers. B Company, the right flank of the Battalion (during the retirement) encountered an enemy cyclist patrol of forty men with light machine-guns in the Miraumont—Puisieux Road. The Company's Lewis guns opened fire and dispersed the patrol, but one gun and a few men were cut off and captured by the enemy moving up the Miraumont Valley. Eventually the Battalion formed a defensive line about 300 yards east of the Bucquoy—Puisieux Road, with Lewis gun posts pushed forward. Three Companies

BUCQUOY: THE RUINED CHURCH.

were in the front line (A, B and C from right to left) and D Company was in support along the road.

The 2/4th Duke of Wellington's (Major L. J. Coombe), having acted as outposts of the 2/7th and 5th Battalions, withdrew through the latter and took up a position in support just west of the Bucquoy—Puisieux Road. The 9th Durham Light Infantry (Pioneers) were about 300 yards west of the Puisieux—Bucquoy Road, in some old trenches. The 187th Infantry Brigade (Lieut.-Col. B. J. Barton) was in Divisional Reserve and had withdrawn to the neighbourhood of Biez Wood.

The moves of the three Infantry Brigades were completed by about 8 a.m.

But the position of the 2/7th and 5th Duke of Wellington's Regt. was by no means a sinecure; neither knew of the whereabouts of the other. The first-named Battalion held a position right out in front of the left flank of the 5th Battalion and the right flank of the 8th West Yorks. (185th Infantry Brigade); the danger of penetration or envelopment was therefore great.

At this hour the positions of the Divisional Artillery and other units, as far as can be gleaned from the official diaries, were as follows:—The C.R.A., on the previous afternoon, when the G.O.C., 62nd Division, had assumed command of the sector, had found himself responsible for a tremendous number of guns consisting of several divisional artilleries.[1] They were all over the place, scattered up and down the line, some batteries being in action, some on the move and others in positions of observation in readiness in rear. The 62nd Divisional Artillery had been diverted to near Monchy-au-Bois, but when morning arrived the tired gunners had taken up new positions, south of Monchy, in the area between Hannescamps and Les Essarts. The wagon lines were south-east of Hannescamps.

Of the 62nd Battalion M.G.C., B Company was with the 185th Infantry Brigade and C with the 186th Infantry Brigade; the two remaining Companies were in reserve west of Bucquoy with the 187th Infantry Brigade.

The three Field Companies, R.E., were situated: 461st Company at Gommecourt, at work on the Gommecourt Salient, providing cyclist road patrols later on in the day; the 460th Company moved

---

[1] General Anderson had under him the VIth Brigade R.F.A., XCIIIrd (A) Brigade R.F.A., 41st Divisional Artillery, CXth Brigade R.F.A., CCXXXVIth Brigade R.F.A. and 62nd Divisional Artillery.

26TH MAR. early in the evening to Fonquevillers where, in conjunction with Labour Companies, work was begun on a line of trenches between Gommecourt and Hebuterne ; the 457th Company was also engaged in this work. The early morning retirement of the Infantry Brigades had somewhat broken up the systems of communications laid by the Signal Company, and it was not until mid-day that the whereabouts of the main Headquarters of all three Infantry Brigades were located and cable lines laid.

Early in the morning Divisional Headquarters moved back to, and was accommodated by 8-30 a.m., in Fonquevillers.

The left flank of the Division was protected by the 42nd Division, which held a line running from the left flank of the 185th Infantry Brigade, thence north of Ablainzevelle and east of Ayette. But the right was entirely exposed and, as was expected, it was not long before the enemy again began to press heavily with the very evident intention of rolling up the southern flank of the Division ; touch had been entirely lost with the Vth Corps.

The attack began shortly before 8 a.m., when the enemy advanced from Achiet-le-Petit westwards, in artillery formation. The machine-guns opened fire and checked his advance 400 yards from the wire in front of the 185th Infantry Brigade. A hostile light T.M., which had been seen coming out of Achiet-le-Petit, came into action about this time ; artillery fire was brought to bear on the Divisional front ; enfilade machine-gun fire raked the trenches of both front-line Brigades and soon the battle seemed everywhere joined.

The right flank of the Division was always the point of anxiety. Here the 5th Duke of Wellington's, who had almost to fight their way back to the positions they now held, had, at about 8-30 a.m. received the welcome addition of a section of four machine-guns from the M.G. Battalion. Two were placed immediately north of Puisieux to cover the Miraumont—Puisieux valley and two to cover the approaches from the direction of Achiet-le-Petit. The enemy at this period was well within range and all four machine-guns came immediately into action. Very soon afterwards the enemy was reported in Puisieux and on the high ground south of that place. "A" Company of the 5th Duke of Wellington's was, therefore, withdrawn and placed facing directly south towards Puisieux to protect the right flank. All the while the enemy was pressing vigorously, but was held back by rifle, Lewis-gun and machine-gun fire. The 9th Durham Light Infantry (under Major Wilson), in the support trenches about 300 yards west of the Puisieux—Bucquoy 26TH MAR. Road, established liaison with the 5th Duke of Wellington's and the 2/4th Battalion was in support of both Battalions. Old trenches north of Puisieux afforded the troops some protection, but the right flank of the Division, though sorely pressed, was stubbornly defended. The enemy's troops seemed countless, they came on unceasingly —Company after Company. Puisieux was full of them, while south of that place they could be seen advancing in great numbers westwards towards Serre, and it was not long before rumours were in circulation that he had reached Hebuterne. The 5th Duke of Wellington's held on as long as possible, frustrating a very determined effort about 11-30 a.m. to outflank the Battalion. But a move was imperative, and gradually, fighting all the way, Companies giving mutual support, the Battalion swung back its right and, in conjunction with D Company and the 9th Durham Light Infantry, took up a position just north of the Gommecourt—Puisieux Road from the south-east corner of Rossignol Wood, joining up with the left of the 2/4th Battalion. All the while the left of the 5th Battalion had been out of touch with the 2/7th, whose whereabouts were unknown. The position occupied at about 2-30 p.m. on the 26th by Colonel Walker's Battalion was maintained throughout the day.

Meanwhile the 2/7th Duke of Wellington's had taken heavy toll of the enemy as he passed south of the Battalion, on towards Puisieux. The Lewis gunners caught numbers of Germans in enfilade and did great execution. Colonel Thackeray, being unaware that the 5th Battalion lay some way behind his right flank, deeming *his* right in danger of being turned, had used B Company to form a defensive flank. At about 10-45 a.m. the enemy seemed to be right round the right flank of his Battalion and he therefore gave the order to retire, Company by Company, to his second position which had been selected along the southern and south-eastern exits of Bucquoy. The withdrawal was carried out with but few casualties, but on the C.O. informing Brigade Headquarters of his movements, he received orders to move back to his old position. This was a difficult task, as the enemy had already occupied part of his old position. Nevertheless, owing mainly to the dash and gallantry of A Company, who rushed an enemy machine-gun section, killed the team and captured two machine-guns, in the main the previous position occupied by the Battalion was reoccupied, though the right flank was extended along an old system of trenches, south of Bucquoy. Touch had been obtained with the 8th West Yorks. on the left and

26TH MAR. when the movement had been carried out the 2/4th Duke of Wellington's were in the gap between the right of the 2/7th and left of the 5th Battalion.

All the while the right flank of the Division was entirely exposed. For some hours (from shortly after 9 a.m.) a huge gap of between 3 and 4 miles had existed between the IVth and Vth Corps. In the old British line of 1917, round Hebuterne, a crowd of men (about 1,000 strong) of various units belonging to the 19th Division, had taken up positions; in the vicinity of Gommecourt another crowd of men of similar proportions was holding disused trenches, which had existed from the days of the Somme Battles of 1916. To fill the gap between the 62nd and the 17th Division (Vth Corps) a New Zealand Division was on its way, but was not expected until the early afternoon. On receipt of rumours that the enemy had reached Hebuterne, an officer was sent out to ascertain the truth and returned with the information that no enemy troops were in the village; isolated cavalry patrols might have reached it (hostile cavalry had been reported on the right flank of the 5th Duke of Wellington's), but Hebuterne was not held by the Germans.

The continuous heavy attacks of that day of fierce fighting will long be remembered by the Division; attacks, pressed with great vigour by troops from whom the final fruits of victory had already been snatched. For by the afternoon of the 26th March the great German offensive, north of the Somme, had almost spent its fury. The Seventeenth German Army, the right flank of the enemy's attack, was exhausted; the Second German Army, in the centre, had become entangled in the old shell holes and trench systems of the Somme Valley, its right flank far in advance of its left; only the Eighteenth German Army, on the left flank, bent upon the capture of Amiens (if possible), still retained a semblance of the dash and fighting spirit, with which it had advanced through the early morning mist of the 21st March.

In obviously disappointed and pessimistic tones Ludendorff said of the Seventeenth Army that, " it had lost too heavily on the 21st and 22nd, apparently because it had fought in too dense formation "—an old German fault. At the Second Army he has a dig, because although fresher, it " was already complaining of the old shell holes. It could get no further than Albert."[1] Finally he ends with words, which, coming from the Chief of the German General

---

[1] Albert was entered by the enemy on the night 26th/27th March.

Staff, are full of significance: "Strategically we had not achieved what the events of the 23rd, 24th and 25th had encouraged us to hope for." 26TH MAR.

It was, therefore, with a fury bordering on despair, that the enemy flung himself into the gap between the flanks of the IVth (62nd Division) and Vth (12th Division) Corps, in a last vain endeavour to drive a wedge between the right Corps of the Third Army. He almost succeeded, but not quite, and the reason he did not do so was largely owing to the fine defence put up by the 62nd Division about mid-day and during the afternoon of the 26th March, when attack after attack was launched against it, but fell back broken and shattered, like waves dashing themselves uselessly against a rocky coast.

On that momentous day—26th—the volume of machine-gun fire which met the Germans, as they advanced against the 62nd Division in the Bucquoy sector was almost certainly the heaviest the enemy had faced throughout the whole war. And the reason was the totally unexpected arrival (and attachment to the Division) of a number of expert machine-gunners, who created appalling casualties and awful havoc amongst the dense grey masses as they advanced upon General Braithwaite's hard-pressed troops.

The General himself tells the story in the following words:

" I was sitting in my hut at Fonquevillers when an enormous figure appeared in the doorway, carrying in his hand an alpine stock about 7 feet high, he himself being about 6 feet 6 inches. This was Ironside, known amongst his friends as " Tiny Ironside," and now General Ironside, Commandant of the Staff College. His question to me was:

" ' Have you any use for one hundred of the best machine-gunners in the world?'

" My reply was:

" ' Have I not!'

" It appears that Ironside, who at the time was Commandant of the Machine-Gun School in France, had been ordered up with every available man and gun and had lost his way (or else the troops he had been told to join had moved) and he found himself near my Headquarters and, knowing I was hard pressed, came to offer his services. It was a perfect Godsend.

" We went out there and then I showed him the position I wanted him to occupy and was also able to show him some excellent

26TH MAR. targets, in fact targets that made many machine-gunners' mouths water."[1]

During the afternoon no less than five attacks were made on the 2/7th Duke of Wellington's Regt. and the 8th and 2/5th West Yorks. They were all bloodily repulsed. The first three reached a line about 400 yards in front of the wire entanglements which protected the frontage of the West Yorkshiremen. Here the enemy's troops not only came under a very heavy frontal fire from machine-guns, Lewis guns and rifles, but, on each occasion were caught in enfilade by the Lewis gunners of the 2/7th Duke of Wellington's, firing from the forward trenches of the latter Battalion. These three attacks were obliterated. The last two did indeed succeed in reaching the wire, but here the same fate met the enemy as on his three previous attempts and only a few survivors crawled back to the German lines.

It was impossible not to admire the bravery of the enemy's troops, but they had opposed to them tough and hardy men who had served their apprenticeship with Failure, Disappointment and Suffering and who, but a year previously, had passed eastwards[2] only a little south of the line they then held, somewhat green as soldiers, somewhat young in knowledge of warfare, yet just as high in spirit as on this day of March, 1918, when tried in the fire of battle, they were found true metal. " It was amazing to see," said a C.O. of his Battalion, " how cheerful all ranks were in this time of strain, partly because they knew what depended on their ' sticking ' it and partly because they could see the damage they inflicted, but mainly because of the sporting spirit[3] that was in them ; the more difficult and desperate the circumstances the more cheery and self-reliant they became."

[1] General Ironside remained with the 62nd Division for some days till General Headquarters found out his whereabouts and ordered him off elsewhere. But as General Braithwaite said : " He had done his job and relieved the pressure on the sorely-tried Division. Indeed his value to the 62nd Division at that time cannot be estimated."

[2] The 62nd Division on the 26th March, 1918, was very near to the positions they had achieved on 1st March, 1917 (three months after arrival in France), during the German Retreat to the Hindenburg Line.

[3] " The sporting spirit " : how many glorious and gallant deeds were performed up and down the line, by officers and " other ranks " because of that spirit ; how often did men face death with a smile upon their lips, their eyes full of that spirit's light, gained upon the playing fields of England ! " There was just a sporting chance "—that wonderful phrase, so typical of British troops and the British temperament, occurs often in the official diaries !

And this being true of one Battalion was true of all, for that 26TH MAR. was the spirit of the men, of that Yorkshire which bred them. It was true not only of the men handling rifles, bombs and machine-guns in the front line trenches, but true also of those units of the Division behind the line, the troops waiting in reserve, the stretcher bearers of the R.A.M.C. carrying back the wounded almost always under rifle and shell fire, of the Sappers digging trenches in rear, should a retirement be necessary, of the Signal Company,[1] struggling to keep communications intact amidst a perfect inferno of shells and untold confusion, of the transport drivers, the ration parties of the Army Service Corps, the Battalion Brigade and Divisional Headquarters Staffs who, not being in the first line of battle, were yet liable to death at any moment:

"He also serves who only stands and waits."

One of the hardest things a soldier has frequently to submit to is that of being shot at, though unable to return the shot. For an Englishman this is a bitter pill to swallow! Yet it happened every day and every month in France and Flanders during those four terrible years of warfare.

Throughout the day the 187th Infantry Brigade (Lieut.-Colonel B. J. Barton) had not been actively engaged. At 1-30 p.m. the 2/4th Battalion K.O.Y.L.I. (Lieut.-Colonel B. H. H. Perry) had received orders to form a defensive flank between Puisieux and Hebuterne, but eventually the line taken up by the Battalion extended from Hebuterne to the west of Rossignol Wood, three Companies being in line, C, A and B, from right to left, with D Company in support. B Company was in touch with the 5th Duke of Wellington's Regt. The 5th K.O.Y.L.I. (Lieut.-Colonel O. C. Watson) and the 2/4th York and Lancs. (Lieut.-Colonel F. St. J. Blacker)

---

[1] The splendid work done by the Divisional Signal Company under Major R. V. Montgomery is thus commented upon by General Sir Walter Braithwaite:—

"In the Retirement, when the Germans first attacked, the Corps Test Box was taken up and burnt and all wires to Corps Headquarters were disconnected. Then came down my Division and we were thrust in to stay the advancing Germans, so everything in the way of communications had to be re-organized afresh. It was more important to get good communications from Divisional Headquarters forward to Brigades, than backwards to Corps, and in this work the Divisional Signal Company excelled itself. Day and night the Signallers were out laying cables and repairing cut telephone wires, and it speaks volumes for the efficiency of that unit that Divisional Headquarters and Brigades were kept in touch throughout all the changing fortunes of that hectic time."

L

26TH MAR. remained in reserve in the positions they had occupied early in the morning.

Dusk had begun to fall over the battlefield (about 5-30 p.m.) and on the left front of the Division the enemy's violent attacks had died down. With the 62nd Division he had joined battle and had suffered heavy losses. But he was evidently not in a mood to accept, without a further effort, the repulse inflicted upon him by the Yorkshiremen, for about 7 p.m., under a heavy machine-gun barrage he made a demonstration against the right flank of the 186th Infantry Brigade. Owing to a misunderstanding the 5th Duke of Wellington's Regt., the 9th D.L.I.[1] and the 2/4th Duke of Wellington's retired, but the Tanks, which had been waiting at Battalion Headquarters, 5th Duke of Wellington's Regt., were at once sent forward, and the three Battalions again advanced to their original positions. Unable to face the Tanks, the moral effect of which was very great, the enemy fled back to his own trenches.

During the night 26th/27th the 2/7th West Yorks. (Lieut.-Colonel C. K. James) moved forward and relieved the 2/5th and 8th Battalions, the relief being completed about 2 a.m. One Company of the 2/5th West Yorks. (C), however, remained in the front line on the left flank of the 185th Infantry Brigade. Both Battalions had had a very trying day, but came out of the line in the best of spirits. The 8th had lost its gallant Commanding Officer—Lieut.-Colonel A. H. James, D.S.O.—who was unfortunately killed early in the day. The 2/5th and 8th Battalions, on relief, moved back to the support trenches on the high ground west of Bucquoy.

Along the front of the 185th Infantry Brigade the night passed quietly.

The 186th Infantry Brigade, after the Tanks had driven the enemy back to his original line, spent a somewhat disturbed night. Patrols were out and several prisoners were captured.[2] The enemy's snipers were active and the right flank of the Brigade was in constant danger of being turned. The maze of old trenches in front of, and east and west of Rossignol Wood, and of which the enemy appeared to have an excellent knowledge, necessitated extreme vigilance.

[1] For the action whereby Private T. Young, 9th D.L.I., gained the Victoria Cross, see Appendix III.
[2] Extract from 186th Infantry Brigade Diary, 26th : " Prisoners captured during the day include the celebrated " Cockchafers " of the 3rd Guards Division, with whom the Brigade had many hand-to-hand encounters in Bourlon Wood during the Battle of Cambrai, 1917.

PRIVATE T. YOUNG, V.C., 9TH DURHAM LIGHT INFANTRY.

Face p. 152.

The huge gap which had existed between the right of the IVth Corps and the left of the Vth Corps had, however, by nightfall, on the 26th, been partially filled. The 4th Australian Brigade began to arrive in the Divisional area about 7 p.m. and (under orders of G.O.C., 62nd Division) took over the defence of Hebuterne from troops of the 19th Division, who withdrew to Bayencourt. By 10-45 p.m. the leading Brigade of the New Zealand Division had moved up towards Serre, filling up half of the gap between the left of the 12th Division (Vth Corps) and the right of the 62nd Division. The New Zealanders occupied a position about 1½ miles west of Serre, with their left flank resting on the high ground east of Colincamps. 26TH MAR.

About 11-30 p.m. orders were received at Divisional Headquarters from IVth Corps Headquarters stating that as a second Brigade of New Zealanders was marching up during the night and was to join up with the Division *south of Puisieux*, the 62nd was to co-operate in this movement by prolonging its line as as to gain touch with the New Zealand Brigade. The 187th Infantry Brigade was warned for this operation, but the orders were subsequently cancelled, as the New Zealanders could not get as far forward as they intended. The 4th Australian Brigade was then ordered to gain touch with the New Zealanders, and this was done at about 7 a.m. on the morning of the 27th, at the Quarries south of Hebuterne.

The 27th March again witnessed fierce fighting along the Divisional front, the enemy resuming his attacks on the 185th Infantry Brigade, east of Bucquoy, and on the 186th Infantry Brigade between Bucquoy and Rossignol Wood. 27TH MAR.

As early as 7 a.m. small parties of the enemy, in fours, were seen by C Company of the 2/5th West Yorks., the 2/7th West Yorks. (185th Infantry Brigade) and the 2/7th Duke of Wellington's (186th Infantry Brigade) advancing westwards from Achiet-le-Petit. Harassing fire was at once brought to bear on them and the Divisional artillery, Lewis guns and machine-guns swept the area over which the enemy was advancing. For two hours the German artillery poured shell into Bucquoy, and on to the front line trenches of the Division. Ever since the night of the 25th, when Divisional Headquarters evacuated the village—Bucquoy had become a very unhealthy place; at all hours of the day and night shells fell amongst the ruined houses, flinging plaster and bricks in all directions, or on to the roads, blowing great holes in the already pock-marked highways. Nevertheless, dangerous as were the trenches held by

27TH MAR. the 185th Infantry Brigade in the eastern exits of the village, the troops, with splendid tenacity, clung to the tumbled earthworks, which at least afforded them protection from rifle and machine-gun fire.

The Lewis gunners of the 2/7th Duke of Wellington's Regt. from their advanced trenches on the right of the 185th Infantry Brigade, again caught the enemy in enfilade and inflicted great loss on his troops as they advanced. Well indeed might Ludendorff complain that the Seventeenth German Army was early exhausted, because of the manner in which it had gone forward, *i.e.*, in massed formation. The colossal losses of the Germans in their Great Offensive of March, 1918, were largely responsible for their final defeat.

Throughout the 27th March the 2/7th West Yorks. gallantly maintained their positions. About noon Colonel James asked for a barrage to be put down, the gunners replying promptly. The Battalion's losses during the day numbered nearly 100 other ranks, but as the Diary proudly states : " The line was not entered in any part and enormous casualties were inflicted on the enemy by rifle, Lewis-gun and machine-gun fire, compelling him to withdraw in disorder."

The Divisional Artillery, still in action between Essarts and Hannescamps, served their guns under a perfect deluge of hostile shells. Their splendid devotion to the infantry in the front line was one of the many memorable things in that fine defence of Bucquoy. Of a gunner officer it was reported that he " sat practically in the open for seventy-two hours by the telephone, receiving and sending messages. He was constantly under shell fire and had to carry the telephone from spot to spot to be able to carry on." Of another gunner officer, responsible for maintaining communication between all batteries of the Brigade and all neighbouring formations taking part in the operations, it was written : " During the whole of this time (26th, 27th and 28th) he was continually laying or mending wires ; where the shelling was most severe he had to go oftenest, and did so with entire disregard of his personal safety. His work (and the results of it) and his behaviour were beyond all praise."

On the right of the Divisional front Brigadier-General Burnett's Brigade (186th) closed with the enemy in bombing contests. The old system of trenches south of and running through Rossignol Wood was a constant source of trouble, for about 12-30 p.m. the right Company (D) of the 5th Duke of Wellington's Regt. was 27TH MAR. attacked, both from across the open and along the old trenches. The attack in the open was easily driven off by rifle and Lewis-gun fire, but the bombing attack up the trenches was very persistent and difficult to hold. To add to the difficulty there was a shortage of bombs. D Company established a block in the trench running south and so kept the enemy back, but he had filtered into Rossignol Wood and from there two snipers got to work on the flanks of the Battalion. During the afternoon several demonstrations by the enemy against the 5th Battalion were broken up by Lewis-gun and artillery fire. But, "about 7 p.m.," states the narrative of the 5th Duke of Wellington's Regt., "the Battalion on our right was seen to be bombed out of its position by the enemy and our right flank again became completely exposed."

The 2/4th K.O.Y.L.I., who, on the previous afternoon, had placed three Companies—C, A and B (from right to left) between Hebuterne and Rossignol Wood, at which place B Company was in touch with the right of the 5th Duke of Wellington's, had spent a day of considerable anxiety and bombing contests with the enemy, for, at 9 a.m. in the morning, the enemy was observed deploying half-way between Serre and Hebuterne. An urgent call for bombs was sent out, but none were available. Presently the enemy attacked A and B Companies, working up the old trenches. Twice B Company, fighting splendidly all the while, was driven out of its position, but on each occasion the enemy's triumph was short-lived, the K.O.Y.L.I. attacking and regaining every foot of lost ground. Whenever the enemy showed himself in the open he was promptly dealt with and heavy casualties were inflicted upon him, but when he bombed his way up the communication trenches there were no bombs to thrust him back again.

At 4 p.m. 77 mm. guns and trench mortars opened on the gallant K.O.Y.L.I., and a little later hostile aeroplanes flew over the trenches, dropping bombs and trying to machine-gun the occupants. Then, at 5-15 p.m., another heavy attack was launched against A and B Companies, which finally drove these two Companies from their positions on the high ground east of Hebuterne. It was this attack which was instrumental in uncovering the right flank of the 5th Duke of Wellington's.

A dangerous gap now existed between the right of the 186th Infantry Brigade and the 4th Australian Brigade in Hebuterne.

D Company of the 2/4th K.O.Y.L.I., which had been waiting

27TH MAR. in reserve all day, was then ordered to counter-attack and restore the situation, and at the same time the 4th Australian Brigade was ordered to send two Companies from their reserve Battalion to man the trenches east of Gommecourt to stop the progress of the enemy in a north-west direction, but apparently orders could not be circulated in time and a defensive line was formed west and south-west of Rossignol Wood.

Two Companies of the 5th K.O.Y.L.I. were then sent forward to reinforce the 2/4th Battalion, and these were ordered to extend the line to the right, where a gap existed.

At 10 p.m. four tanks, assisted by the 5th K.O.Y.L.I., attacked Rossignol Wood and returned, reporting the Wood empty.

A counter-attack, in order to gain the original line held by the 2/4th K.O.Y.L.I., was ordered to take place before dawn on the 28th, and for this purpose two Companies, 5th K.O.Y.L.I. and 2/4th York and Lancs. Regt. were placed at the disposal of the O.C., 2/4th K.O.Y.L.I. The following story of what happened in this affair is taken from the Battalion Diary of the 2/4th K.O.Y.L.I.

28TH MAR. "The counter-attack was launched at 4-15 a.m. Two tanks, which had been left in the south-east corner of Rossignol Wood, were found to be occupied by the enemy, and proved very strong points which were not reduced. The formations for this counter-attack were as follows:—Remnants of A and B Companies on left, D Company on right—1st Wave; one Company (2/4th) York and Lancs. on left, one in centre and one of 5th K.O.Y.L.I. on right—2nd Wave; one Company (2/4th) York and Lancs. on left, one Company 5th K.O.Y.L.I. in centre and one on right—3rd Wave. D Company and the 5th Battalion Companies gained their objectives. They were then cut off and nothing was heard of them after 8 a.m." The Battalion Diary of the 5th K.O.Y.L.I. corroborates these details—A, B and C Companies push well forward and regain objectives (being our original front line). D Company was held in reserve. Later A, B and C Companies are cut off by the enemy and are missing.

Two gallant C.O.'s had become casualties during the night of 27th and in the early hours of the 28th. Lieut.-Colonel O. C. Watson, D.S.O.,[1] of the 5th K.O.Y.L.I., was killed during the counter-attack at 4-15 a.m. on the 28th, while Lieut.-Colonel St. J. Blacker, of the 2/4th York and Lancs. Regt., was wounded a few

[1] See Appendix II. for account from the "London Gazette," of Colonel Watson's action and death, which gained for him the Victoria Cross.

THE LATE LIEUT.-COL. O. C. S. WATSON, V.C., 5TH K.O.Y.L.I.
KILLED AT ROSSIGNOL WOOD, 28TH MARCH, 1918.

" He held his life as nothing."—*London Gazette*.

Face p. 156.

hours earlier, before midnight on the 27th. Major Shearman 28TH MAR. assumed temporary command of the former Battalion and Capt. C. M. Hill temporary command of the latter.

The official accounts of the fighting which took place on the night of the 27th and early hours of the 28th are conflicting and incomplete. No " situation " maps are with the Diaries and, in many instances, the co-ordinates are not given. It was a period of extreme stress and the keeping of accurate records was practically impossible.

Desperate fighting again took place on the 28th March. The attacks launched this day against the 62nd Division were part of the concerted action of eleven German divisions, hurled against the British line from Bucquoy to Avion, just south of Lens, in a determined effort to break through.[1] The attack involved the right of the First British Army.

The attack on the 62nd Division began at 8 a.m. with a heavy barrage put down, not only upon the front line trenches, but on the back areas about Gommecourt, Pigeon Wood and Biez Wood. For two hours this bombardment continued with unabated fury. The 185th Infantry Brigade still held the left of the Divisional Sector, with the 2/7th Battalion West Yorks. in the front line, and although the Battalion suffered from shell fire, the enemy made no infantry attack on the West Yorkshiremen.

South of Bucquoy, however, the 186th and 187th Infantry Brigades, as well as the 4th Australian Brigade at Hebuterne, were subjected to furious attacks throughout the day.

General Braithwaite had sent a message to his troops on the previous afternoon : " Men are doing splendidly and I know how tired they are, but we have got to stick it."

And " stick it " they did !

The 2/7th Duke of Wellington's Regt., observing a large body of the enemy advancing towards their right, opened a long-range fire with eight Lewis guns and broke up the advance ; this was at 9 a.m.

About 9-30 a.m. the enemy was observed massing between Fork Wood and the ridge south-west of the Wood. At this hour a very heavy barrage was falling on the area occupied by the 5th Duke of

---

[1] " The Seventeenth Army.........attacked in the last days of March in the direction of Arras, making its principal effort on the north bank of the Scarpe. It was to capture the decisive heights (Vimy Ridge) east and north of Arras ; the next day (29th) the Sixth Army was to prolong the attack from about Lens and carry the high ground in that area. I attached the greatest importance to both these attacks."

28TH MAR. Wellington's Regt., 9th Durham Light Infantry and 2/4th Duke of Wellington's Regt. The Divisional Artillery was signalled to fire on this concentration and, with a battery of machine-guns belonging to the 62nd Battalion M.G.C., inflicted very heavy casualties on the enemy. But the latter was not to be denied and, an hour later, in great strength and with grim determination, he attacked along the whole front of the 5th Duke of Wellington's Regt. and 9th Durham Light Infantry. All up and down the line from just south of Bucquoy, thence northwards across the Scarpe to east of Vimy, the enemy hurled thousands of men that day at the British line; at one place six waves of German troops, advancing shoulder to shoulder, were counted. They were brave, those Germans, but as a famous General once said: "It was not war." They were decimated ere ever they reached the British wire.

Along the 62nd Divisional front the enemy did not succeed in reaching the trenches of the 5th Duke of Wellington's Regt. and of the 9th Durham Light Infantry. Time after time, the records state, the enemy massed troops and advanced only to meet the same fate, the Lewis guns and accurate rifle fire were too much for him and, "during the rest of the day the enemy were seen crawling back towards Fork Wood." In front of one Company alone, belonging to one of the two Battalions attacked, lay 200 German dead.

In conjunction with these heavy attacks across the open, a very determined bombing attack was made by the enemy east of Rossignol Wood. In this attack, one platoon of D Company—No. 13—of the 5th Duke of Wellington's Regt. became isolated. Many gallant efforts were made to reach the platoon which, at 1·5 p.m., was reported as still holding out, and at last the attack succeeded, only to find, alas! that Second-Lieut. A. Cawthra and his comrades had been overwhelmed and none remained alive.

At 3·15 p.m. the enemy again massed for an attack south-west of Fork Wood, but again the Divisional Artillery and machine-guns tore gaps in the ranks of the assembling Germans and no attack developed.

A little later the 2/4th York and Lancs. Regt. reported the enemy again in possession of Rossignol Wood and endeavouring to bomb west and east along both flanks. East of the Wood the 5th Duke of Wellington's established a bombing block and formed a defensive flank—D Company being withdrawn into the line with B Company. Riflemen were then concentrated to keep down the enemy's snipers.

West of Rossignol Wood, the 187th Infantry Brigade had like- 28TH MAR. wise been heavily attacked. Several attempts made to push through the line of the 2/4th York and Lancs. Regt.[1] met with no success. The remnants of the 2/4th K.O.Y.L.I., in the line, numbering only just over 200 officers and men, were subjected to heavy shelling. Of the 5th K.O.Y.L.I. only D Company now remained.

West of the 187th Infantry Brigade, against the 4th Australian Brigade, at Hebuterne, the enemy had also made several determined attacks, both across the open and up the old system of trenches, where his bombers made progress. By 2 p.m. he had driven the 5th K.O.Y.L.I. from the Ridge, east of Hebuterne, and from Rossignol Wood.[2]

At 11 a.m. the 41st Division had been ordered up to man the hastily-constructed system of defences, known as the Purple Line, running north and south, east of Gommecourt. An officer of the 124th Infantry Brigade (41st Division) had reported at Rottemoy Farm for orders and, with the concurrence of 41st Divisional Headquarters, was ordered to recapture Rossignol Wood. The attack was to be made from the north. There was, at this period, one Battalion belonging to the 41st Division holding the trenches west of the Wood and, through a mistaken order, this Battalion, instead of moving round the Wood and attacking it from the north, attacked due eastwards, with the result that it became involved in fighting with enemy posts, which had worked forward from the left flank of the 4th Australian Brigade in the direction of Nameless Farm. By the time the attack and results of this attack became known, darkness had begun to fall and the situation at Rossignol Wood was critical. The 8th West Yorks., then in 185th Brigade reserve, west of Bucquoy, were ordered to counter-attack as early as possible and placed for this purpose under the orders of the G.O.C., 187th Infantry Brigade. The G.O.C., 4th Australian Brigade, was also ordered to co-operate by driving the enemy from the trenches south-east of Gommecourt, using, if necessary, all his reserves. If the attacks of the 8th West Yorks. and 4th Australian Brigade succeeded the 5th Duke of Wellington's Regt. was to advance its right flank and conform.

It was 7 p.m. before these orders could be issued and just dark.

[1] On 28th March, Major L. H. P. Hart assumed command of the Battalion *vice* Lieut.-Colonel Blacker, wounded.

[2] During the 28th Lieut.-Colonel C. K. James, D.S.O., O.C., 2/7th West Yorks., assumed temporary command of the 187th Infantry Brigade, the Brigadier having been evacuated, sick.

28TH MAR.

The 8th West Yorks. moved down for the purpose of making the attack, but the ground was unknown to them and no reconnaissance was possible. The Australians, who had better opportunities of preparing their attack, became involved with the enemy (before the West Yorkshiremen were ready) in a bombing fight, and succeeded in driving him back 500 yards down the trenches south-east of Gommecourt. But it was 2-30 a.m. on the morning of the 29th before the West Yorks. launched their attack and, though the Battalion did not succeed in capturing the Wood itself, owing to the heavy machine-gun fire, the northern end of the Wood was reached.

The attack on Rossignol Wood had failed, but the situation had been greatly eased and the gap between the 186th Infantry Brigade and the Australians had been satisfactorily filled. Two prisoners were captured by the 8th West Yorks. The Diary of the 2/4th York and Lancs. Regt. (187th Infantry Brigade) recorded that that Battalion " took over 30 yards of trenches in the Wood, captured by the West Yorks. and the West Yorks. were then moved back."

28TH/29TH MAR.

On the night 28th/29th the 185th Infantry Brigade was relieved by the 42nd Division and the West Yorkshiremen were withdrawn to the vicinity of Rottemoy Farm, where they were in a good position to reinforce the 187th Infantry Brigade, should it be necessary.

Throughout the night no further attacks were made by the enemy; he had spent his fury, and had found the British line unbreakable, not only along the front of the 62nd Division, but also along the whole front of attack astride the Scarpe. " With this day's battle (28th)," said the Official Despatches, " which ended in the complete defeat of the enemy on the whole front of the attack, the first stage of the enemy's offensive weakened and eventually closed on the 5th April."

The 26th, 27th and 28th of March were days of which the 62nd Division might well be proud. The repeated attempts of the enemy to break through the line and roll up the flanks had nowhere succeeded. Gaps in the line had indeed been forced, but when the enemy attempted to exploit them his troops were caught in enfilade and were swept away ere ever they reached the wire. Ever since the afternoon of 25th, when the 185th and 186th Infantry Brigades, dead tired, having marched all the previous night, but " cheery " beyond words, moved down the two roads running eastwards from Bucquoy, played into action by their bands, the right flank of the Division had been in perpetual danger and it was no small feat to maintain it during the subsequent days of heavy attacks by night and by day. Well deserved was a message received on the 29th from IVth Corps Headquarters : " The Corps Commander congratulates 42nd, 62nd and New Zealand Divisions and the 4th Australian Brigade on their magnificent behaviour during the last few days' fighting. Numerous heavy attacks by the enemy have been completely repulsed with heavy loss and the capture of prisoners and machine-guns. He heartily thanks the troops for their courage and endurance, and is confident that they will continue to hold the line against all attacks." 28TH/29TH MAR.

The enemy did not again attack in force. Constant bombing and sniping, patrol work and machine-gun activity occupied the attention of all troops in the front line. Sniping was very active on both sides, but the Division seems to have maintained more than its own in this deadly work. One N.C.O., belonging to the 2/7th Duke of Wellington's Regt., claimed to have killed thirty-one Germans in one day.

On the night of the 31st March/1st April the 186th Infantry Brigade was relieved by a Brigade of the 37th Division and marched back to Souastre and Henu. The following night the remainder of the Division (less the artillery) was relieved by 37th Division and moved back into the reserve area in the neighbourhood of Pas, Marieux and Authie. 31ST MAR./ 1ST APRIL

The strain of the past week had been terrific.[1] In France and

---

[1] General Braithwaite thus pays tribute to the fine work of his Brigadiers and Os.C. Battalions during those strenuous days :—
" General Taylor was away from the 187th sick, and as his successor had not arrived, the Brigade was temporarily in command of one of the colonels, but he also was sick and not up to the strain, so General Burnett of the 186th Brigade, in addition to his own work, reorganized the 187th Brigade on the 27th of March in a most masterly way, handing the reorganized troops over to Colonel C. K. James (7th West Yorks. Regt.), whom I appointed to the command until the arrival of Brigadier-General Reddie. Again both Walker (Lieut.-Colonel) and his Second-in-Command, both of the 5th Duke of Wellington's, although wounded, declined to leave their Battalion and carried on their functions, wounded as they were,—a magnificent example to their gallant men. I would like also to say something about Lieut.-Colonel A. H. James of the 8th West Yorks., known throughout the Division as ' James VIII.', in contradistinction to his namesake, C. K. James, who commanded the 7th West Yorks., and who was known as ' James VII.'. The Division sustained a very great loss in the death of ' James VIII.' during this period. He was killed as he would have wished to be killed—in command of his Regiment on the 26th of March. His loss was felt not only in his Battalion, but in his Brigade and throughout the Division. He had brought his Battalion to a high pitch of efficiency. He was a very gallant, honest, fearless soldier, one we could ill afford to lose. O. C. Watson (Lieut.-Colonel) was another fine soldier who was killed during this time. He had been very badly wounded at Bullecourt, but insisted on going back to the Division at

31st Mar./
1st April

Flanders the troops were under no delusions as to the momentous issues of the great German offensive; they knew it meant all or nothing to the enemy, and they determined it should be nothing! Very heavy losses were expected, for the numbers of the German divisions opposed to them were fairly accurately known. But they went into the fight optimistic and with high spirits grand to see. Those who sat at home in England would have been astonished at the optimism prevailing in the British front lines.[2] There was more pessimism in one town in England than in the whole of the British trenches along the Western Front!

Back in the reserve area the 62nd set to work to reorganize and refit. Terribly exhausted were some of the men; for about a week on end the 186th Infantry Brigade (as an instance) had been in the front line, bearing the brunt of the enemy's determined efforts to turn the right flank of the Division, but the staunch devotion of the Yorkshiremen robbed the Germans of victory. The small amount of ground gained by the enemy was but poor recompense for the heavy losses in men he had sustained, for between Bucquoy and the western banks of the Ancre, opposite Thiepval, the British line for the last five days of the Great German Offensive of March, 1918, remained practically the same; between 27th and 31st March, less ground had been given on this front than on any other part of the line from Arras to where the British and French lines met, south of the Somme. The 62nd Division, with the 42nd and New Zealand

the first possible opportunity. This gallant officer was killed in a counter-attack on Rossignol Wood. At first the attack was successful, but his men were eventually outnumbered, and he saw that retirement was necessary. The assault which he led was at a critical moment, and undoubtedly saved that part of the line for which he was responsible, and when retirement became necessary, he ordered his men to go, but remained himself in a communication trench to cover the retirement, though he faced almost certain death by so doing. In the words of the extract from the *London Gazette*, in which he was awarded a posthumous V.C. ' both in the assault and in covering his men's retirement, he held his life as nothing, and his splendid bravery inspired all troops in the vicinity to rise to the occasion, and saved a breach being made in a hardly-tried and attenuated line. Lieut.-Colonel Watson was killed while covering the withdrawal.' To lose two such men as ' James VIII.' and O. C. Watson in the same battle was a dire blow to the Division. In addition three commanding officers were wounded : Lieut.-Colonel Freddie Blacker for the third time. The Division owed much to Brigadier-Generals Burnett and Hampden and Lieut.-Colonel C. K. James, who commanded the Brigades during this period. Better leading or more cool and courageous handling no troops ever had."

[2] The losses of the 62nd (W.R.) Division during March, 1918, were ninety-eight officers and 2,084 other ranks, killed, wounded and missing. Most of these were during the period 25th—31st March. Two C.O.'s were killed and three were wounded.

Divisions, should be particularly proud of the stand made north of 31ST MAR./ 1ST APRIL
the River Ancre.

The splendid support given by the Divisional Artillery to the hard-pressed infantry in the first line trenches has already been referred to, whilst again and again the fine efforts of that latest formation—the 62nd Battalion M.G.C.—can be detected in the description of those periods when the machine-gunners caught the enemy troops as they advanced against the Division. Behind the line the pressure was not less severe. At Divisional Headquarters the strain was very heavy. Night and day the " G " Staff knew no rest in a situation which changed almost from hour to hour.[1] On the "A" Staff, fronted with the difficulty of replenishing the constant diminishing stocks of ammunition and stores, was imposed a task of extreme gravity. It was no easy matter to procure even the barest necessities, for dumps had been blown up or stripped clean, transport was scattered or had become intermingled with transport of other divisions, and the ordered system of refilling had received a rude shaking ; it was a period during which one could only " beg, borrow or steal," whenever and wherever an opportunity presented itself ; and if opportunities did *not* present themselves they had to be made. On the 29th March the Diary of the A.A. and Q.M.G., 62nd Division, (Lieut.-Colonel H. Lea) contains the following entry : " Large demands for bombs owing to bombing attacks of both sides at Rossignol Wood. Demands met, but with some difficulty. If the Divisions had not moved from XIIIth Corps area with full echelons, ammunition situation would have been at times critical."

On the 28th March, Fonquevillers, where Divisional Headquarters were situated, was so heavily shelled that a move became necessary and Divisional Headquarters were established in Souastre.[2]

[1] On 29th March the G.S.O.2, Battalion Major F. W. L. Bissett, M.C., D.C.L.I., was wounded.

[2] " The first Divisional Headquarters on March 25th was at Bucquoy, near the Railway Station, but we were very soon shelled out of that during the night. *Gommecourt* :—We had not been there more than a few hours, before we were shelled out of *that*, and every line cut, and we went back to Fonquevillers (where we remained 26th, 27th and 28th of March), which was a possible Headquarters, and had the advantage of being within easy reach of all Brigade Headquarters and the front line, an essential in the type of battle we were fighting. On the 28th, however, the shelling was so bad that the wooden walls of the Headquarters Hut were pitted by shrapnel like smallpox, and when it came to an orderly being hit while he was actually handing a letter to the G.O.C., it was time to find more sheltered Headquarters, where the work could be carried on in a little more security, and so, on the 29th, Divisional Headquarters found its final resting place at Sousatre."

Chapter XV.

THE PERIOD OF ACTIVE DEFENCE

1918.

> "At the outset of this period, the most pressing need after filling up the gaps in our divisions, was to close the breaches which the German advance had made in our successive defensive systems."
>
> Official Despatches.

FOR only a very few days was the 62nd Division out of the line. The German Offensive in Picardy had spent itself by the 5th April, but on 9th the Offensive in Flanders began and no one knew whether it might not break out afresh south of Arras. The splendid defence of Bucquoy by the 62nd had placed the Division high in favour at General Headquarters. It had earned the distinction of being mentioned in official despatches, and at a time when every soldier was needed in the front line trenches, the period allowed for reorganization and refitting was cut down to the minimum.

6TH/7TH APRIL.

On the night of the 6th/7th April the 62nd moved back into the front line relieving the 42nd Division; the 185th Infantry Brigade taking over the right and the 186th the left sub-sectors of the Bucquoy sector; the 187th Infantry Brigade was in Divisional Reserve.

April was a comparatively quiet month, which in many ways was a blessing. Much work was necessary, both in the front line and on the communications, for which purpose every available man who could be spared joined the working parties which, by day and by night, were employed in strengthening the defences and in digging new defensive lines, of which, between April and July, Sir Douglas Haig stated, " 5,000 miles of trenches were constructed." Truly a prodigious performance.

24TH/25TH APRIL.

On the nights of 23rd/24th and 24th/25th of April the 37th Division relieved the 62nd, the latter moving back to Authie and area, in Corps Reserve. The Diary of 62nd Divisional Headquarters, at this period, gives an admirable insight into the state of

24TH/25TH APRIL.

preparedness of the Army. The entry is dated the 25th April: " The Division, whilst in Corps Reserve, will be prepared to move
(a) From 9 p.m. to 9 a.m. daily at one hour's notice;
(b) From 9 a.m. to 9 p.m. daily at two hours' notice.

The rôle of the Division is to regain any portion of the Purple Line in the Right Divisional Sector that may be lost, or, in the case of a hostile attack on a fairly large scale, the Red Line between the Corps Right Boundary and J.14 central. The 187th Infantry Brigade is placed under the orders of the G.O.C., New Zealand Division, in case of necessity." The reasons for this state of preparedness were that the Battles of the Lys were not yet ended, and the Second Battle of Kemmel Ridge was actually taking place when the above entry was made.

15TH MAY.

Until the 15th May the Division was out of the line, but on the 16th the 186th Brigade moved up into the left sub-sector, relieving the 63rd Infantry Brigade (37th Division). On 17th the 185th Brigade took over the right sub-sector, the 187th Brigade remaining in Divisional Reserve. Headquarters of the 62nd were established at Henu.

Although up and down behind the whole front line of the British Armies on the Western Front intense activity prevailed, the troops in the forward trenches were far from idle. The German Offensive on the Lys ended on the 29th April. Then began the period of Active Defence, during which the Germans suffered enormous losses. At all times of the day and night, the guns pounded the enemy's forward and back areas. These " harassing shoots," as they were called, took very heavy toll, not only of his infantry, but of his artillery. Trench mortar batteries, Stokes guns, Lewis guns and machine-guns fired " concentrations " on the enemy's trenches and soon the *morale* of the German soldiery began to suffer considerably.

Adopting similar tactics the enemy appears to have shelled the British lines with a degree of intensity which caused such entries to be made in the 62nd G.S. Diary as : " Artillery activity above normal." Such phrases occur frequently during the month of May, but apart from one or two minor affairs there are no records in the Divisional Diary of an attack on a large scale, either on, or by, the enemy.

18TH MAY.

The first of these " affairs " apparently took place early on the morning of the 18th May, when, at 6 a.m., a small party of twelve Germans was observed in Bucquoy cemetery. A patrol belonging to the 2/7th Duke of Wellington's Regt. pushed forward to engage 18TH MAY. this hostile party and successfully dispersed it; the Germans retired leaving one dead man behind.

On each of the next five days the enemy literally drenched the Divisional Area with gas shell, "mustard gas" being used freely.

At 11-15 p.m. on 23rd May the 2/7th West Yorks. Regt. carried 23RD MAY. out a "minor enterprise" on an enemy post in the neighbourhood of Bucquoy. The enemy outnumbered the West Yorkshiremen, who were eventually forced to retire, though not before they had killed three Germans in a hand-to-hand fight. The 2/7th had one man wounded.

A little later—at 12-30 a.m. on 24th—the enemy attacked a party of the 8th West Yorks. who were working in the front line; one officer and fourteen other ranks were wounded and one officer (Lieut. E. Pepper) and fourteen other ranks were missing.

The 2/5th West Yorks. carried out a daylight raid on the 25th on an enemy post south-west of Bucquoy. The raid began at 2-45 p.m. and fourteen prisoners, two light machine-guns and one Granatennerfer were captured and a dug-out in the enemy's lines destroyed. Obviously annoyed by the success of the Yorkshiremen, the enemy pounded the trenches of the 185th Brigade all the afternoon and, at 8 p.m., attempted a raid on the trenches of the 2/5th West Yorks., but was repulsed.

Until the end of May the artillery of both sides continued to shell one another unmercifully, and the infantry in the front line trenches had a bad time.

The above is a fair survey of trench warfare at this period. It was costly in the extreme. During May, the 62nd lost nineteen officers killed, wounded and missing and sixty-two other ranks killed, 392 wounded and fourteen missing. Unfortunately the killed included that very gallant officer Lieut.-Colonel C. K. James, 2/7th West Yorks. Regt., who was wounded and died on 19th, a great loss to the Battalion, Brigade and Division.

On 1st June instructions were received that two more battalions 1ST JUNE. of the Division—2/7th West Yorks. Regt. (185th Brigade) and 2/7th West Riding Regt. (186th Brigade), were to be formed into training cadres and, after reinforcing the remaining units of both Brigades, the surplus men and officers were to be sent down to the Base. The 1/5th Devons. and 2/4th Hants. Regts. were to take the place of the two Battalions.

Thus again, the Order of Battle of the Division was disturbed.

1ST JUNE. Bitter indeed was the pill to swallow, for both battalions had fought most gallantly from the very time they landed in France in January 1917. But the training of new troops was essential, and the cruel blow suffered by the 2/7th West Yorks. and 2/7th Duke of Wellington's Regts. was somewhat softened by the knowledge that, having fought well and achieved much, they were now to be used in preparing fresh arrivals in France to take their places in the front line.

A few days later the 1/5th Devons. and 2/4th Hants. arrived, the former being posted to the 185th Brigade and the latter to the 186th Brigade.

The 2/7th West Yorks. and the 2/7th Duke of Wellington's Regts. were relieved in the front line for the last time on the 15th June, and, on the following day, the Training Staff Cadres of both Battalions proceeded by rail from Mondicourt for Boulogne *via* Abbeville. On the 19th June the surplus personnel proceeded to the Base by road.

24TH JUNE. On the 24th June the relief of the 62nd Division by the 37th Division began, the former passing back into General Headquarters Reserve "to be prepared to move at 9 hours' notice to join the XXIInd Corps."

Divisional Headquarters were at Pas, the 185th Brigade at Authieule, Amplier and Terramesnil; the 186th Brigade at Henu and Thievres and the 187th Brigade at Couin. The Divisional Artillery was at Sarton and Orville, the D.A.C. being at Amplier.

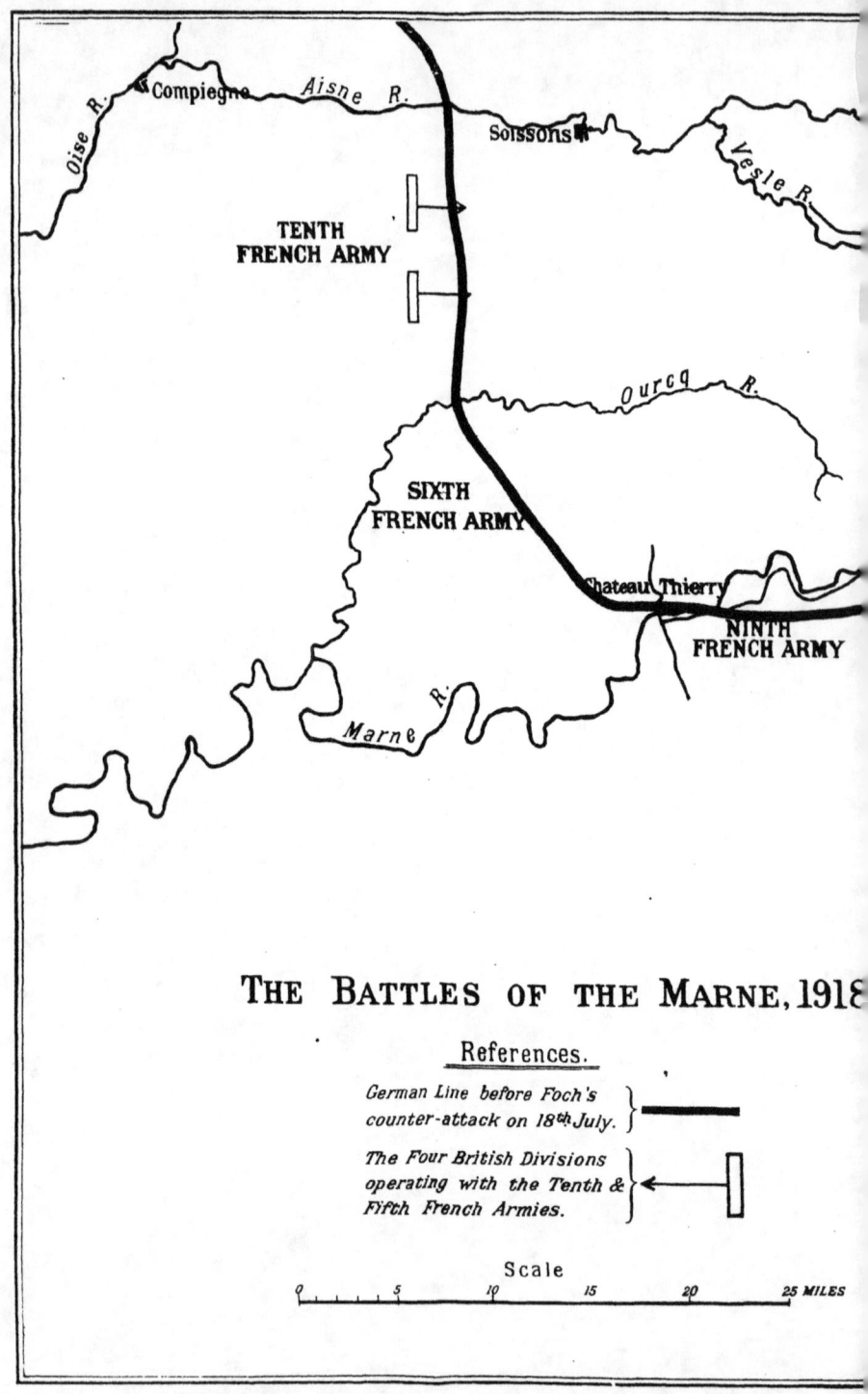

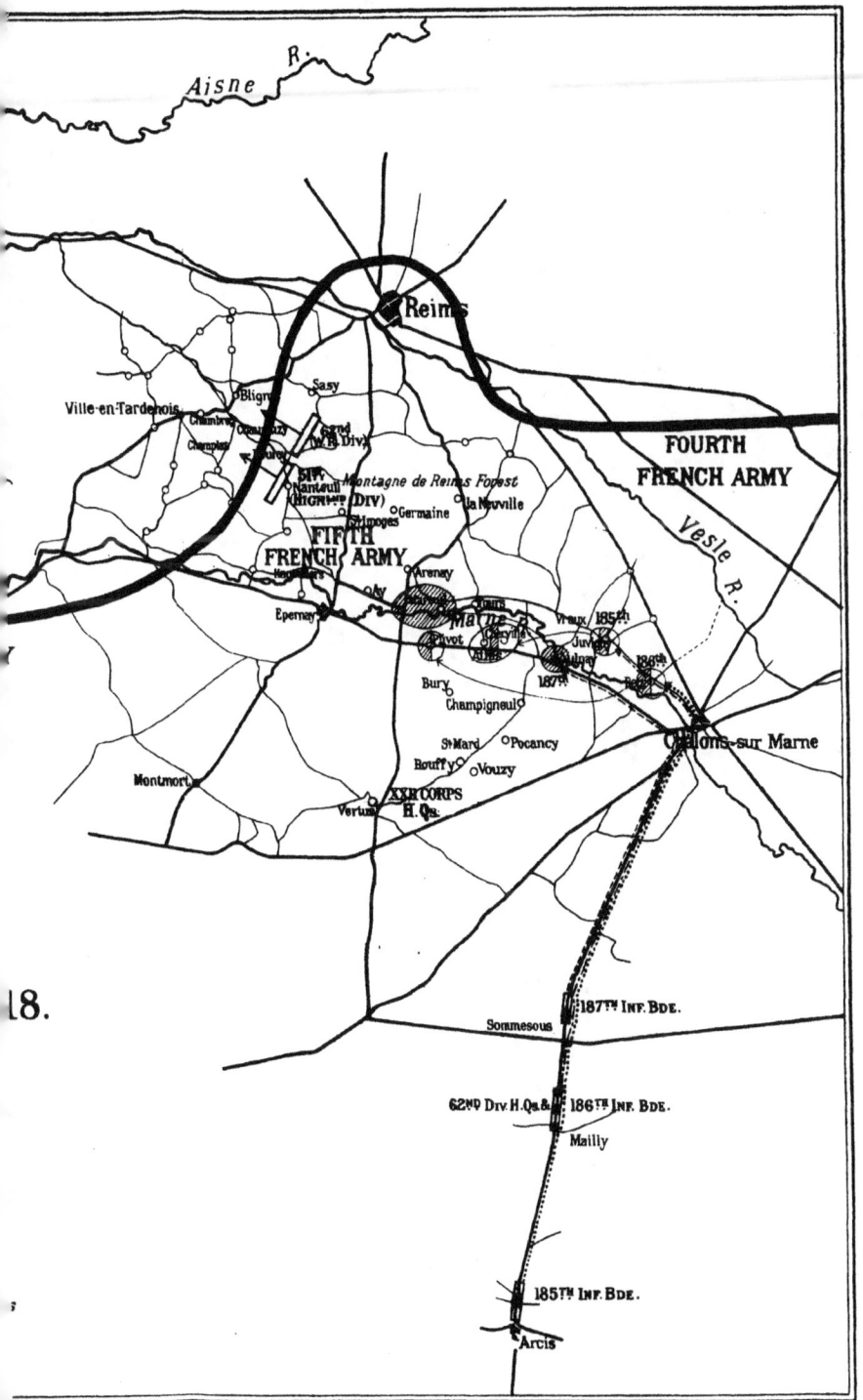

DOWN TO THE MARNE.

Chapter XVI. 1918.

THE DIVISION MOVES DOWN TO THE MARNE

AMIDST all the changing episodes of the war there were some upon which men still look back with pleasurable recollections and gratitude. And to those who served with the 62nd Division in all its periods of hard fighting and rest (and survived them) the quiet peaceful days which followed relief from the Bucquoy sector at the end of June, 1918, will long be remembered. Divisional Headquarters were at Pas—the IVth Corps Rest Area—and around, in the villages and towns, the remaining units of the Division were billeted and, to the joy of all, the gunners were with them. Rare indeed were such occasions, for usually long after the tired and exhausted infantry had been withdrawn from the line to "rest," the guns remained behind to "carry on." A more unselfish existence it is not possible to imagine. But on this occasion, to the unbounded satisfaction of all ranks, the sorely-tried gunners had been relieved, and therefore back in the Rest Area the Division not only set to work to train hard, but also to *play hard.* Comfortable billets and glorious summer weather, drill and parades in the morning, sports in the afternoon, performances by the, now famous, "Pelican Troupe," which played to crowded houses in the evening, all combined to make this rest period one to live in the memory. And with death their constant grim companion in the front line trenches, how men lived and laughed away from them!

JUNE.

Thus a fortnight passed. A fortnight—and then came rumours of a move, this time to "an unknown destination": rumours, followed quickly by "Operation Orders." With the 51st (Highland) Division, the 62nd was to move south, to join the Fifth French Army.[1]

The battles of the Marne, 1918, were about to begin and British troops were once again to fight amidst the cornfields of the Marne valley. But on this occasion the troops would be Territorials and

[1] The Official Despatches state that the 15th, 34th, 51st and 62nd Divisions constituted the XXIInd Corps under Lieut.-General Sir A. Godley. But the 15th Division went to the XXth French Corps and the 34th Division to the XXXth French Corps, both of the Tenth French Army. The 51st and 62nd Divisions, constituting the XXIInd British Corps, joined the Fifth French Army, after having first of all detrained in the Fourth French Army Area.

JUNE.

men of the new army, worthy successors of the old Regular army, many of which lay buried beneath the very ground over which English and Scottish battalions, with the French armies, were to once more drive the Germans back to the Aisne river.

The units of the 187th Infantry Brigade were holding their sports when verbal orders for the move were received from Third Army Headquarters, and at once the administrative staff set to work to prepare the " programme," no light task seeing that something like forty trains, each of forty coaches, would be required to transfer the Division to its new front. Entrainment was to begin at 4 p.m. on the 14th July.

The circumstances which gave rise to the transfer of British troops to the French Area are briefly as follows :—The great German offensive south of Arras on March 21st had been followed, in April, by similar operations on the Lys front and important places had been gained by the enemy before his advance had been definitely stopped. Thereafter followed the period of " Active Defence," during which the reorganization of the British and Allied armies took place. Minor operations, in which artillery bombardments played a great part, prevented the enemy making a further attempt upon the British front, but south, in the areas held by the French armies, it was evident that the Germans intended launching a similar offensive to those of the 21st March and 9th April. " The British General Staff," said Sir Douglas Haig, " had always held the opinion that before the resumption of the enemy's main offensive on the Arras—Armentières—Montdidier front, the attack on our northern flank in Flanders would be followed by a similar attack on the southern flank of the Allied armies. This view had proved correct. Though probably delayed by his unexpectedly extensive commitments in the Lys battle at the end of May, the enemy had designed his plan of operations on the lines which we had foreseen and had launched a violent surprise attack on the Aisne front. In this attack certain British divisions, which had been sent there to rest, became involved from the outset."[1]

Prisoners taken by the French, within a few hours of the German offensive on the Aisne front, gave information of the coming great attack on the 27th May. On this date no less than twenty-eight German divisions, supported by tanks, attacked the Sixth French Army on a front of 36 miles north-west of Rheims. By

[1] 8th, 21st, 25th and 30th Divisions, subsequently reinforced by the 19th Division.

nightfall the enemy had forced the line of the Aisne on a wide front and had crossed the Vesle west of Fismes. By the evening of the 30th the centre of his attack had reached the Marne, but the rate of his advance in the British sector (between the Vesle and the Ardre valley) had begun to slacken. For the next few days, however, fighting was still intense, the enemy gaining the north bank of the Marne from Dormans to Chateau Thierry and advancing astride the Aisne to the outskirts of the Villers Cotterets Forest, and across the high ground north-east of Attichy. On the eastern flank of the salient created by the enemy's advance the British forces, at this date under command of the Fifth French Army, withdrew gradually to the line Aubilly—Chambrecy—Boujacourt, where they were able to concentrate. For some days the enemy's attacks continued, culminating, on the 6th June, in two determined attempts on the important position known as the Montaigne de Bligny, which commands the valley of the Ardre. All these attacks were most gallantly repulsed and the enemy's advance definitely stayed. It was of the part played by the British troops in this attack that the French General, under whom they served, wrote :—" They have enabled us to establish a barrier against which the hostile waves have beaten and shattered themselves. This, none of the French who witnessed it will ever forget."

On the 7th June the enemy made a surprise attack on the French between Noyon and Montdidier. The attack failed, but the strain now imposed on the French armies by these two attacks was considerable and the Germans might reasonably be expected to exploit the situation with all the means in their power. Indeed German General Headquarters was, at this period, desperately in need of a victory with which to buoy up the German people.

At French Headquarters it was accepted as a certainty that the enemy was about to attack in strength east and west of Rheims, and it was feared the attack might spread even into the Argonne, endangering a wide sector of the French position. Marshall Foch thereupon withdrew the whole of the French forces (eight divisions) from Flanders and transferred them south to the French front. " He asked that four British divisions might be moved, two of them to areas south of the Somme and two to positions astride that river, so as to ensure the communications between the French and British armies about Amiens and to enable him to move four French divisions farther east to his right flank. After carefully weighing the situation I agreed to this proposal and immediate orders were given for the movement. On the 13th July a further request was received from Marshal Foch that these four British divisions might be placed unreservedly at his disposal, and that four other British divisions might be despatched to take their places behind the junction of the Allied armies. This request was also agreed to, and the 15th, 34th, 51st and 62nd Divisions, constituting the XXIInd Corps,[1] under the command of Lieut.-General Sir A. Godley, were accordingly sent down to the French Front."[2]

14TH JULY.

On the 14th July entrainment of the 62nd Division began, the first train leaving at 4-42 p.m. The 187th Infantry Brigade entrained at Doullens North, and 185th at Doullens South and the 186th Infantry Brigade at Mondicourt. The Divisional troops were split up amongst Brigade troops and the Divisional Artillery entrained at all three stations. Entrainment continued through the night and,

15TH JULY.

at 6-12 a.m. on the 15th July, Divisional Headquarters left Mondicourt.

The Division was in first-class fettle, and was in splendid form when the orders to move south arrived. The Divisional Artillery, especially, during this period of rest had benefited greatly and, after the Division had entrained, General Braithwaite received a very complimentary letter from General Geddes, commanding R.A., IVth Corps, in which he said " I told the Corps Commander that I have seldom seen horses in such magnificent condition, or a better turn out of men, horses and vehicles. They might have been proceeding for a ceremonial show in London, instead of going to take part in a battle."

On this same day—15th July—the Germans made their great attack on both sides of Rheims. The Seventh German Army attacked west and the First and Third German Armies east of the city. " The Seventh German Army was to cross the Marne east of Chateau Thierry and at the same time to advance on both sides of the river in the direction of Epernay, while making Chalons-sur-Marne their principal objective. The attack of the Army Group left untouched the enemy positions between the Ardre and east of Rheims, thus acquiring a considerable breadth, which seemed favourable to success. The junction of the two attacking groups in the neighbourhood of Epernay might lead to very important results."[3] In short, Ludendorff hoped to pinch off Rheims and the territory

[1] See previous footnote.
[2] Official Despatches.
[3] Ludendorff.

south of it. But this attack had been foreseen by Marshal Foch, who 15TH JULY. had made every possible preparation to meet it. West of Rheims the enemy crossed the Marne east of Chateau Thierry, and pushed his line southwards almost to the north-western edge of the Foret de Montaigne de Rheims. But east of Rheims the First and Third German Armies had made but little progress. The Fourth French Army retired to its second line of defence, leaving only machine guns to prevent the enemy advancing too rapidly : but on its second line the Fourth French Army held the Germans firmly.

"On the 16th," said Ludendorff, "we gained ground up the 16th JULY. Marne and towards the Ardre." A pocket, 10 miles wide, had indeed been gained south of the river, but Foch regarded it without concern ; his efforts were concentrated on a counter-attack between Chateau Thierry and Soissons, where he knew the Germans were least expecting a heavy blow. And so, all unknowingly, Ludendorff played into the hands of France's great general and had laid up for himself a store of trouble and affliction from which he was never to recover.

It should be remembered that at this period the Germans were still superior in strength to the Allied forces in France and Flanders.

Thus momentous things were happening even while the trains conveying the 62nd Division were running southwards, and when the Division arrived at its detraining stations the eve of great events had almost arrived.

The journey south occupied about thirty-eight hours, but the change of scenery and the prospects of an entirely different kind of warfare, to say nothing of a glimpse of Paris, through which the long trains passed, raised in all ranks an extraordinary degree of enthusiasm.

Divisional Headquarters reached Mailly-le-Camp (about 20 16TH JULY. miles south of Chalons-sur-Marne) on the 16th and at 5 p.m. detrained, establishing Headquarters at Vraux ; here also the 186th SEE MAP Infantry Brigade detrained. The 185th detrained at Arcis and the NO. 11. 187th at Sommesous. On detrainment the Brigades moved in motor buses to the following billets areas :—185th Infantry Brigade, Juvigny-sur-Marne ; 186th Infantry Brigade, Recy ; 187th Infantry Brigade, Aulay-sur-Marne. The Division was now in the Fourth French Army Area.

[1] The map shows the German line on the 15th July and should be studied in conjunction with the map showing the operations of the 62nd (W.R.) and 51st Divisions after their arrival and entry into the battle.

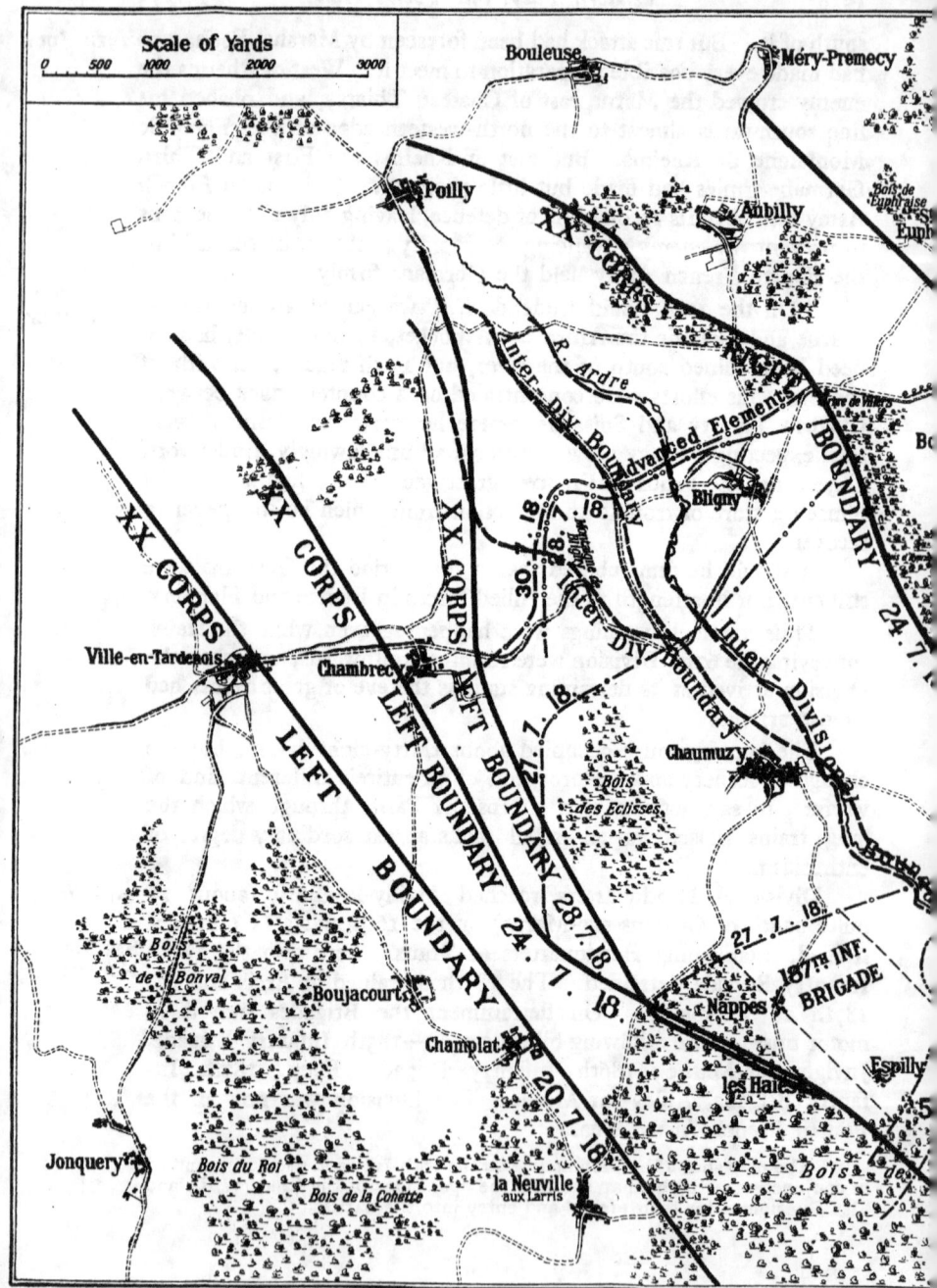

THE BATTLE OF TARDENOIS: CAPTU

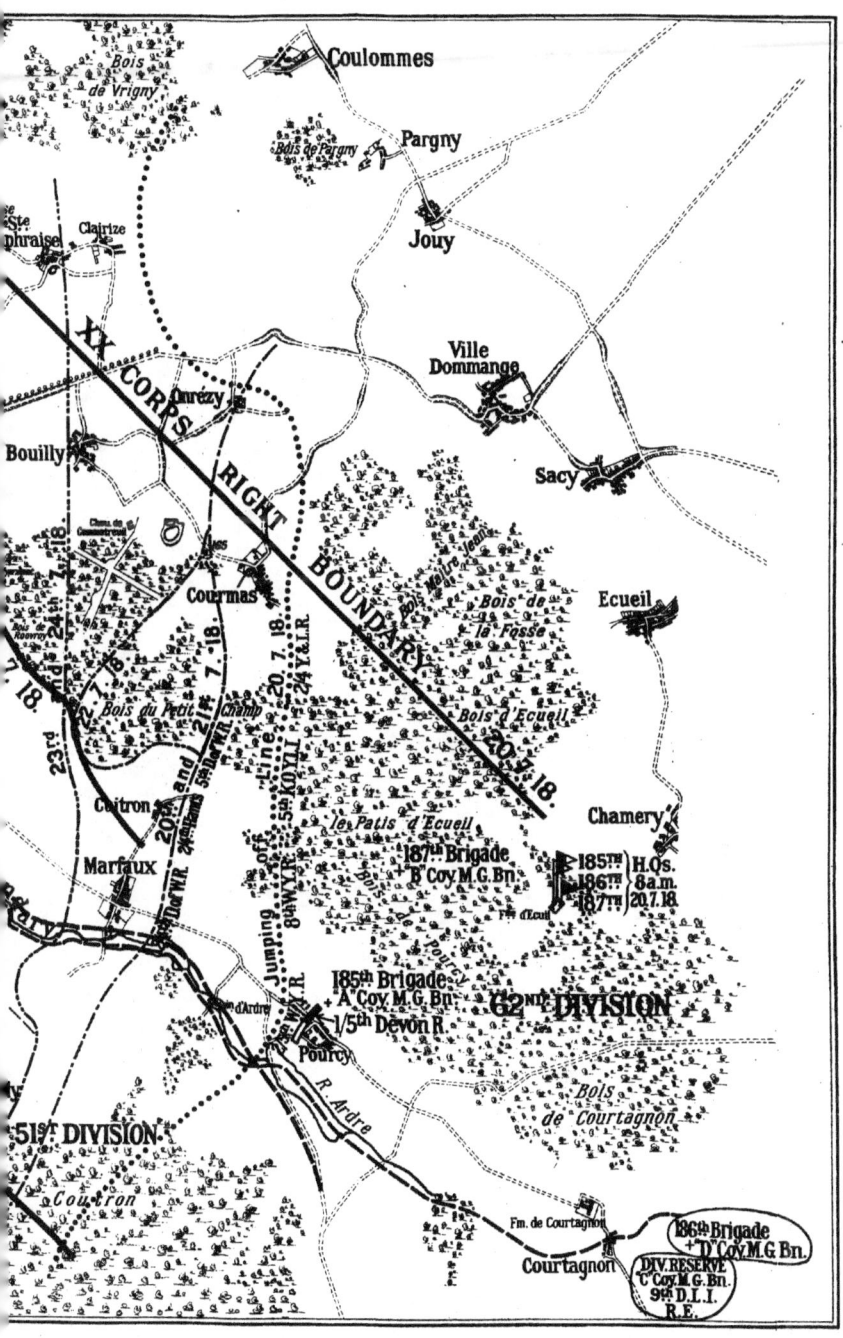

Chapter XVII.

1918.

THE BATTLE OF TARDENOIS: CAPTURE OF MARFAUX.

"We had now to deal with the heavy counter-offensive of General Foch against our sharp Salient between Soissons and Rheims. English divisions were also taking part."

Ludendorff.

ON arrival at Mailly-le-Camp General Braithwaite motored to Chalons and there reported to Fourth French Army Headquarters. He was told that as all attacks on the Army front, *i.e.*, east of Rheims, had been repulsed and the enemy brought to a standstill, the XXIInd British Corps was to join the Fifth French Army, and that the 62nd Division was to move on the following day to the Fifth Army Area. Orders then had to be sent out to divert the bus convoys, which were carrying the troops from detraining stations to their billets, into the new area. Eventually all the convoys were traced and the battalions which had not settled down into billets were pushed on into the new areas, whilst the three Brigade Headquarters and units which had already arrived in billets in the Fourth Army Area spent the night where they were. Orders were issued for the remaining units to march at 5 a.m. next morning to concentrate in the Fifth French Army Area.

The confusion which had arisen placed a heavy burden on the Administrative Staff, while the considerable distance between the detraining stations and the front line inflicted unnecessary fatigue on the units as they moved forward. Apparently the French were none too sure that the enemy might not push through and to prevent any possibility of a dislocation of their plans, fixed the detraining stations some distance from the forward area.

The move by road began at 5 a.m. on the 17th and, on completion, the 62nd Division was disposed as follows:—Divisional Headquarters and Headquarters, 185th Infantry Brigade, at 17TH JULY.

17TH JULY. Tours-sur-Marne, the units of the Brigade being at Plivot; the 186th Infantry Brigade was at Athis and Cherviole, and the 187th Infantry Brigade at Bisseuil and Mareuil.

Divisional troops for whom no lorry transport had been provided and who, in consequence, had to march between 20 and 30 miles, were not completely concentrated in their new billets until the 18th, while some units, including the last Battalion to detrain, did not 19TH JULY. arrive until the early morning of 19th July. But finally these tired units and the Divisional Artillery were billeted as follows :—Artillery : in Pocancy, St. Mard, Roofy and Vouzy ; 62nd Battalion M.G.C. and R.E. Companies, Champigneuil and Champagne ; 9th Durham Light Infantry, Bury.

Fifth French Army Headquarters were at Montmort and British Corps Headquarters at Vertus.

Apparently the general situation along the front of the Fifth French Army was as follows :—In the German attack of 15th July, the IInd Italian Corps, the centre corps of the Army, had been forced back down the valley of the Ardre as far as Nanteuil. A vigorous counter-attack had, however, relieved the latter place and, at present, it was held by the French. On the right of the Italian Corps the Ist Colonial French Corps had thrown back its left flank to conform to the movement of the Italians. At the junction of the Fifth and Sixth French Armies, the enemy had succeeded in penetrating some distance down the valley of the Marne towards Epernay, and the Vth French Corps of the Fifth Army had been obliged to fall back. It was therefore anticipated that the rôle of the British Corps would be to relieve or reinforce the IInd Italian Corps, which consisted of 1st Italian Division on the right (Headquarters at Serniers), 120th French Division in the centre (Headquarters at St. Imoges), and 14th French Division on the left (Headquarters at Hautvillers). Only the 14th French Division was comparatively fresh.

18TH/19TH JULY. About 10 p.m. on the night 18th/19th the 187th Infantry Brigade moved up to the Ferme D'Ecueil, to be at the call of the 1st Colonial French Corps should the enemy attack.

19TH JULY. At 12.30 a.m. on the 19th a staff officer from XXIInd Corps Headquarters arrived at 62nd Divisional Headquarters with orders for the 62nd to concentrate behind the IInd Italian Corps by noon, 19th July, preparatory to attacking through the Italian Corps in a general advance along the whole army front on 20th July. These orders cancelled the relief of the 1st Italian Division on the night 19th/20th July.

The 62nd Concentrates

19TH JULY

What had happened?

On the 18th General Foch had launched his counter-attack between Chateau Thierry and Soissons. The Tenth, Eighth, Ninth and a part of the Fifth French Armies (in the order given from left to right) dealt the German armies a surprise blow. Ludendorff had not counted upon a counter-attack falling on this part of his line and had left only a few divisions in front of the Tenth French Army. He had imagined that his own attacks had drawn all the French reserve towards the Marne and Chalons.

It was at this stage, when the enemy was reeling under the sledge-hammer blows dealt him by Foch that the 62nd and 51st Divisions on the Rheims side of the salient, and the 15th and 34th Divisions between the Oise and the Aisne came into line, to help pinch off the huge salient between Rheims and Soissons.

At 2-45 a.m. on the morning of the 19th July orders were received for the 62nd Division to march at 5 a.m. and concentrate in the following areas:—185th Infantry Brigade at St. Imoges; 186th Infantry Brigade, Germaine; 187th Infantry Brigade (already there) at Ferme d'Ecueil; 62nd Battalion M.G.C. and the Field Companies, R.E. at La Neuville; Divisional Artillery at Avenay and Ay.

At 12 noon Divisional Headquarters moved from Tours to Germaine. Broadly, the scheme of attack in which the 62nd and 51st Divisions were to take part was up the valley of the Ardre river to a final objective 7 kilometres (roughly 4½ miles) from the starting point; the attack to be supported by French and Italian artillery. The scheme was decided at a conference held at IInd Italian Corps Headquarters, at which the British Corps (Sir A. Godley) and IInd Italian Corps commanders, the G. O.'s C., 62nd and 51st Divisions and French G. O.'s C. were present. On conclusion the G. S. O.'s 1. of both British Divisions set out for XXIInd Corps Headquarters at Vertus for written orders and to make final arrangements. The long journey to Vertus delayed matters considerably, so that when at last orders were received at 62nd Divisional Headquarters it was nearly 5 o'clock in the evening and a detailed reconnaissance of the positions to be attacked was impossible. The scheme of attack was explained to Brigadiers at Divisional Headquarters at 5-30 and draft orders issued, but it was 9 p.m. before final orders were sent out and " Zero " hour was at 8 a.m. on the following morning.

SEE MAP No. 12.

The 62nd was to attack on the right and the 51st Division on the left, the dividing line between Divisions being the River Ardre; the 2nd Division Italian Corps was attacking on the right of the 62nd Division.

19TH JULY.

General Braithwaite decided to attack on a two-Brigade front, 187th on the right, and 185th on the left; on the leading Brigades reaching their first objective the 186th from Divisional Reserve, was to pass through the 185th and 187th and capture the second and final objective.

A machine-gun Company was attached to each Brigade; one M.G.C., the Pioneer Battalion (9th Durham Light Infantry) and the three field companies, R.E., less a few parties detailed for bridging the Ardre and preparing the road through Marfaux, were in Divisional Reserve.

Fighting, vastly different from anything previously experienced, now faced the Division. Trench warfare, for the time being was done with. It could hardly be called warfare in open country, for the attack would, in places, have to go through thick forests and, as will be read later, the troops, in moving up to their assembly positions, tramped through almost impenetrable woods, in which the enemy lurked, making strenuous efforts to hold up the advance of the Yorkshiremen. Guerilla warfare would aptly describe much of the fighting which subsequently took place.[1]

The valley of the Ardre varied from 2,000 to 3,000 yards in width. Much of it was gently undulating corn land, with the crops ripe for cutting, and of sufficient height to act as excellent cover for attacking or defending troops. The villages of Marfaux, Chaumuzy, and Bligny lay on the slopes to the river, bordered by steep ridges and spurs, heavily wooded on the crests, whilst Cuitron, Espilly and Nappes were perched high up on the steep sides of the hills.

At 8 p.m. on the evening of 19th July the 187th Infantry Brigade received orders to attack the enemy's positions in Courmas and Bois du Petit Champ at 8 a.m. on the following morning. The situation of the Brigade was then :—187th Infantry Brigade Headquarters (Brig.-General A. O. Reddie)—Chamery; 2/4th (Hallamshires) York and Lancs. Regt. (Lieut.-Colonel L. H. P. Hart)—Nogent; 5th K.O.Y.L.I. (Lieut.-Colonel F. H. Peter)—Bois de Pourcy; 2/4th K.O.Y.L.I. (Lieut.-Colonel C. A. Chaytor)—Sermiers. Half-an-hour later the troops had begun to advance, the 2/4th K.O.Y.L.I. being the first to move, followed by the Hallamshires and the 5th K.O.Y.L.I. The 2/4th York and Lancs. Regt. was to be on the right of the attack, the 5th K.O.Y.L.I. on the left, and the 2/4th K.O.Y.L.I. in support.

[1] Speaking of the thickness of the woods, General Braithwaite said : "I have seen nothing thicker since I fought thirty-five years ago in the Burmese Jungle."

Some little confusion occurred at the beginning of the move 20TH JULY. owing to the guides being Italian, and lack of interpreters, but eventually the battalions were well on the way, and by 4-30 a.m. on the morning of the 20th, were in their assembly positions; 187th Infantry Brigade Headquarters had moved up to Ecueil Farm.

Headquarters, 185th Infantry Brigade (Brig.-General Viscount Hampden) from Tours and the units of the Brigade from Plivot had set out at 5 a.m. on the morning of the 19th to march to St. Imoges. The dusty roads, crowded with transport and traffic, mostly French, tried the troops to the utmost, and tired, thirsty and hungry when they reached their destination, they sank, almost exhausted, to the ground. They were to bivouack for the night in the thick woods about St. Imoges.

The three Battalions had hardly made themselves comfortable and the officers' cooks were engaged in providing the best possible meal, when all C.O.s were called to Brigade Headquarters in the woods east of St. Imoges. Here the situation, as far as known to the Brigadier, was explained, and orders for the attack on the following morning given out. Battalion commanders were told to march off as soon as possible to reach Courtagnon by 12 midnight, where guides provided by the French, then holding the line, would meet them and conduct them to their assembly positions. The frontage allotted to the Brigade was from the Bois de Rheims, on the right, to the River Ardre, on the left; the 8th West Yorks Regt. (Lieut.-Colonel England), on the right; 2/5th West Yorks. (Major R. Stewart), on the left, and the 1/5th Devon Regt. (Lieut.-Colonel H. V. Bastow), in support. The positions of assembly were:—8th West Yorks Regt. Bois de Pourcy; 2/5th West Yorks Regt. and 1/5th Devons, round Pourcy.

No details exist in the Battalion Diaries of the difficulties of that terrible march by night, through almost pitch-black forests, to the positions of assembly. Only one report—by the C.O., 1/5th Devons—gives any impression of the hard task set to troops already tired out by the day's march :—" My Battalion," he said, " marched at 10 p.m. from St. Imoges. Guides were met at the Farm Courtagnon; these led the Battalion by woodland tracks to positions of assembly near French Regimental Headquarters. Tracks very steep and rough; heavy shell fire experienced *en route*. Casualties, one officer and twenty-three other ranks wounded, and two other ranks killed. The Battalion formed up at the point of assembly on 20th July at 5-30 a.m. Men very tired by hard climb and rough road."

20TH JULY. But the following account from the private diary of an officer, serving with the 8th West Yorks, gives a very vivid impression of that exceedingly difficult march. " By 10 p.m. we were well on our way with the platoons at intervals of 100 yards. It was a march which will long be remembered, for the bright moonlight made the long straight road into a shining white ribbon, dividing the eerie blackness of the Forest of Rheims.

" Leaving the main road we plunged into the darkness of the wood along a country lane, which soon became only a track. ' They have halted in front, Sir,' shouted the connecting file just ahead. . . . . However, it was a real genuine halt and the column disappeared into the hedge-rows, except for the limbers and the small unfortunate crowd of Lewis gunners, who were now getting their guns, spares and panniers of ammunition, as it had been decided to send back the limbers from this point.

" We now reached one of the worst stages of the journey. The track, hitherto quite respectable, now became a mere narrow space between trees, and later on, into a mere nothingness. Thick blackness was everywhere excepting a faint illumination showing where the tops of the trees were. On and on we stumbled in single file, colliding with trees and with our neighbours and plunging into deep holes full of sticky mud. At one place we passed some French poilus, but could only recognize them by their words of welcome. After despairing of ever getting out of this maze of blackness we began to discern some faint light ahead, and in time we dragged ourselves out into the clean and wholesome moonlight. A rest just outside a gas-shelled, ruined village and again this long single file tried to rejoin its forces.

" Once through the village we again left the road and having climbed up a steep path found ourselves once more in the woods. By this time each Company was moving independently with its own French guide. It was not long before we were on the hard road, disentangling ourselves from Italians, French, another unit of our Division, motor lorries, French transport, ammunition wagons, guns, limbers and mules ; countless mules—mules carrying rations, mules carrying water, mules carrying ammunition and more (spare) mules. We sat down by the wayside and waited . . . and then resumed our journey under the guidance of our very impatient guide. (I discovered later that his impatience was justified, seeing that he had no idea as to our destination !)

" The unfortunate Battalion then became mixed up at some

cross-roads with a crowd of units from different Divisions and of seemingly different nationalities.

" The scene was awesome. French guides, interpreters, company commanders, vied with each other in apt description of the situation, and present and future fate of the responsible authors. The men were feeling too done to comment much beyond an occasional muttered curse.

" Again and again a kind of a raid had to be organized in order to rescue one of our men who had been whirled into the running stream of humanity and mules. . . Our guide implored us to double, but this was just a little beyond us, as we could scarcely limp along. But the fears of our guide were justified for the road began to be heavily shelled. . . Once more we plunged into the horrors of those forest depths and, in the early hours of the morning these dark woods, with their muddy paths and their foul stenches of gas and decaying bodies of horses, began to tell on the energy and spirits of the men. I walked, or rather stumbled along in a kind of mental haze. . . .in a pestilential blackness with a hazy moonlight above the trees, we stumbled on and on and on, through trees, over trees, into trees. When I could think, it was about our attack at dawn. . . There is no energy left for grim jokes or curses, and the only sounds are the sobs of some youngster who found his load of rifle, ammunition, pack, rations, bombs, equipment, one or two panniers and other impedimenta almost too much for his boyish strength. . . It was some time before I could realise that my guide was informing me that we had finished the journey."

A halt was called and whilst the Company Commander went forward to interview the French Company Commander, whose position the former was supposed to take over, the men dropped exhausted and fell fast asleep immediately. Eventually, it transpired that this Company (D) of the 8th West Yorks. was to be in the third wave of the attack; and so it had to be hurried out into a place secure from observation.

From the edge of the Bois de Pourcy, the battered village of Marfaux could be seen away on the left flank ; Cuitron lay opposite the centre, and Bois de Petit Champ on the high ground, whose southern slope was to form the right flank of the 8th West Yorks. In front of the Battalion stretched a golden panorama of cornfields—a wonderful sight in the early morning light.

Just before 8 a.m. the attacking troops were in position : 187th Infantry Brigade (Right) with the 2/4th York and Lancs. on the right,

20TH JULY. the 5th K.O.Y.L.I. on the left and the 2/4th K.O.Y.L.I. in reserve; the 185th Infantry Brigade (Left) with the 8th West Yorks. on the right, the 2/5th West Yorks. on the left and the 5th Devons in reserve. Each attacking Battalion was to move forward on a two-company front.

The 186th Infantry Brigade (Brig.-General J. G. Burnett), which had been ordered to pass through the 187th and 185th Infantry Brigades (when the latter had attained their first objectives) and capture the second and final objectives, had received its final orders at 2-30 a.m. on the morning of the 19th July to concentrate in the woods immediately south of Germaine. Having dumped their packs and surplus baggage at Athis, the Battalions set out to march *via* Tours-sur-Marne and Avenay to their given destinations.

The Brigade was more fortunate in that General Burnett received preliminary orders for the attack on the following day, at 12 noon, his Brigade having reached the woods south of Germaine at 11-30 a.m. It was possible, therefore, for his C.O.'s and Company Commanders to reconnoitre the road between Germaine and Courtagnon; the position of assembly for the Brigade was in the wood east of Courtagnon.

The 186th Brigade was to attack with all three Battalions in line; 5th Duke of Wellington's Regt. (Lieut.-Colonel J. Walker) on the right, 2/4th Hants. Regt. (Lieut.-Colonel F. Brook) in the centre and the 2/4th Duke of Wellington's Regt. (Lieut.-Colonel P. P. Wilson) on the left.

At midnight 19th/20th July the Brigade set out from Germaine. Traffic on the roads was very congested and the assembly positions were not reached until about 5 a.m. The three Battalions do not appear to have experienced the same formidable difficulties in reaching their assembly positions as confronted the 187th and 185th Infantry Brigades.

To each Brigade one Company of the 62nd Battalion M.G.C. (Lieut.-Colonel G. H. Harrison) was allotted—B to the 187th; A to the 185th and D to the 186th. C Company was in reserve with orders to concentrate at Courtagnon by 4 a.m. on 20th. The 9th Durham Light Infantry were in Courtagnon Wood as reserves. The Field Companies, R.E., were at Neuville, but the Signal Company, during the night of 19th/20th had the unusual experience of laying lines over unknown ground in darkness, with the result that they suffered badly from the traffic, until made safe later by poling. But by early morning of 20th the Company had linked up

THE 1/5TH DEVONS RESTING.

communications between Divisional Headquarters at St. Imoges and Ferme D'Ecueil (Brigade Headquarters of the 187th and 185th Infantry Brigades).

The Divisional Artillery was in the process of moving up, and was therefore not available for the barrage, which was arranged by the French Artillery. But gun positions had been reconnoitred by the afternoon of the 19th by the C.R.A. (Brig.-General A. T. Anderson) and his Battery Commanders. R.A. Headquarters opened at St Imoges (at Divisional Headquarters) at 7 a.m.; the 310th Brigade, R.F.A., (Lieut.-Colonel D. J. C. Sherlock) was in its position of assembly, along the road from Etas de Mont Rieul to St. Martin, by 6 a.m., but at 7 a.m. the 312th Brigade, R.F.A. (Lieut.-Colonel A. G. Eden) was in column of route along the road " immediately north of Montaneut " (the diary has it) with some Italian Artillery, the head of the column being at the cross roads.

Thus disposed, the 62nd Division awaited " Zero " hour.

Staff officers had twice visited the 120th French Division to arrange for the artillery barrage, but the positions of the French troops in the front line being uncertain, the barrage was arranged so as to fall 1,000 yards ahead of the forming-up positions of the 62nd Divisional infantry and to keep on this line for an hour. It was 1 a.m. on the 20th before the final barrage scheme was received at 62nd Divisional Headquarters and it had therefore to be accepted as it was. To quote from the Divisional Narrative :—" The attack as far as the ' Halt ' in the barrage was to be made under a creeping barrage of French and Italian Artillery, lifting 100 metres each six minutes. From this line the 62nd Divisional Artillery, which was to follow the infantry and come into action near the line of departure, would support the attack, reinforced by such other guns which were still within range."

These artillery instructions are important, for it will be seen later that the range of 1,000 yards ahead was far too great, leaving the enemy's machine-gun nests quite untouched.

When 8 a.m. arrived all three Infantry Brigades had reported their positions of assembly, with the three Brigade Headquarters at Ferme D'Ecueil.

At 8 a.m., punctually, the two assaulting Brigades moved forward to the attack. It was a brilliant morning, full of sunshine which flooded the cornfields, over which part of the attack was moving forward. " Surely," said an officer, " there was no war in this pleasant country." But the standing crops in the undulating

20TH JULY. valley, the vineyards on the slopes leading up to the heights and the dense woods along the ridges, concealed from view hostile positions of great strength, and death lurked in the shimmering haze covering those peaceful fields and quiet uplands.

The 2/4th York and Lancs. Regt. (Hallamshires), the right attacking battalion of the 187th Infantry Brigade, with D Company (Capt. Kirk) on the right, A Company (Capt. Ellse) on the left and C Company (Capt. Smith) in support, whose forming-up line had been the fringe of the wood on the north-east side of the road running from the edge of the Bois D'Ecueil, went forward in great form. " Despite the trying march up and little rest," said the C.O., " the Battalion ' jumped off ' in good spirits." At ten minutes past eight a heavy enemy barrage fell in front of Cormas and D Company suffered considerable casualties, but the advance continued steadily. Courmas was taken and D and C Companies passed rapidly on towards the Chateau de Commetreuil and Wood. But as the troops dashed across the open ground a strong volume of machine-gun fire from the Chateau and eastern edge of the Wood swept the ground over which the Hallamshires were advancing and more casualties were suffered. The Chateau seemed to belch fire from every quarter and to avoid being hung up and possibly endangering the flank of the left Battalion, the two Companies of Hallamshires passed on towards Bouilly, which they cleared of the enemy, capturing several machine-guns and twenty prisoners, including one officer.

The 5th K.O.Y.L.I., on whom rested the responsibility of clearing the western edge of the Bois du Petit Champ, experienced little difficulty until they came to the south-eastern edge of the Chateau Commetreuil Wood. But here the centre Company came under heavy machine-gun fire which swept down the Chateau Drive. Hostile machine-gun fire from a clearing at the south-west corner of the Wood also impeded the advance. Of this Company three officers were killed and one wounded. The left Company had fought its way through the Bois du Petit Champ but was likewise held up by heavy frontal and enfilade machine-gun fire. The remnants of both Companies were withdrawn and reorganized and attached to the Reserve Company of the Battalion.

The two right platoons of the right Company of the 5th K.O.Y.L.I. seem to have had considerable excitement. The two left platoons of the Company were held up at the south-east edge of Chateau de Commetreuil Wood. The two right platoons (Nos. 6 and 8) advanced towards the Wood west of Cormas. Here Second-Lieut.

P. Moore, who was in command of these two platoons, under the impression that the Wood was in possession of the Hallamshires, went forward with his runner. The latter was immediately shot down. Moore then returned to his men, and taking a party of ten, again attacked the Wood. Five of his men were killed and four wounded and only one remained. The Germans then retired to the north-east corner of the Wood, but Moore went after them, rushed the machine-gun, killed the gunners and took two prisoners and the machine-gun. With the latter he cut off the enemy, retiring along the track running north-east from Point 165. Here he captured two more Germans and another machine-gun. The gun he turned on the still-retreating enemy and worked it until it stopped firing, then, having no knowledge of the working of a machine-gun he busied himself in collecting all the troops he could find and continued the advance towards Builly. He reached the forked road just south-east of the village, but his party was too weak to take and hold the village, and he retired and consolidated along the road on the north-eastern side of the Chateau Lake.

The Reserve Company (Capt. Oliphant), after heavy fighting, reached the junction of the Chateau drives where a line was established along the south-eastern edge of the Wood.

Heavy fire from concealed machine-gun nests in the Chateau drives and from the west made the situation untenable and finally a further withdrawal was made.

The 2/4th K.O.Y.L.I., the supporting Battalion of the 187th Infantry Brigade, had unfortunately to endure heavy shell fire for an hour and a half before " Zero " hour, so that when 8 a.m. arrived they had already lost one Company Commander and several other ranks wounded. At " Zero," however, the Battalion went forward, following the Hallamshires (2/4th York and Lancs.) at about 500 yards distance, A Company on the right, C on the left and B Company following in rear. The heavy barrage falling about 100 yards around the Wood on the front of advance was passed through with hardly a casualty. A Company advanced in artillery formation from the road and, on reaching the ridge south-east of Courmas, extended, as the enemy's machine guns from the Bois de Rheims had begun to sweep the front of advance. On the Courmas—Onrezy Road an enemy machine-gun was captured and the crew put to flight. The Company was now in line with the Hallamshires, who were being held up by enfilade fire. Another machine-gun was captured on the Courmas—Onrezy Road, the crew killed, and the German officer

20TH JULY. in command, taken prisoner. A Company then moved on in the direction of Bouilly, but machine-gun fire caused many casualties and again the advance was held up.

C Company also advanced in artillery formation until the enemy's machine-gun fire forced the Company to extend in open order. Eventually the Company reached a small copse and a cornfield west of Courmas. From this position, though swept by machine-gun fire, the advance was continued in sectional rushes. Four officers were wounded in the cornfields (for the enemy was cunningly disposed and his machine guns could not be located) including Second-Lieut. Swaby, who had been cut off with the remainder of the Company. Shortly afterwards, B Company, which had been in support, but was finally ordered into the front line, captured a machine-gun nest of four guns.

The 186th Infantry Brigade should now have passed through the 187th, but as the former did not appear, a further attempt to advance was not thought advisable, for there does not seem to have been much information as to what was happening on the front of the 185th Infantry Brigade.

Accordingly the 2/4th York and Lancs. Regt. formed a defensive flank along the Courmas—Bouilly Road and with a strong point at the cross roads between Bouilly and Onrezy. Touch was gained with the 86th French Infantry at Bouilly and the 2/4th K.O.Y.L.I. were consolidated on the left of the Hallamshires.

On the whole the attack of the 187th Infantry Brigade had made fair progress. Courmas was held and good positions for continuing the attack on the following day secured.

Meanwhile on the left flank, the attack had not progressed so well. Here, the 8th West Yorks on the right and the 1/5th West Yorks. on the left of the 185th Infantry Brigade had a most difficult task, for it entailed an advance over more open ground against positions stuffed with machine-guns and covering every approach to the villages of Marfaux and Cuitron, which stood on high ground.

The objective allotted to the 185th Infantry Brigade was the high ground along the line Chaumuzy—Bligny—Aubilly. On the capture of this line the 5th Devons were to pass through and capture the first objective—the line Sarcy—Le Gros Termie.

Under the barrage, which, though no one knew it, was falling much too far ahead, the 8th and 1/5th West Yorks. went forward to the attack at 8 a.m. Of the 8th West Yorks—A Company (Capt. G. G. Kinder) on the right and B Company (Capt. J. E. Appleyard) on the left, in artillery formation, led the advance of the Battalion, C Company being in support and D Company in reserve. 20TH JULY.

As the two attacking Companies went forward from the edge of the Bois du Pourcy a wide stretch of golden cornfields lay between them and the battered villages of Marfaux, on the left, Cuitron in the centre, and the Bois du Petit Champ on the right. It was not long before the enemy's machine-guns joined their barking to the scream of the shells of the French barrage passing overhead. And soon men began to fall rapidly. Cross-fire, from the edges of the woods high up above the right flank, and from Cuitron and Marfaux villages, swept the front of the attack and it was very evident that the barrage had affected the enemy not at all, for everywhere his machine-guns poured a perpetual hail of bullets into the waves of the advancing Yorkshiremen. And the worst of it was that these guns could not be located; they were very skilfully hidden amidst trees and corn. " It was an invisible foe which we were pitted against," said an officer of the Battalion, " and very few of us ever caught sight of a Bosche." The two front Companies of the 8th West Yorks. had soon lost so many officers and men that the support and reserve Companies were advanced into the line. The commanders of both A and B Companies had already been killed.

Isolated parties of the Battalion seem to have reached a point about 100 yards from Marfaux, but finally had to withdraw. Something of the nature of the fighting may be gathered from a private account written by the officer who commanded D (the Reserve) Company.

"At one period of this blazing hot summer morning I had reached a small brook fifty yards from the first house in Cuitron village. Birkell, Company Sergeant-Major; Connor, my orderly, and a few men of our Company, about seven in all, formed our little party. On either side we could still see a few unwounded men, the sole remnants of four Companies, carrying on with this unequal struggle against a dozen or so enemy machine guns. . . The house, some 100 yards just to our front, seemed to be the real obstacle and I thought it might be quite possible to crawl along the ditch and into the copse and so engage them from the rear. Thus it was that C.S.M. Birkell, Connor, a Lewis gunner with gun, and myself, continued crawling through the corn and into the marshy copse near this unfriendly house. We had almost reached the far side of the copse when we bumped into trouble. The Lewis gunner was our first casualty. Birkell was killed by a sniper who seemed

20TH JULY. only a few yards away and somewhat in our rear. Connor was the next to be hit by another sniper just a few yards away who must have been hidden in a small clump of trees. I crouched in a small pool of water at the corner of the copse, not knowing where my enemies were. I lay ' doggo ' in this two feet of water, surrounded by rank undergrowth and rushes, with the hot sun scorching the little of me which was above water. Any slight movement I made was immediately rewarded by a sharp crack from my attentive sniper and a neat little furrow curved along the rim of my shell-hole refuge. They suddenly began to shell this corner of the copse. Heavies and gas shells followed each other in quick succession and I became covered with wet, muddy earth and almost choked with poison gas. This nightmare ceased after about twenty minutes." And then this officer decided to make a move. Everything was quiet, the enemy's snipers seemed to have left the vicinity. In crawling away, he met two of his men, both wounded. The three were joined by another wounded man. In a little while, the orderly was found, shot through the chest and arm. " I looked at my garrison of wounded and decided to make an attempt to get back to our own lines." And so they set out, crawling warily, through the rushes. Before the party had covered twenty yards, two more men were met, one badly wounded. After a slow and very painful crawl through the rushes and pools of water, the party had gone some forty yards, when— " crack "—snipers had again found them. Three of the party were again wounded, steel helmets were hit, water bottles smashed, boots, entrenching tools, rifles, all suffered from Bosche markmanship, though not a German could be seen. " Still we crawled on and on, helping each other over bad places, before we reached the edge of the copse and out again into the cornfields." But there was still that horrible house at the corner of Cuitron to pass, and as the party came level with it, enemy machine-guns opened fire and joined in with the snipers. A friendly shell hole provided rest and shelter for a little while and then, when darkness had fallen, the party moved on once more and finally reported to Battalion Headquarters soon after midnight.

A fate similar to that which met the 8th West Yorks. was shared by the 2/5th Battalion, attacking on the left of the former. With D Company on the right and A on the left, C in support and B in reserve, the Battalion moved off at 8 a.m. with Marfaux as its objective. The poor effects of the barrage were at once apparent in the volume of machine-gun fire which swept across the cornfields and open spaces as the Battalion went forward. The village and the woods near it all contained machine-gun nests. One wood on the immediate left of the battalion was a source of trouble during the whole attack. This wood, instead of being captured by the 51st Division (on whose front it was), was ignored by the Scotsmen and, as it had received no attention from the barrage, the German machine-guns had everything their own way and were able to bring a heavy enfilade fire to bear on the West Yorkshiremen as they made splendid, but vain, efforts to reach Marfaux. With great gallantry the Battalion managed to reach a position just short of the village, but it was impossible to go further. The support and reserve Companies numbered only about thirty men each. The situation reports for the two attacking Companies are interesting :—" A Company reports that only about twenty men of A Company left, wants instructions." This message was sent back at 10-7 a.m. The O.C., D Company, reported : —" Am occupying two shell holes south-east of Chaumuzy, only six men of ours left and eight men and one officer of the Devons ; in touch with Hants. on right (150 yards), but nobody on left. What am I to do ? At present holding on and consolidating." This message was sent at 11 a.m.

20TH JULY.

But the Brigade assumed the positions gained to be held :—
" Do not move from your present positions without endeavouring to inform these Headquarters."

The 5th Devons had already suffered casualties numbering one officer and twenty-three other ranks wounded and three other ranks killed, by shell fire, when the Battalion reached its assembly positions, and though tired by their long night march the men were in excellent spirits.

The Battalion was in support of the 8th and 2/5th West Yorks. and, at 8 a.m., with orders to move by the centre on Cuitron as their line of march, keeping to the woods and in touch with the two attacking Battalions as long as possible, the two leading Companies C and D, joined by A and B Companies, set out. " The leading Companies," said the C.O., " made fair progress in support of the 5th West Yorks. Regt., who both appeared to come under hostile machine-gun fire on leaving Pourcy and the woods at Le Pates D'Ecueil. My second line—A and B Companies—were severely handled by enemy barrage on edge of woods and all came under severe machine-gun fire on debouching into the open."

About 11 a.m., it appeared obvious that the attack could not develop successfully, as the 51st Division across the Ardre was held

20TH JULY. up owing to the very heavy shelling in front of Bois de L'Aulnay and Marfaux, and the 2/5th and 8th West Yorks. were, as already shown, in a similar position. Colonel Bastow, therefore, after reporting the position to Brigade Headquarters at Ferme D'Ecuiel, sent A and B Companies (less two platoons in reserve at Battalion Headquarters) to support the 2/5th West Yorks., who had got within fair distance of Marfaux but could get no further. On again reporting his position to Brigade Headquarters the C.O. of the Devons was ordered to push out outposts and " hang on " to the ground won. Finally the Devon men linked up with the 2/5th and 8th West Yorks., though the operation was considerably hampered by an enemy barrage.

In the meantime, at about 11-45 a.m. Divisional Headquarters had decided, in view of the situation, not to reinforce the frontal attack on the line Marfaux—Cuitron, but to move its reserve Brigade (186th) to the right in order to exploit the success of the 187th Infantry Brigade and to attack Marfaux and Cuitron from the flank and rear, through the Bois de Rheims. To this end, orders were despatched to the G.O.C., 186th Infantry Brigade, but unfortunately two Battalions of General Burnett's Brigade had already become involved in the fighting in front of the two villages, and flank and rear attacks as intended by Divisional Headquarters, could not be carried out.

The 186th Infantry Brigade had set out from Germaine at midnight, to march to its positions of assembly in the north-east corner of Bois de Courtagnon, some 4,000 yards from the front line. At " Zero " hour the three infantry battalions were formed up :—5th Duke of Wellington's on the right, 2/4th Hants. in the centre and 2/4th Duke of Wellington's on the left, the left flank of the latter being on the northern bank of the River Ardre.

As the Brigade moved forward, the Marfaux—Pourcy Valley and the Bois de Rheims were under heavy fire from hostile artillery. A little later, as the battalions drew near the firing line, the whole country over which the advance had to be made was swept by heavy rifle and machine-gun fire. The deadly machine-gun nests, hidden in the standing corn or admirably concealed in bushy banks, covered the whole of the approaches to Marfaux and Cuitron.

The 5th Duke of Wellington's, accompanied by Lewis guns, limbers, S.A.A., and bomb carts, after advancing in rear of the 187th and 185th Infantry Brigades, soon found that things had not gone as well as had been hoped for with the assaulting Brigades, B, C and Headquarters Companies, therefore, struck off in a north-west

A British Sentry in the Forest of Rheims.

direction, through the Bois de Courtagnon to Ecueil Farm, thence 20TH JULY. through the Bois D'Ecueil to the village of Courmas. Here they found the position still obscure and nothing definite was known of the situation of the 187th Infantry Brigade's attack, though reports were in circulation that Bouilly had been captured. Courmas and the Bois D'Ecueil were, at this period, under such heavy shell fire that a more sheltered position was taken up in the southern edges of the Bois D'Eceuil, overlooking the village and the valley. A and D Companies had meanwhile advanced behind the 185th Infantry Brigade along the Courtagnon—Pourcy Road, thence in a northwesterly direction through the Bois de Pourcy. Heavy hostile artillery fire caught these two Companies at the northern edge of the Bois de Pourcy and 25 per cent. casualties were suffered in a very little while. The position in front of them was obscure, and it was evident that the 185th Brigade was held up in front of Marfaux and Cuitron and could make no headway. The West Yorks. Battalions had established a few posts on the forward slopes west of the Bois de Pourcy, but the main line remained in the wood. The two Companies, therefore, taking advantage of whatever cover offered itself, remained during the morning in the shelter of the western edge of Bois de Pourcy, north of the Marfaux—Pourcy Road. Thus, throughout the whole day the 5th Duke of Wellington's was split up, B and C Companies not gaining touch with A and D Companies until 21st.

The 2/4th Hants., the centre Battalion of the 186th Infantry Brigade, in coming up with the 185th Infantry Brigade and finding the latter at a standstill, gallantly endeavoured to continue the advance. B and D Companies, with A Company in support, made strenuous efforts to force their way through to Marfaux and Cuitron, but the enemy's machine-gun fire decimated their ranks. Major Molyneux, who led the attack, was wounded early in the fight. Despite the bravery of all ranks, it was impossible to reach Marfaux. Small bodies did, indeed, manage to reach the outskirts of the village, but this position, without strong support (which was not forthcoming) was untenable and the Hampshiremen dug in at about 500 yards east of the village. This position was maintained throughout the day.

The 2/4th Duke of Wellington's also met with serious opposition on the left flank of the attack. The Battalion, on clearing the Ferme de Courtagnon, broke into company artillery formation—two Companies in the front line and two in support. On approaching Pourcy, machine-gun bullets from the direction of Cuitron, swept the advance,

20TH JULY. and the Companies opened out in extended order. Nothing could be seen of the 51st Division on the left and, on the right, the 2/4th Hants who, owing to the nature of the ground had been forced for a time to follow in rear of the 2/4th Duke of Wellington's, had not yet come up on the right flank; both flanks were thus " in the air."

Eventually, however, the right of the Battalion came up with the 185th Infantry Brigade, then about 600 yards from Marfaux. At this point the two waves on the right, *i.e.*, the two right Companies, seem to have merged into one and joined up with units of the 185th Brigade, with which they made another attempt to go forward in the direction of Marfaux.

But the two waves on the left, *i.e.*, the two left Companies, did not gain touch with the 186th Brigade and, though advancing slowly, pressed on along the northern bank of the Ardre River. Several strong points and a farm—Min.d'Ardre—gave considerable trouble. The platoons on the left flank stormed and took the farm; another platoon rushed a strong point north of the farm and, killing the occupants, captured two machine-guns. A platoon on the right, close to the road, attacked a second enemy point, taking fourteen prisoners and two machine-guns.

The two right companies, with the 185th Infantry Brigade, continued to work their way through the southern edge of the Bois de Pourcy, though meeting with heavy opposition from machine-gun fire.

The records state that :—" Nearly fifty per cent. of the Battalions by this time had become casualties, but with splendid spirit they gradually worked their way forward."

The two left Companies had, by now, become split up into small parties. Isolated units, eager to capture Marfaux, had pressed forward to within 70 yards of the village. One platoon on the northern edge of Marfaux actually succeeded in entering the village, but the enemy was too strong and, in turn, these—the gallant Duke's, were forced to retire to the line held about 200 yards east of the village.

By 3 o'clock in the afternoon, the whole attack had practically ceased. Dead-tired—but unbeaten—the Yorkshiremen set to work to reorganize and keep a firm hold on their gains. Heavy casualties had been suffered, but the enemy had been forced to give ground, and the knowledge that British troops were pitted against him, as well as French and Italians, had shaken his defence. The bravest men in the German Army, during the latter half of 1918, were the machine-gunners; they alone held up the allied attacks and once they gave way the German line gave also.

No material change took place in the Divisional line until the evening, when the 185th Infantry Brigade was ordered to withdraw behind the line of the 186th Infantry Brigade. The Pioneers (9th Durham Light Infantry) were also assembled behind the 187th Infantry Brigade, in support, available for operations on the next day.

Quite unlike anything the Division had hitherto experienced in France, was the desperate fighting which took place on the 20th July. The enemy clung tenaciously to all his positions. Everything was in his favour—his machine-guns were skilfully concealed and well handled, and his snipers were everywhere where vantage ground could be made use of. The barrage which, had it come down on the right positions, must have shaken him, was wide of the mark. And yet, the Yorkshiremen, fighting under extraordinary disadvantages and difficulties, clung equally tenaciously to every foot of ground gained. Their pluck and endurance were inspiring. Prisoners (three officers and fifty other ranks) had been taken from four German Divisions, *i.e.*, 103rd, 123rd, 50th and 86th, which showed that the enemy was as strong, if not stronger, than the two British Divisions opposed to him.[1]

On the night of 20th the British line ran roughly east of Espilly, Marfaux and Cuitron, thence through the Bois de Rheims, west of Courmas, southwards to the cross roads between Bouilly and Onrezy.

About 10 p.m., orders were received from Corps Headquarters to continue the attack on the following day. The 62nd Division was to complete the capture of the remainder of the Bois de Rheims and the Bouilly Ridge, as far as the path west-south-west from the northern end of Bouilly village. The 187th Infantry Brigade was detailed to carry out the attack.

But it was not until about 5 o'clock on the morning of the 21st that the 187th Infantry Brigade received orders to capture the Bois de Petit Champ and the Bouilly Ridge.

The main attack was to be carried out by the 9th Durham Light Infantry (Lieut.-Colonel E. Crouch) supported by the 5th K.O.Y.L.I. In conjunction with the attack the 2/4th York and Lancs. Regt. was directed to clear the Chateau de Commetreuil grounds. The attack on the Bouilly Ridge was to be by way of Bois de Rouvroy and Bois d'Avermont.

The attack was to be made under a creeping barrage, lifting 100

---

[1] The estimated casualties of the 62nd Division on 20th July (less three battalions) were forty-six officers and 775 other ranks.

21ST JULY. metres each ten minutes, with frequent halts; the six minute lifts through thick woods had been found too fast.

The records of this attack are very brief. But apparently the 5th K.O.Y.L.I., who, on account of the shortage of time, were ordered to guide the 9th Durham Light Infantry to the forming-up line (*i.e.*, the front held by the K.O.Y.L.I.), owing to the similarity of two clearings in the woods and the thickness of the latter, misjudged the position, with the result that the line actually taken up by the Durhams was 600 metres further back than was intended. This meant that the Battalion at " Zero " hour would be that distance further from the creeping barrage.

At 10-30 a.m. the barrage came down and the attack started, but by the time that the 9th Durham Light Infantry debouched from the woods and rushed down the hill, a perfect inferno of machine-gun fire swept the line of advance. The three attacking companies of the Durhams, *i.e.*, B on the right, A in the centre, and C on the left, succeeded in reaching the woods on the opposite side, but here the advance was held up and no further progress could be made. The Battalion Diary states that the enemy had "hundreds of machine guns."

The Battalion had advanced 600 yards on a wide frontage and very gallantly had made its attempt to carry out orders, but no troops could withstand that murderous machine-gun fire, and consolidation was ordered of the ground gained.

Meanwhile the 2/4th York and Lancs. Regt. had made an equally brave but unsuccessful attack on the Chateau and grounds. B Company of the Battalion attacked the Chateau, but again the enemy's machine guns were so numerous, and put up such a stubborn resistance, that an advance was impossible. After several hours hard fighting the gallant Hallamshires succeeded in capturing several machine guns and a few prisoners, but were forced to withdraw to their original line along the Courmas—Bouilly Road.

As there were no fresh troops available to carry on the attack, General Braithwaite decided to break off the action and orders were dispatched to the 187th Infantry Brigade to consolidate the ground gained and pull the 9th Durham Light Infantry out of the line as soon as possible.

On the left of the 62nd Division, the 51st, which had attacked at 8 a.m., had made but little progress. The 2nd French Colonial Division, on the right, had also attacked and had gained ground in the direction of St. Euphraise and the Bois de la Vallotte; it had also retaken Bouilly from the enemy.

During the afternoon the position of the French division on the right of the 62nd Division became clearer and, in consequence, it was possible for Divisional Headquarters to consider the whole situation, which is admirably summed up thus in the Divisional Narrative :—
" Although the 187th Infantry Brigade, on the 20th, had pushed through to Bouilly, the western half of the Bois du Petit Champ was evidently completely in the enemy's hands. No progress could be made on the line Marfaux—Cuitron until the enemy was cleared from the spur at the south-west corner of the Bois du Petit Champ, from which the whole valley down to the river was commanded. The 187th Infantry Brigade was holding the line east of the Chateau de Commetreuil, thence west to Courmas and through the wood jutting north from the Bois du Petit Champ. The Brigade had suffered heavy casualties and had no Battalion fit for the attack. The 186th Infantry Brigade was holding the front from 187th Infantry Brigade to the River Ardre with two Battalions, with the third Battalion in support, which had not already been heavily engaged. The 185th Infantry Brigade had pulled two Battalions out (of the line) during the previous night, but still had the third Battalion lying out beside Marfaux and this could not be extricated untill after dark. It was decided to clear the Bois du Petit Champ on 22nd July and, once the spur at the south-west corner of this Wood was in our possession, capture Marfaux and Cuitron the following day by frontal attack. The 186th Infantry Brigade was ordered to carry out the first operation—the clearing of the Bois du Petit Champ—on the 22nd."[1]

21st July.

At 8 p.m. the Corps Cyclist Battalion was put at the disposal of the G.O.C. Division, and was ordered to report to the G.O.C., 186th Infantry Brigade and come under the latter's orders.

The night of 21st/22nd July passed without incident, the 5th K.O.Y.L.I. relieving the 9th Durham Light Infantry without interruption. The Pioneers, on relief, withdrew to the Bois D'Ecueil.

The small operation ordered for the 22nd July was far from easy. It is one thing to attack an area where the enemy's defences can be seen, but quite another thing to advance through thick, almost impenetrable woods, against an unseen foe. The Bois du Petit Champ was known to be sheltering enemy machine-gun nests as well as

---

[1] " It was a most infernal place and had defied all efforts of the French and Italians. The plan for its capture, which was entirely successful, was General Burnett's and, I think, must stand for a long while as an example of forest fighting conducted admirably."

General Braithwaite.

21ST JULY. considerable numbers of the enemy; as a test of courage, therefore, the intended attack was severe.

The plan of attack, as given in the diary of 5th Battalion Duke of Wellington's Regt., is thus described:—" The Battalion received orders to capture the Bois du Petit Champ, part of the Bois de Rheims, as far west as the track between Courmas and Chaumuzy— the idea of the attack being for A and D Companies to advance along the north, and for B and C Companies along the south, limits of the objective, on a one-platoon front of 50 yards. The leading platoons to endeavour to push forward to the furthest limit of the objective, one platoon to be dropped from the rear of the attacking columns at distances of 30 metres. These platoons to form strong points capable of all round defence. After the strong points had been established by platoons, the latter to send out section patrols to search the wood for any enemy posts or personnel between themselves and adjoining posts."

It will thus be seen that the attack was to take place on a narrow front along, and just inside, the two edges (northern and southern) of the Wood.

The attack was to be supported by an artillery barrage of all available 18-pounders and French 75's, creeping at the rate of 100 yards every ten minutes till clear of the final objective. The "Heavies" were to bombard selected areas, and machine-gun fire was to be maintained on the southern slopes of the hill and south of it. French machine guns covered the northern slopes of the hill.

" Zero " hour was timed for 12-15 p.m.

For sheer excitement and deadly danger this attack was probably unequalled by any operation in which the 5th Duke of Wellington's had hitherto taken part.

22ND JULY. By 11-30 a.m. the attacking troops were in position—A and D Companies on the right, B and C on the left. At " Zero " the barrage came down 250 yards in front of the existing front line for 10 minutes and remained stationary. The barrage lifted, and then began an extraordinary man-hunt in the depths of a forest.

A Company was the first to draw covert and had hardly set foot in the wood when opposition was met with. It was, however, soon overcome and the first prisoners taken. Advancing cautiously, the Company pressed on and had got 250 yards into the wood when, suddenly, it bumped up against a strong point, held by a party of twenty Germans, with four machine-guns. Then ensued a desperate struggle, but here again resistance was broken down and the garrison

"Then Began an Extraordinary Man-hunt in the Depths of a Forest."

and the machine-guns in the post were captured. Again, A Company pushed on through the thick trees and undergrowth and a further 200 yards had been covered when another strong point made itself evident by a sudden burst of machine-gun and rifle fire. But this second post shared the same fate as the first and six more machine-guns and a party of from thirty to thirty-five Germans were added to the list of captures. D Company had taken a hand in this capture, for A had become weakened by casualties.

22ND JULY.

The two Companies (A and D) now pressed on together. Yet another 300 yards were traversed, during which isolated machine-gun nests, mostly consisting of single guns and a small crew, were captured, when a volume of very heavy fire came from a strong point about the centre of the wood. It was so skilfully hidden that the " Dukes " were unable to locate it and a halt was called. But still it was impossible to determine the position of the post. A retirement was then ordered and the two Companies fell back 300 yards and consolidated their positions in a series of posts from the northern to about the centre edge of the wood. Two platoons of the 1/5th Devons, who had been sent up by 186th Infantry Brigade Headquarters, helped to consolidate the positions. The two Companies now sent out patrols to gain touch with the two Companies (B and C) operating on the southern edge of the wood.

C and B Companies (going forward in that order) had encountered opposition ere ever they reached the wood. A strong point, about 50 yards from the point of assembly, just inside the forest, opened fire as the men advanced and, for a while, the Duke's were held up. The rear company (B), however, joined in the attack and by an encircling movement from both flanks, the strong point was captured and the garrison of fifty Germans and eight machine-guns were taken. At the southern edge of the wood a series of five enemy strong points were next met, but these were all quickly dealt with and the garrisons and machine-guns captured. These strong points yielded about twenty machine-guns and eighty prisoners. C Company finally reached its objective at the north-west edge of the wood, having suffered severely on the way, though several small isolated posts were taken *en route*. The Company had, however, hardly set to work to consolidate the ground gained, when a strong enemy counter-attack was launched from the north. The enemy threatened envelopment and the gallant Duke's fought hard to prevent him closing in on the forward post. But eventually, C Company was surrounded and the most forward post, held by Second-Lieut.

22ND JULY. Storry, fell into the hands of the enemy. Hard and bitter fighting then ensued. With fixed bayonets, the Germans charged the two remaining posts of the Company. A Lewis gun was brought into action and the enemy was bloodily repulsed. For a little while he retired, obviously shaken. Presently, however, he came on again, using stick bombs freely and got so close and was in such superiority in numbers, that the position became untenable. With fine courage, Capt. J. B. Cockhill withdrew his few remaining men to a shell hole in the open, on the southern edge of the wood. Here the gallant survivors were not only subjected to a heavy rifle and machine-gun fire from the wood but from the valley at Cuitron. To make matters worse, a shell burst in the shell hole, putting the Lewis gun out of action. It was hard luck, but there was no other course open, but to retire still further, in a westerly direction, followed closely by the enemy. At length, after a running fight, two officers and six other ranks reached B Company's posts and the enemy, evidently contented, gave up the pursuit.

Meanwhile B Company had made a strong point about 700 yards in the wood away from the jumping-off point and, assisted by a Company of the 1/5th Devons, consolidated a line from the southern edge of the forest. The post was placed here in order to meet A and D Companies, who eventually gained touch with B and the remnants of C Company. The new line was consolidated at nightfall and held by the Battalion with the assistance of the 1/5th Devons.

The day's fighting had been costly. Colonel Walker's Battalion had lost five officers and 150 N.C.O.'s and men, but had captured two officers and 206 other ranks, all belonging to the 53rd Prussian Regt. : forty-one machine guns were also taken. The enemy stated that the attack was a surprise, a relief having taken place only an hour before " Zero."[1] The Germans had been holding the wood with two Battalions and a third Battalion was in close support.

The artillery barrage was very accurate and effective, and inflicted many casualties on the enemy. But at the outset of the operation the enemy's reply was weak and only when his gunners became aware of the situation did they place a heavy bombardment on the edges of the wood and all approaches thereto.

Of the remaining units of the 186th Infantry Brigade, the 2/4th

---

[1] The 5th Duke of Wellington's were "heartily congratulated by the Corps, Divisional and Brigade Commanders on their particularly fine fight, which had had the effect of greatly reducing the enemy's power of resistance." *Battalion Diary.*

Hants. continued to hold its position, but the 2/4th Duke of Welling- 22ND JULY. ton's sent forward two fighting patrols, each consisting of one officer and twenty other ranks, to reconnoitre Marfaux. Splitting up into small parties the patrols endeavoured to enter the village from the north and south, but the enemy was on the alert and put up a strong resistance, and eventually, having suffered 50 per cent. casualties, the survivors retired as best they could, crawling through the standing corn. During the evening a prisoner was taken by the Battalion; he stated that Marfaux was held by one battalion and was full of machine-guns.

The 187th Infantry Brigade (during the 22nd) spent a comparatively quiet day. The 9th Durham Light Infantry (Pioneers) were transferred to the 186th Infantry Brigade. The success of the 186th Brigade relieved the constant danger to the left of the 187th and in the evening the latter pushed forward the left flank of the 5th K.O.Y.L.I., who succeeded in gaining touch with the 5th Duke of Wellington's in the Bois du Petit Champ. The 2/4th York and Lancs. Regt. spent the day in consolidating their position along the Courmas—Bouilly Road and part of the old French line in front of Courmas.

Just after midnight on the 22nd/23rd, Divisional Headquarters appear to have received a report from the 186th Infantry Brigade Headquarters of the enemy's counter-attack against the 5th Duke of Wellington's which had resulted in the loss of the spur at the southwest corner of the Bois du Petit Champ. As the possession of this spur was of paramount importance for an attack on Marfaux and Cuitron, ordered for the morning of the 23rd, by the 186th Infantry Brigade, an alteration in the plan of attack was immediately necessary.

The previous orders issued to the 186th Infantry Brigade were :— The Brigade would attack the Marfaux—Cuitron line, under cover of an artillery barrage. For this operation the 9th Durham Light Infantry, the Corps (New Zealand) Cyclists and a company of French Tanks was placed at the disposal of the Brigade. The Durhams were to attack on the right, along the side of the hill, and to capture Cuitron and the spur immediately south of Bois du Petit Champ. The New Zealand Cyclists, to whom was attached one Company of 2/4th Hants., were to attack with their left on the Ardre and to capture Marfaux and the Ridge 500 yards west of it. The Tanks were to advance in the gap between the 9th Durham Light Infantry and New Zealand Cyclists, to protect their inner flanks and assist in the reduction of any strong points encountered. The 51st Division was

o

22ND JULY. attacking in line, with the 186th Brigade, south of the Ardre River. Attacking units were to be in their assembly positions by 2 a.m. and " Zero " hour was 6 a.m.

The receipt of the report concerning the enemy's counter-attack on the 5th Duke of Wellington's Regt. necessitated the addition of two Companies of the 8th West Yorks. (185th Infantry Brigade) to the attacking troops. These two Companies were given the task of again clearing the southern and western edges of the Bois du Petit Champ. All the Divisional Artillery, also, with the exception of one 18-pounder and a 4·5 Howitzer Battery, was taken off the frontal barrage and ordered to support the attack of the 8th West Yorks.

The first objective for the attack was the line of the villages Marfaux—Cuitron ; the second objective the spur running down to the Ardre about 400 metres north-west of the two villages.

The attacking troops reached their assembly positions without difficulty, but whilst waiting to go forward, the 9th Durham Light Infantry had about seventy casualties from the enemy's shell fire.

The two Companies of 8th West Yorks. detailed for the attack on the Bois du Petit Champ were, as a matter of fact, the whole Battalion, for even with a few reinforcements just arrived from " Echelon B," the Battalion was only just strong enough to be organized into two small Companies—termed No. 1 and No. 2. These two Companies were disposed—No. 1 on the right, No. 2 on the left.

There was no time for a reconnaissance and Colonel England (commanding 8th West Yorks.) and Colonel Walker (commanding 5th Duke of Wellington's) led the two Companies to their assembly positions.

23RD JULY. At 6 a.m. the advance was begun. Almost from the outset No. 2 Company was held up by a machine-gun nest and suffered severe casualties. Within half-an-hour all No. 2's officers were out of action and the command of the company devolved upon No. 306966 Sergeant James Horner, who with great skill and gallantry handled his men well, leading them, after some stiff fighting, to the outside of the wood and establishing a post which afterwards proved of great value.

No. 1 Company was more fortunate, though its adventures were no less exciting. The Company advanced in small sections, keeping touch as much as possible. The left section worked along the wood overlooking the valley.

" Careful direction and the keeping of position soon became

impossible. The thick undergrowth, some quite impassable, pre- 23RD JULY vented any intelligent observation. Sections charged each other but did not fire when the mistake was noticed. Our own scouts sometimes carefully stalked each other. Then the Bosches decided to join in the game. A machine-gun would spit out from some cunningly-concealed position. At times an ingenious sniper would fire at us from his fortalice in some tree-top. However, we were getting on and had already secured a few prisoners. . . . Once, we had gone forward, only to find a whole crowd of Bosches behind us. We changed direction to avoid being cut off. This game of hide-and-seek continued for hours. The wood was certainly held in strength. The nervous excitement of scrambling through undergrowth, sometimes meeting a terrified Hun, popping up from some hole, or sometimes finding oneself in the centre of an amazed group of attacking Germans, was rather wearying."

But No. 1 Company had done its main task, it had cleared the edge of the wood of enemy machine-guns and, as a result the attack of the 186th Infantry Brigade, which followed, was able to go forward without being enfiladed by murderous machine-gun fire. Eventually the Company consolidated the edge of the wood and remained there during the night 23rd/24th. Meanwhile the 9th Durham Light Infantry on the right of the two Battalions attacking Cuitron and Marfaux, after C and A Companies had suffered seventy casualties from hostile gun fire, had withdrawn to the wood, there to await " Zero " hour. The narrative of this attack by the gallant Pioneers is very brief indeed and is given in extenso :—" At 5 a.m. the Battalion formed up and attacked at 6 a.m. A Company had thirty more casualties before leaving the wood (these in addition to the previous seventy). Attack was completely successful and the village of Cuitron was captured, with eighty-five prisoners and nine machine-guns in all. Much booty was captured and eight French 75 mm. guns were retaken. B Company was attached to C Company for this attack. The Corps Cyclists (New Zealanders) attacked on our left and took Marfaux. All ground captured was consolidated and held. Casualties were one officer wounded; fifteen other ranks killed; ninety-three wounded and eight missing."

The attack of the 77th French Division, which started at 11 a.m., succeeded in gaining the Bois de Rouvroy, half of the Bois D'Hyermont and the Chateau de Commetreuil. During the afternoon there was some doubt about the situation along the western edge of the Bois du Petit Champ. The attack of the 8th West Yorks. had gained

23RD JULY. the south-west corner of the wood and spur, and the 77th French Division was in possession of the southern end of the Bois de Rouvroy, but it appeared probable that there were Germans still in the pocket between these two places. During the late afternoon, French troops with some platoons from the 187th Infantry Brigade cleared this pocket and gained touch with the 8th West Yorks. on the south-west corner of the wood. During the night of the 23rd/24th the 8th West Yorks. succeeded in occupying the strong point on the spur, capturing two Minenwerfers and a searchlight mounted on a cart.

24TH JULY. On the same night the 62nd and 51st Divisional Headquarters moved up to Hautvilliers. The 24th July was a comparatively quiet day, though Marfaux and Cuitron were heavily shelled by the enemy.

At night, the enemy's aircraft was particularly active and carried out a great bombing attack on Epernay. Divisional Headquarters were then at Hautvilliers, the residence of Comte de Chandon (of champagne fame). The Chateau was half-way up the Montaigne de Rheims, and Epernay lay below. The Divisional Staff had just finished dinner when the noise of a great number of aeroplanes going over took everybody out on to the terrace, where a strange and awesome sight was seen. Relays of hostile aeroplanes passed over the Chateau every quarter of an hour, going towards Epernay. As if seated in the gallery of a theatre, the Divisional Staff watched the gradual destruction of Epernay, the hostile aircraft hovering far above, up and down from Epernay to Chalons, and the loud explosion of bombs was almost continuous. One bomb fell on the railway station, igniting a French ammunition dump, which kept on exploding for the next twenty-four hours. Another bomb set fire to a French petrol dump, 25 kilometres away, on the far side of Chalons; the glare was so intense that it was possible to see to read all night.

After five days in the line, during which Brigades and Battalions had been almost continuously engaged with the enemy, casualties had become heavy, *i.e.*, ninety-eight officers and 3,053 other ranks. The total number of prisoners captured had been seven officers and 428 other ranks.

The Divisional front was shortened on the 24th, the right boundary of the XXIInd Corps being altered to :—Southern edge of the Bois du Petit Champ—Western edge of the Bois du Rouvroy—Bois D'Hyermont—Bois de Dix Hommes—the Corps to hold the spur at the south-west corner of the Bois du Petit Champ with one Battalion.

Men of the Duke of Wellington's Regt. resting in a Shell-hole after the Capture of Marfaux.

This reduction in the Corps front enabled the Divisional front to be reorganized, for owing to the continual attacks, and Battalions of all three Brigades being put into the line to reinforce, units had become intermingled. 24TH JULY.

The 187th Infantry Brigade was pulled out entirely into Divisional Reserve. The 186th Infantry Brigade then took over the front line, gradually relieving troops of the 185th Infantry Brigade so that the latter could reorganize and become the supporting Brigade. This reorganization took place during the night of the 24th/25th July.

On the 25th July a preliminary conference took place to discuss further operations on the Corps front. 25TH JULY.

It had become evident that a further advance up the valley was not possible until the high ground south of the Ardre had been captured. It was therefore decided to attack on the southern side of the river, the 51st and 62nd Divisions operating in a combined attack. North of the Ardre the 62nd Division was still to hold to its positions, but was to send one Brigade to operate with the 51st Division. The Corps Commander suggested the 26th as a convenient date for this operation, but both the 51st and 62nd Divisional Commanders urged postponement until the 27th, in order that the Brigade in reserve, which was to make the attack, might have an opportunity of a complete 24 hours' rest. To this the Corps Commander agreed.

Marfaux, Cuitron and Pourcy were heavily shelled on the 26th, but otherwise the day passed without incident. The Divisional Commanders called a conference and described details for the impending attack. The scheme of operations finally issued to the Brigadiers comprised an attack on a three-brigade front—Brigades of the 51st Division on the left and right and a Brigade of the 62nd Division in the centre. Of the former Division, the 152nd Infantry Brigade was to attack on the right and the 153rd on the left; the 187th Infantry Brigade of the 62nd was to operate between the two Brigades of the 51st. The 186th Infantry Brigade (north of the river) was also ordered to be ready to throw forward its front and keep in touch with the right Brigade of the 51st Division as the attack progressed. On the left of the 51st Division, the 14th French Division was attacking Paradis and La Nouville. The advance was to be supported by an artillery and machine-gun creeping barrage in depth. 26TH JULY.

The ground over which the right and centre Brigades were to advance, was commanded from the edge of the Bois de Cuitron, and

26TH JULY. the attacking troops might possibly be subjected to enfilade fire. Moreover, the advance on the left would have to be made through woods, thick in places, which would undoubtedly thin out the troops on the flank and behind them in the centre and right. An advance, at first in echelon, was therefore ordered.

Such was the general plan of attack.

Orders received subsequently by the 187th Infantry Brigade Headquarters may be summarized briefly as follows :—The Brigade was to attack on a three-battalion front—5th K.O.Y.L.I. on the right, 2/4th York and Lancs. in the centre and 2/4th K.O.Y.L.I. on the left. The positions of assembly were in the Sunken Road running south-south-west from Bois de l'Aulnoy between the northern and southern Brigade boundaries. B Company, 62nd M.G. Company was allotted to the Brigade to assist in the attack. The 187th T. M. Battery was to concentrate at Brigade Ammunition Dump for carrying stores forward, but two Sections with their mortars would be kept in readiness to support the attack at any position where their services were required.

" Zero " hour was 6 a.m. on the 27th July.

During the night of 26th/27th the three Battalions moved up to their assembly positions, taking over from troops of the 51st Division. The 5th and 2/4th K.O.Y.L.I. seem to have reached their jumping-off places without incident, but the Hallamshires were caught at Pourcy in a severe burst of hostile shell fire and casualties were suffered by the Headquarter Company.

27TH JULY. At " Zero " hour the guns opened fire and put down a barrage 200 metres west of the jumping-off line. As the troops of the 153rd Infantry Brigade (51st Division), attacking on the left of the 187th Brigade, had to fight their way through the Bois de Cuitron before coming into line with the Yorkshiremen, the creeping barrage moved forward from in front of the former Brigade at " Zero " plus ten minutes, moving at the rate of 100 metres per six minutes until " Zero " plus fifty minutes. By this time the left flank of the 187th Infantry Brigade was sufficiently protected and the three Battalions began their advance.

At 6-10 a.m., the enemy put down a weak barrage along the Brigade front, but it was of a scattered nature and did not in any way hold up the advance, which began at 6-50 a.m. Apart from isolated machine-gun fire, but little opposition met the K.O.Y.L.I. and Hallamshires as they pressed forward up the valley ; neither on the right and left flanks were the 152nd and 153rd Infantry Brigades held up in their advance. By 7-40 a.m., reports from ground observation had reached Divisional Headquarters that the 187th Infantry Brigade had attained the ridge between Espilly and Nappe and, five minutes later, Brigade Headquarters confirmed this information, adding that Espilly had been captured (2/4th K.O.Y.L.I.) and passed through practically without opposition. A little later Nappes was reported taken, and the Hallamshires had established a line in front of the Bois des Eclisses. In the latter a solitary German was captured. He had been left behind with a telephone to report the progress of the British troops. For during the night 26th/27th, the enemy had withdrawn practically along the whole front.[1]

At 9-44 a.m., the 187th Infantry Brigade had gained the second objective, *i.e.*, the track through Bois de Coutron in the north-west corner of the Bois, thence west of Nappe, thence along the ridge to Quesnay, thence to the Ardre immediately west of Mig-de-Voipreux.

The Brigadier then asked for instructions whether he should go on or consolidate on the line gained. He was ordered to concentrate on the second objective as the artillery barrage would not allow for a further advance at this period, and the situation on the left was not clear. But a little later (at 10 a.m.) the G.O.C., 51st Division (whose Headquarters were with the 62nd Divisional Headquarters at Hautvilliers) received information from the 152nd and 153rd Infantry Brigades that their flanks were in touch with the 62nd and French Divisions and, after a short consultation, it was decided, subject to approval from Corps Headquarters, to push on at 1 p.m. to the general line north-north-east corner of Bois de Coutron—Chaumuzy —small copse west of Bois de Rouvroy.

Meanwhile, north of the Ardre, the 186th Infantry Brigade on the right of the 152nd Infantry Brigade, had advanced in conformity with the scheme of operations. The 2/4th Hants. pushed forward posts as far as the Moulin de Voipreux, on the left, and finally on the right joined up with the left flank of the 2/4th Duke of Wellington's Regt., on the spur south of the Bois du Petit Champ. The Hants. were greatly assisted in establishing the line laid down for them

---

[1] Ludendorff gives his line on the morning of the 27th July, as extending from Vrigny, south-west, across the Ardre to just north of Ville-en-Tardenois thence to Fere-en-Tardenois. " In the night of the 26th, the withdrawal of the front north of the Marne was accomplished according to plan and in perfect order."

27TH JULY. by the work of an N.C.O. (Corporal Williams) who, in the early morning, " carried out a daylight patrol as a result of which the objective was reached without loss."

At 11 a.m., orders for a further advance at 1 p.m., were issued. The 187th Brigade was to advance to the spur running from south of the Bois des Eclisses to Chaumuzy, the 186th to advance north of the river to the line Moulin Chaumuzy—Copse west of Bois de Rouvroy; to the 152nd Infantry Brigade was given the objective Chaumuzy—Moulin Chaumuzy. Brigadiers were ordered first to send forward strong reconnoitring patrols, followed by stronger forces, which would seize and occupy the objectives. The 185th Infantry Brigade was to send one Battalion (the 2/5th West Yorks. were detailed) to Espilly, to come under the orders of the 187th Brigade, the remainder of the Brigade to act in close support of the 186th Infantry Brigade. All machine-guns north of the Ardre were to work with the 186th Brigade, those south of the river with the 187th Brigade. One Brigade of Field Artillery was attached to each of the forward Infantry Brigades and, from the diaries, it appears that the 312th Brigade, R.F.A., supported the 186th and the 310th Brigade, R.F.A., the 187th Brigades.

The advance began on the right by the sending out of patrols from the two front Battalions of the 186th Infantry Brigade, *i.e.*, 2/4th Duke of Wellington's (right) and 2/4th Hants. Regt. (left). The 5th Duke of Wellington's and the 9th Durham Light Infantry were to follow in support. Harassing fire was falling on the ground over which the advance was moving, but, gradually pushing their way forward, the 2/4th " Dukes " established themselves in position with their right on the edge of the Bois de Rouvroy, running down the spur to the valley, the 2/4th Hants. then carried on the line to the northern banks of the river near Chaumuzy. The 5th " Dukes " and 9th Durham Light Infantry supported the advance.

Across the river the 187th Infantry Brigade similarly advanced without serious opposition. The 5th K.O.Y.L.I. (right) obtained touch with the 152nd Infantry Brigade in Chaumuzy, the 2/4th K.O.Y.L.I. with the 153rd Infantry Brigade on the left, north of the Bois de Coutron.

The 461st Field Company, R.E., in the line, now set to work with the Battalions to consolidate the new positions gained.

At 12 noon, the Corps Cavalry Regt. had been placed at the

disposal of the 62nd Division and began to move forward. A Divisional Staff Officer was sent to meet the O.C. Mounted Troops at Pourcy, with orders that when the infantry had passed the Chaumuzy line, he was to push forward rapidly and seize the line Arbre de Villers—Bligny—La Montaigne de Bligny. The cavalry set out for Nanteuil at 2-45, and a little later reports reached Divisional Headquarters that the Chaumuzy line had been occupied by the infantry. Meanwhile the 185th Infantry Brigade had been ordered to move forward with the 186th Infantry Brigade in rear of the cavalry and take over the line gained by the mounted troops, before dark : the 186th Brigade on the right of the Ardre and the 185th Brigade on the left. But the cavalry were held up on a line 500 metres south of Bligny—Montaigne de Bligny, the enemy showing considerable resistance.

27TH JULY.

It was dusk when the 186th Brigade went forward to take over the line held by the mounted troops and just dark when the 2/4th Duke of Wellington's and 2/4th Hants. gained touch with the cavalrymen and took over the line which ran from the south-west edge of the Bois de Dix Hommes—The Ardre, 1,000 metres north of Chaumuzy.

But before the 185th Brigade was able to reach Chaumuzy, darkness had set in and, as the situation north of the village was still uncertain, only one Battalion (1/5th Devons) was ordered to pass through it. No opposition was, however, met with and at 1-30 a.m. on the 28th, outposts were established by the Battalion 600 yards north-west of the village. As soon as the situation in front of Chaumuzy was known, the 8th West Yorks. pushed on and established themselves on the left of the 1/5th Devons. The 2/5th West Yorks., who had marched up from Espilly, took up support positions in the valley by Padre Farm, east of Chaumuzy.

At nightfall on the 27th July the situation as known to Divisional Headquarters was :—Very little resistance had been met with as far as Chaumuzy ; the cavalry had been unable to reach the Bligny—Montaigne de Bligny line and that the enemy was holding this line with rearguards, and he had machine-guns in the Bois de Dix Hommes.

In view of the situation the 186th and 185th Infantry Brigades were ordered to continue the advance at dawn on the 28th. The 186th Infantry Brigade to drive the enemy out of Bligny and secure the Red Line north of that village, the 185th Brigade to seize the

27TH JULY. Montaigne de Bligny. At daylight, the Corps Mounted Troops were to send out patrols to Aubilly, Sarcy and Chambrecy in order to gain touch with the enemy. If a further advance was necessary, the 187th Infantry Brigade was to pass through the line. These orders were issued at 10-30 p.m.

On this date Divisional Headquarters moved to Nanteuil, from which place it was possible to see practically the whole of the battlefield.

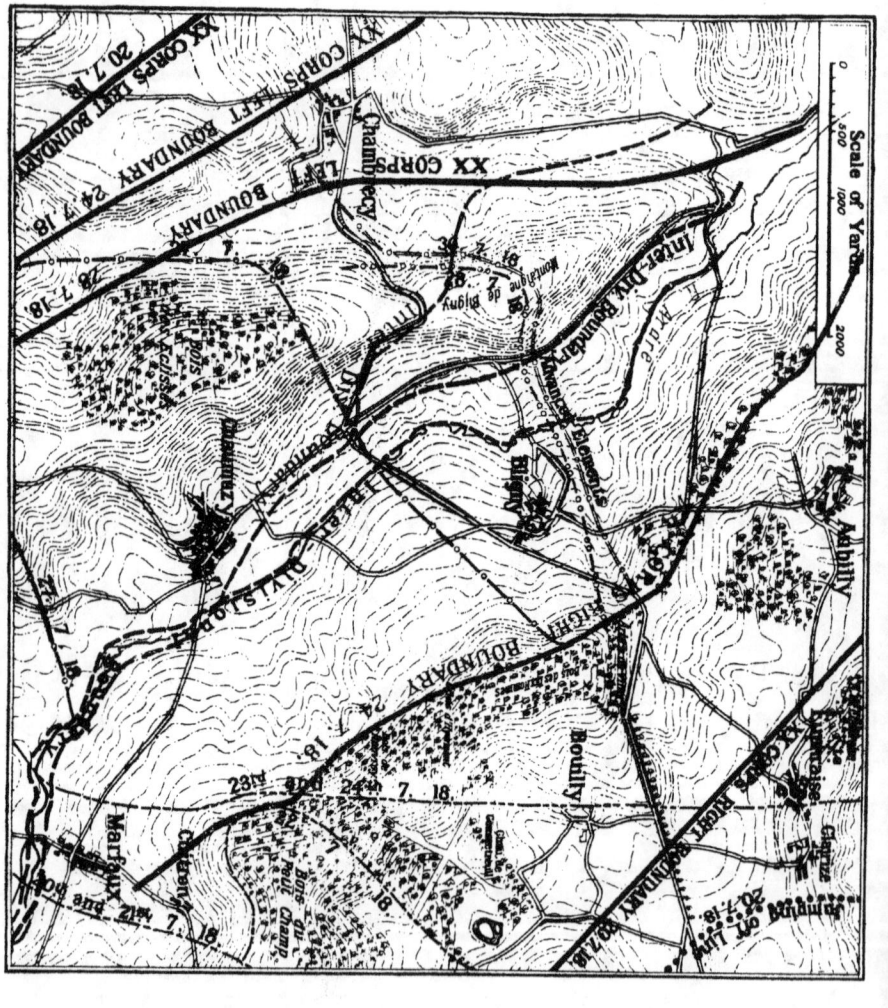

THE CAPTURE OF BLIGNY AND MONTAIGNE DE BLIGNY.

Chapter XVIII. 1918.

THE CAPTURE OF BLIGNY AND MONTAIGNE DE BLIGNY.

28TH JULY.

THE operations of the 28th July were a fitting termination to the splendid efforts of the 62nd Division, which began in the early hours of the 20th. For it was on this day that the 8th West Yorks. won for itself (and therefore the Division to which the Battalion belonged) the deep gratitude of the French, which culminated in the award to the Battalion of the Croix de Guerre, an honour rare in the annals of the British Army.

Before dawn on the 28th the attacking Battalions of the 186th and 185th Infantry Brigades had made final arrangements for continuing the advance.

More closely defined, the objectives of the 186th Infantry Brigade (Brig.-General J. G. Burnett) were a line between Bligny and the Arbre de Villers and Bligny and the trench line west of it. The 2/4th Duke of Wellington's on the right were to attack the former, and the 2/4th Hants., on the left, the latter. The River Ardre was the dividing line between Brigades.

SEE MAP No. 13.

The objective of the 185th Infantry Brigade (Brig.-General Viscount Hampden) was the old French line on the Montaigne de Bligny, and for this purpose the Brigadier had ordered the 2/5th Devons to attack on the right and the 8th West Yorks. on the left; the dividing line between the two Battalions being the Sarcy—Chaumuzy Road.

"Zero" hour was at 4-30 a.m.

The 2/4th Hants. (Lieut.-Colonel F. Brook) had an exciting advance. The Battalion received its orders at about 2-30 a.m. but, as the Battalion Diary states, "It was impossible to get attack organized by that time (4-30 a.m.,) and the start was late. Both officers and men were completely worn out, but they made a magnificent effort to get forward." Three Companies—A, B and D—were ordered to capture Bligny, and C Company was to go through and establish posts on the line of the final objective.

28TH JULY.

A heavy barrage had been put down on the line of advance, and the ground over which the Hants. were to go forward was swept by intense machine-gun fire. It was not surprising, therefore, that at first the Battalion was hung up, the men taking shelter in the sunken road which runs south-west of Bligny. But the Hampshiremen were not to be baulked, for during the morning Lieut. Holbrooke and twenty men, divesting themselves of all equipment with the exception of rifles and a bandolier of ammunition apiece, began to crawl forward towards Bligny. It was a perilous task, but by dint of carefully taking advantage of every piece of cover, the little party eventually reached the north-eastern edge of the village; here they established themselves.

At 4 p.m. patrols, under Second-Lieut. Brierley, Second-Lieut. Viscount Uffington and Corporal Williams, were sent out from the sunken road and succeeded in establishing four posts on the objective. Under cover of these posts the whole Battalion was able to move forward and by 6 p.m. the whole of the objective allotted to the Battalion had been gained, an achievement which drew from the Brigadier the following message to Colonel Brook: "Tell your officers and men they have done splendidly."

Meanwhile the 2/4th Duke of Wellington's (Lieut.-Colonel P. P. Wilson), dead-tired from the previous day's operations had, at 4 a.m., taken up their assembly position between the Bois de Dix Hommes and the Bligny—Chaumuzy Road. In this position they were much exposed and suffered heavily from an intense bombardment and from machine-gun fire coming from the Bois de Dix Hommes, Arbre de Villers and the high ground north of the old French line. "The men were suffering from extreme exhaustion," said Colonel Wilson, "and the advance became most difficult." But no one thought of giving in. The men forced themselves along and by sheer perseverance and dogged determination one platoon, having marched round by the Bois de Dix Hommes, managed to reach the objective. At this period touch was not established with the French on the right but the position gained was held. Another platoon, by creeping forward first round the eastern and then the northern exits of Bligny, reached its objective also. No further movement was possible until dusk, when the 2/4th Dukes, as a whole, advanced and consolidated the old French line—their objective.

Thus both Battalions of the 186th Infantry Brigade, with magnificent pluck and perseverance, had made good their objectives.

West of the Ardre the attack of the 185th Infantry Brigade had meanwhile met with splendid success. On the right of the Brigade 28TH JULY. front, the 1/5th Devons. (Lieut.-Colonel H. V. Bastow), whose right lay along the bank of the Ardre, started the attack at 4-10 a.m. and met with little opposition until the cross-roads about 1,300 metres north of Chaumuzy were reached. Here machine-gun fire swept the advance, coming principally from the direction of Bligny. But by taking advantage of whatever cover presented itself, the Battalion pushed gallantly on and, at 7 a.m., reached its objective. Touch was not obtained with the left flank of the 186th Infantry Brigade for, as already narrated, the Hants. were held up until later in the day. Colonel Bastow, therefore, obtained permission to send up A Company of 2/5th West Yorks., with instructions to form a defensive flank on the right of the Devons. On the arrival of the Company of the 2/5th West Yorks. (about 10-30 a.m.) the position was established and effectively protected the right flank of the Devons.

On the left of the Devons, the 8th West Yorks. (Lieut.-Colonel N. A. England) were in their assembly positions, on the immediate left of the Chaumuzy—Sarcy Road, and just clear of the village by 3 a.m. At 4 a.m. the Battalion, in artillery formation, moved off to the attack—D Company (Capt. T. P. Reay) on the right, C Company (Capt. N. Muller) on the left, B Company (Lieut. H. R. Burroughs) behind D Company, and A Company (Capt. C. M. Hirst) in rear of C Company. " The men went forward in splendid style "—the Battalion Diary stated.

It is worth recording that the 8th West Yorks. had only just been reorganized for, in the early hours of the 27th, a very wet and tired party of ten officers and 200 other ranks—reinforcements —arrived for the Battalion, which now had the necessary numbers to reorganize into four companies of three platoons each. But platoon sergeants had mostly to be drawn from young lance-corporals who were quite strangers, while the Lewis-gun teams could be given no more than two trained gunners. Also there were among the reinforcements " many youngsters just out from England who had not yet received their baptism of fire." These facts should be borne in mind.

By 4 a.m., when the Battalion moved forward, the rain had stopped altogether. It was still dark, with only the faintest suggestion of approaching dawn. A chilly mist hung over the country and a damp passage resulted through the corn.

" D Company, with its right on the road, led the way, and our

28TH JULY. section (the story is from a narrative by the commander of B Company) followed not very far behind, as they wound their way through corn and pasture. It was now growing light enough to see something of our surroundings. On our left there loomed out a spur topped with occasional trees, across the road on our right was a miniature prairie, yellow with ripened corn, which ceased only when it reached the Bois de Bligny, on the higher ground, whilst far away in the distance was a dim incline of some prominent hill. This far-off knoll then, and its encircling trenches, formed our goal this morning. It still looked a good 2 miles to the Montaigne de Bligny...... We were getting along in great style and not a sign of the enemy had been seen...... We then reached the Bligny—Chambrecy road which cut across our front. In the crossing we had to clamber over a rather high bank, but we were soon over this obstacle and into the cornfields. The Montaigne grew more and more distinct with such details as a small wood half way up its steep slopes and several isolated trees became easily distinguishable. It was now broad daylight and the mists were clearing. There were no enemy to be seen and the battle so far was progressing well.

"The sharp report of a Mauser rifle rang out 'crack'! Then rifles and machine-guns spluttered and cracked from scores of hidden emplacements in the hill sides. Two guns were spurting out destruction from the high ground on the left. Were we going to be caught again within a deadly zone of machine-gun cross-fire? Our advance received a decided check. The delay did not last long, for each section changed its hitherto steady marching programme to one of quick rushes and short rests......Forgetting their fatigue, section after section darted up in the corn, rushed a few yards, dropped down and opened fire, all obeying orders which rang out from the impromptu section commander, above the spluttering of the machine-guns and the crack of the snipers, and all in the face of a heavy enemy fire coming from a hill with steep and treacherous sides. But we were making headway, though only a slow one, against this strong resistance.

"Then up the road on which our right flank was resting and where we joined up with the Devons., a cavalry patrol galloped majestically towards us and amidst the cheers of our men dashed past us...... Snipers and machine-guns began to thin our ranks. Some sections lost heavily and grew small in numbers. One heroic Lewis gun section consisted of one Lewis gunner, his gun and a pannier of ammunition, which he hauled along when not firing at the Bosches to keep them down until his pals made their rush forward."

But still the line crept gradually forward. Nothing seemed able to stop that darting up in the corn of twenty resolute sections. The enemy's fire became less certain; his markmanship was poor, and finally it wavered. That strange feeling of exultation which suddenly comes to attacking troops swept over the West Yorkshiremen and, rushing on with the bayonet, they came to close grips with the enemy and completed his discomfiture. The Germans fought well, but the grim Yorkshiremen fought better. The enemy broke and fled, hurried on by fire from his own machine guns which had been turned on him as he scrambled back up the steep hill in frantic haste to get away from the fate which pursued him.

The Battalion Diary records that, on the first check when the hitherto silent hillside suddenly became like a sheet of fire—" Capt. Muller (commanding C Company, on the left front of the Battalion) realizing that the success of the operation depended upon the immediate capture of the high ground on his front, led his Company forward, and after a short but stiff struggle gained the position. The whole line then pressed on and drove the enemy from the crown of the hill."

The usual clearing operations had to be carried out as the attack progressed. " The dug-outs were searched, the wood was cleared and a few of our sections had won through to the crest. Sections reassembled and carried on up the hill, through the vines, and over the side and into the old disused trenches, where a few lingering Bosches were captured."

The line was then consolidated and held, two Companies of 2/5th West Yorks. (Lieut.-Colonel R. H. Waddy) being attached to the 8th West Yorks. and two Companies of the same Battalion to the 2/5th Devon Regt., in close support.

Thus the Montaigne de Bligny fell to the victorious 8th West Yorks.[1] of the 62nd Division. It was a grand fight. Nothing could have been finer than the way in which all ranks went forward and, after the first check, resolutely set to work to sweep the enemy from the side of the hill. Many of the troops, it will be remembered, were new to active warfare, but the splendid example of their seasoned

---

[1] In this operation the 8th West Yorks. lost Capt. N. Muller—killed—three officers wounded, two officers missing; thirteen other ranks killed, ninety-three wounded, nine missing, two gassed.
The Battalion captured sixty-nine prisoners and nine machine-guns.

28TH JULY. comrades taught them almost in a flash how to fight and how to win.

Afar off British and French Staff Officers who were watching the battle must have been thrilled by the sight of these brave men fighting their way up a steep hill in the face of fierce opposition.

Dealing with the operations of the 29th July, the Divisional narrative stated : " The continuous and arduous nature of the fighting precluded any further advance during the day, partly owing to the exhaustion of the troops and partly to the tenacity of the opposing forces, now reinforced by a comparatively fresh Division—the 240th —which had received, and certainly obeyed, orders to hold on at all costs.

" During the night (28th/29th) the 187th Infantry Brigade took over the ground gained by the 186th Infantry Brigade, which now went into Divisional Reserve. French and British artillery moved forward to be in close touch with the infantry brigades.

" To conform to an attack made by the 77th French Division through the Bois les Honleux, the 187th Infantry Brigade pushed forward liaison posts and patrols along the valley of the Ardre to keep in touch with the French troops on their right. Liaison was closely maintained throughout so that our troops were able to supply the French units with rifles and small arm ammunition taken from our casualties, when their own supply of ammunition had run out and a dangerous attack was imminent.

" Mounted patrols succeeded in getting up the Ardre Valley as far as the Copse, about 1,500 yards north-west of Bligny, but a heavy counter-attack drove the French out of the Bois les Honleux and our most advanced elements withdrew in conformity to the old French line.

"At 8 p.m. the 2/5th West Yorks. Regt. successfully carried out a small attack to complete the capture of the Montaigne de Bligny, and this was the final incident of note in the operations under review."

29TH JULY. On the morning of the 29th it was found that the enemy still occupied a strip of the old French line on the left of the Montaigne de Bligny, about 150 yards in length.

This attack was carried out by D Company of the 2/5th West Yorks., two platoons of which were to establish a position on this strip of wood, and two platoons to pass through and gain a position 150 yards north-west of this point in order to obtain direct observation over the village of Sarcy. The first objective was quickly taken, but the two platoons detailed for the second objective

The 8th West Yorkshires moving back from the Front Line after they had Captured the Montaigne de Bligny.

apparently lost direction and were captured by the enemy. 29TH JULY.

At night the 51st Division took over the front held by the 185th Infantry Brigade as far east as the Chaumuzy—Sarcy Road, the 8th West Yorks. moving back into support, in the valley south of Chaumuzy.

About four o'clock on the afternoon of 29th, 62nd Divisional Headquarters received warning from Corps Headquarters that the Corps was being withdrawn for entrainment to another area. One artillery brigade of the Division was to be pulled out on the night 29th/30th and the remainder of the Division on the night 30th/31st July.

The Brigade of artillery, withdrawn on the night of 29th/30th, 29TH/30TH was the 310th, which marched back to its wagon lines at Ferme D'Eceuil, after having supported the small attack by the 2/5th West Yorks.

On the 30th, the day the Division was relieved, the Staff was able to watch an enemy counter-attack launched against the French in the Bois de Honleux, and as General Berthelot's troops were running short of small-arm ammunition the 62nd sent some up to the Frenchmen. The Divisional Artillery was also turned on to the Bois de Honleux, forcing the enemy to retire, which made it possible for the French to stabilize their line.

For the past ten days, the gunners, like the infantry of the Division, had had to accustom themselves to an entirely new kind of warfare. Batteries were constantly on the move and had no more protection than they could dig for themselves in between actions. Communication in the thickly-wooded country was especially difficult.

Both artillery Brigades were in action by 6 p.m. on 20th July, and with the exception of C/312, which had gun positions about 800 yards west of Courtagnon Farm, supported the attack from the Patis d'Ecueil. But on the 21st, in the attack on Cuitron, and on the 22nd, when an attempt was made to clear the Bois de Petit Champ, the guns supported the infantry with splendid devotion. During the attack on 23rd, which resulted in the capture of Marfaux and Cuitron, the barrage put down by the 310th (Lieut.-Colonel D. J. C. Sherlock) and 312th (Lieut.-Colonel A. G. Eden) Brigades, R.F.A., were described by the infantry in the front line as "magnificent." Some batteries fired as many as 600 rounds per gun and prisoners captured were in a great state of depression, declaring their losses from artillery fire had been enormous. This was not

P

29TH/30TH JULY.

to be wondered at, seeing that large bodies of the enemy moving about frequently presented fine targets, of which the gunners took every advantage.

On the night of the 24th, the Divisional Ammunition Column, parked close to the Rheims—Epernay Road, about 2 miles east of Courtagnon, was particularly unfortunate. The enemy was very active dropping bombs from his aeroplanes and a number fell amongst the horses, killing twenty-six and wounding twenty. The famous shire team of roans—the pride of the D.A.C.—lost heavily. In the two artillery Brigades, nine horses were killed and a number of men wounded.

The guns were frequently very heavily shelled by the enemy's artillery and on the 26th, Headquarters of the 310th Brigade had to move several hundred yards, Colonel Sherlock himself assisting in removing wounded men under very heavy fire.

After the successful attack of the 27th, when the villages of Espilly and Nappe fell, the batteries advanced, one at a time, and before dark the 310th had taken up new positions in the Bois du Petit Champ and the 312th close to and west of Pourcy; the C.R.A.'s Headquarters were at Nanteuil. By this time the C.R.A. (Brig.-General A. T. Anderson) had, in addition to the 62nd Divisional Artillery, twelve batteries of French Field Artillery and six French heavy batteries—no small command.

At dawn on 28th, the 312th Brigade moved forward to positions west of Marfaux, supporting the 185th Infantry Brigade in its successful attack on the Montaigne de Bligny. On this day also the guns did magnificent work.

The 310th Brigade moved to positions north of Cuitron in the early morning of 29th, and during the day had many moving targets with direct observation, firing about 1,500 rounds per battery. Shortly after mid-day, A/310 and C/310 advanced, in full view of the enemy, to positions near Moulin de Chaumuzy, and engaged machine-guns which were annoying the infantry. The 312th Brigade also moved forward two batteries in close support: B/312 came into action near Chaumuzy, under heavy fire.

30TH JULY.

At night on the 29th, as already stated, the 310th Brigade withdrew to its wagon lines, and on the morning of 30th, at 10 a.m., the 312th Brigade, having fired in support of a French advance, marched back to St. Imoges.

In speaking of his gunners, the C.R.A. said: " They took to it as readily as if they had done nothing else all through the War and, in spite of the difficulties of ammunition supply and keeping up communications in a thickly-wooded country, they were always ready to open fire up to time, and to support the infantry in their rapid advances. This could only be achieved, however, by the unremitting exertions of every officer, N.C.O. and man, who were fighting and toiling night and day without shelter of any sort and with never more than a chance hour or two of sleep at a time, from the 20th to the 30th July."

30TH JULY.

The devotion of the artillery to the infantry and the affection of the latter for their gunners were never more marked than during those days on the Marne in 1918.

Throughout the whole operations the 62nd Battalion Machine-Gun Corps (Lieut.-Colonel G. H. Harrison) admirably supported the infantry and co-operated with the artillery in covering fire. The machine-gunners fought under entirely new conditions. Hitherto, used only to indirect fire, barrages, etc., they were suddenly confronted with a new phase of warfare in which conditions changed rapidly, calling for quick decisions and initiative on the part of section officers. But once the change was appreciated (and it was marvellous to see how quickly the gunners grasped the principles of fighting continually on the advance in both hilly and wooded country) their co-operation with, and assistance to, the infantry was really splendid. In the attack on Marfaux and Cuitron (on 22nd July) the two villages and the Sunken Road between them and the cornfields were kept under a heavy covering machine-gun fire, which kept generally 300 metres ahead of the artillery barrage, and not only were the enemy's machine-guns reduced to inactivity, but the moral effect on the attacking infantry of the Division was good. On the 27th also, the Machine-Gun Companies lent splendid support in the attack on, and capture of, Bligny and La Montaigne de Bligny.

The Administrative Staff (Lieut.-Colonel H. Lea, A.A. and Q.M.G.) and the units upon whom fell the responsibility of supplying the needs of the Division during this strenuous period of fighting seem, from the Divisional Record, to have done remarkably well.

There are no complaints in the Divisional Diaries and the Army Service Corps Companies of the Divisional Train (Lieut.-Colonel H. H. Wilberforce) never failed to respond to all calls upon them. It is interesting to note the following supply arrangements during the operations : " Supplies were loaded at Railhead and dumped immediately. Divisional Train supply wagons on return from units refilled immediately from dumps and remained full

30TH JULY. overnight, the mobility of the Divisional Supply Service being thus transferred from the M.T. Company to the Divisional Train, thereby releasing the supply lorries for other duties."

The peculiar nature of the operations precluded the Field Companies of R.E. and the Pioneers from their normal duties during trench warfare. From the 23rd to 25th July the three Field Companies were principally occupied in consolidating ground gained, but the roads were but little damaged, the water supply was good and there were no obstacles (to move) other than those provided by the nature of the country, to impede the movement of infantry. The Signal Company, however, had a difficult task in maintaining communications. As to the Pioneers, they had been put into the line as infantrymen, their numerous duties also not being necessary, and right well did they serve the Division.

Evacuation of the wounded from the forward areas during the operations was, considering the difficult country and the somewhat novel conditions under which the medical officers and their staffs worked, extremely good. On the night of 19th/20th July, the A.D.M.S. (Colonel H. Collinson) and the Os.C. Field Ambulances had no light task in getting their C.C.Ss. fitted up, for although the C.C.Ss. had motor ambulance convoys and an advanced depot of medical stores were on the way, they were not immediately available. But the Tent Division of the 2/3rd W.R.F.A. managed to open a temporary C.C.S. at Sezanne, and the Tent Division of a Forward Ambulance of the 51st Division opened at Hopital Auban Moet, Epernay, an advanced operating centre for serious cases, which was, subsequently, taken over by Nos. 50 and 48 C.C.Ss.

The 62nd Division Main Dressing Station opened at St. Imoges and a walking wounded dressing station of the 2/2nd W.R.F.A. at Champillon.

With only their mobilization stores of stretchers and blankets and a very small stock of splints, dressings, etc., and with a distance of about 50 kilometres from the Main Dressing Station to the C.C.S. at Sezanne, the work of medical units was difficult. The situation was, however, met in the following manner: "As a temporary arrangement, centres were established on the main Rheims—Epernay Road at which walking wounded were collected; here, passing lorries were stopped and cases loaded and transferred by stages to Champillon and on to Sezanne. In spite of all precautions, however, a certain number of walking wounded got into the Hopital Auban Moet, at Epernay, and also into French hospitals, but it does not appear that this could have been avoided, particularly as the N.C.O. —and a man, who acted as control in Epernay, were both killed by an enemy bomb on the night 20th/21st July."

30TH JULY.

In a few days, however, the medical arrangements became easier, and with the assistance of the French Medical Services,[1] who were most helpful to Colonel Collinson and his staff, the wounded and sick were adequately looked after and evacuated to the Base. A novel method of marking the routes for stretcher bearers and walking wounded, by means of tying bandages round trees, was very efficient and worked splendidly.

For the first time since the 62nd Division landed in France in January, 1917, troops belonging to other County Regiments had fought side by side with the Yorkshiremen; they had been welded into the Brotherhood of the men from the West Riding. With pardonable pride in their own achievements and a greater regard for the splendid reputation the Division had won for itself it is possible that the Yorkshiremen looked, at first, on these new divisional units with something akin to fear lest they should fail to keep bright the glorious record of the past. For the feeling of *esprit de corps* ran very high indeed in the Division. But the Hants. and the Devons. responded nobly to all calls made upon them, just as the Londoners of the 2/20th Battalion London Regt. were, in the future, to help add further lustre to the brilliant record of what was probably the finest Territorial Division which ever trod the soil of France.[2] What is there a Yorkshireman cannot do? And what is there he cannot do again and again when aided by the Londoners and the men of Devonshire and Hampshire?

> " There is but one task for all
> For each one life to give.
> Who stands if Freedom fall?
> Who dies if England lives?"

[1] The A.D.M.S. at the end of his report made the following acknowledgment to the French Services authorities: "The A.D.M.S. expresses his extreme indebtedness to the French Medical Services for the valuable assistance they gave in the way of cars and stretchers. This help was extended freely and ungrudgingly and at a critical time was of incalculable value."

[2] Some time after the War was over, an officer of the 2/20th London Regt. when writing the history of his Battalion said that in a very little while after joining the 62nd Division—"The Battalion soon had cause to congratulate itself on its new Brigade and Division."

Chapter XIX.

1918.

THE ADVANCE TO VICTORY.

"At last, at last we flung them back
Along their drenched and smoking track,
We hurled them back, in blood and flame,
The reeking ways by which they came."
                                C. G. D. Roberts.

SPEEDED on their way by a touching tribute from General Berthelot,[1] commanding the Fifth French Army—"Vos amis Français se souviendront avec émotion de votre brillant bravoure, et de votre parfaite cameraderie de combat"— the 51st and 62nd Divisions, forming the XXIInd Corps, left the Marne and moved by train back to behind the British line between Amiens and Ypres.[2]

Certain operations in the war will always be remembered with pride by the Divisions which took part in them, but to the four British Divisions operating with the French Armies between Soissons and Rheims, when Marshal Foch began his famous counter-attack on 18th July, 1918, belongs the signal honour of having assisted in dealing the enemy a blow from which he never fully recovered. Nay more! a blow which marked the turning-point of the war. And that the 62nd was one of those four Divisions, is the proud memory of every Yorkshireman.

---

[1] For the full text of General Berthelot's Official Order of the Day to the XXIInd Corps, see Appendix IV.

[2] "On 31st July, after we had gone out, General Berthelot said he would like to review as many of the troops as he could, just outside Moreuil. There was, as may be imagined, great preparation. We had only come out of the line the night before, but we determined to show our Allies a clean Brigade. The review was to consist of one Brigade from the 51st and one Brigade from the 62nd, General Berthelot, commanding the Fifth French Army, taking the salute. The 186th Brigade represented the 62nd Division, and the way the 186th were helped during the night to make themselves and their transport clean and smart by other troops, which were not taking part in the review, is worthy of mention, as showing the 'Esprit de Division' which existed amongst all ranks. An amusing part of the show was, as there was no time to clean everything thoroughly, the Brigadier had all the brass hubs of the wheels on the side General Berthelot would stand, polished 'up to the nines,' the hubs on the other side remaining in the state that ten days' continuous fighting had made them."—General Braithwaite.

The official despatches, dealing with the situation at the end of July, 1918, opens with the following paragraph : " The definite collapse of the ambitious offensive launched by the enemy on the 15th July, and the striking success of the Allied counter-offensive south of the Aisne, effected a complete change in the whole military situation. *The German Army had made its effort and had failed.* " The period of its maximum strength had been passed, and the bulk of the reserves, accumulated during the winter, had been used up. On the other hand, the position of the Allies in regard to reserves had greatly improved. The fresh troops made available during the late spring and early summer had been incorporated and trained. The British Army was ready to take the offensive, while the American Army was growing rapidly and had already given convincing proof of the high fighting quality of its soldiers."

Five days after Marshal Foch had launched his successful counter-attack of 18th July, the Allies held a conference. At this conference the British, French and American Armies were asked to prepare plans for local offensives, " to be taken in hand as soon as possible, with certain objectives of a limited nature." On the British front the objectives were the disengagement of Amiens and the freeing of the Paris—Amiens Railway by an attack on the Albert—Montdidier front. Farther south and east the French and American Armies were to act in a similar manner, freeing other strategic railways which, so long as they could not be used by the Allies, constituted a source of danger and difficulty.

Certain other projects for offensives along the British front in the direction of La Bassée and Hazebrouck were, for the time being, set aside, the disengagement of Amiens being deemed the most important and likely to produce significant results.

It is well, however, to remember that the Amiens operations had been the subject of discussion between Sir Douglas Haig and Marshal Foch before the German offensive on the Marne on 15th July, and that as early as the 13th July, the Fourth Army Commander, General Rawlinson, had been ordered to prepare for it at an early date.

The official despatches on this plan are so important that again a quotation is given from them, which shows the important results arrived at : " It would depend upon the nature of the success which might be obtained in these difficult Allied operations whether they could be more fully exploited before the winter set in. It was subsequently arranged that attacks would be pressed in a converging direction towards Mézières by the French and American Armies, whilst at the same time the British Armies, attacking towards the line St. Quentin—Cambrai, would strike directly on the vital lateral communications running through Maubeuge to Hirson and Mézières, by which alone the German forces on the Champagne front could be supplied and maintained."

"As a secondary result of the advance of the British Armies towards the all-important railway centre about Maubeuge, the group of German Armies in Flanders would find their communications threatened from the south, and any operations which it might be possible for the Allies to undertake in that theatre at a later date would be powerfully assisted thereby. *It was certainly of vital importance to the enemy to maintain intact his front opposite St Quentin and Cambrai, and for this purpose he depended on the great fortified zone known as the Hindenburg Line.*"

Of the whole Allied Front from the Swiss Frontier to the Belgian Coast, that terrible triangle formed by Amiens, St. Quentin and Cambrai was of the greatest importance. In 1916 and 1917 the Allied line had pressed forward over that bloody stretch of tortured country: in March, 1918, the line had been beaten back almost to the point of breaking: now it was to go forward again—for the last time! No river in all France or Flanders witnessed more desperate or vital struggles than the wide banks of the Somme.

"By the beginning of August," said Ludendorff, "we had suspended our attacks and reverted to the defence on the whole front." Thus ended the enemy's ambitious offensive! And of his "Friedensturm," the Chief of the German General Staff, writes: "The attempts to make the nations of the Entente inclined to peace before the arrival of the American reinforcements by means of German victories had failed. The impetus of the Army had not sufficed to deal the enemy a decisive blow before the Americans were on the spot in considerable force. It was quite clear to me that our general situation had thus become very serious."

The date of the British and French advance east of Amiens was fixed for the 8th August. But before that date the enemy had been completely hoodwinked as to where the blow would fall. Preparations for a great attack in Flanders were simulated. Thus it was that while the enemy was occupied in reorganizing his line to meet the changed conditions and almost certain Allied attacks, the Battle of Amiens opened, " while still occupied with these thoughts," said Ludendorff " the blow of the 8th August fell upon me."

8TH AUG.

At 4-20 a.m. on the 8th August, in a heavy mist, rendered more impossible to the enemy's observers by a thick smoke barrage, British, Australian, Canadian and French troops broke into the enemy's line from south of the Ancre (just south of Albert) to Moreuil (south of the Amiens—Roye road). Taken completely by surprise, the enemy was quickly overcome and the Allied troops swept on, advancing some 6 or 7 miles. At nightfall over 13,000 prisoners and between 300 and 400 guns had fallen to the British Army, while the First French Army (on the right of the British) had taken 3,350 prisoners and many guns. The night of 8th/9th August was made hideous by deafening roars, as the enemy exploded his ammunition dumps; the sky was red from the glare of burning villages, the shriek of shells, hurtling through the air, adding to the horrible din of the battlefield.

9TH AUG.

On the morning of the 9th the attack was continued and until the night of the 12th the enemy was given no rest. He had, however, heavily reinforced his front and was ready to oppose any further advance from the line gained by the Allies, the old Roye—Chaulnes defences. But the first blow had staggered the enemy. Twenty German Divisions had been defeated heavily by thirteen British infantry and three cavalry Divisions, assisted by one Regiment from the 33rd American Division and some 400 Tanks. Nearly 22,000 prisoners and over 400 guns had been taken from the Germans and a line 12 miles deep had been driven into their line. Little wonder that, at last, the befooled German soldiery began to realize that the promise made to them of an early and favourable peace was a myth.

18TH/19TH AUG.

Between the 14th and 17th August the enemy withdrew from his positions about Serre, whilst north, in the Lys Salient, he was obviously preparing for a withdrawal; and the capture of Outtersteene village and ridge on 18th and 19th hurried these preparations.

The next thrust at the enemy was to be made between the Somme and the Scarpe Rivers. From here a successful attack between Albert and Arras, in a south-easterly direction, would turn the line by the Somme, south of Peronne, and be a step forward towards the strategical objective—the St. Quentin—Cambrai line.

North of the Ancre the ground had suffered comparatively little from shell fire and was suitable for Tanks. It was arranged, therefore, that on the morning of 21st August, a limited attack, north of the River, in order to gain the general line of the Arras—Albert Railway, should be made. If successful, the 22nd was to be spent in bringing forward troops and guns to the line of the railway and also in bringing forward the left of the French Army between the Somme and the Ancre. The principal attack would be launched on the 23rd by the Third Army and a Division of the Fourth Army immediately north of the Somme, the remainder of the latter Army was to cover the flank of the main operation by pushing forward south of the River. As soon as the Third Army had forced the enemy to fall back from the Mercatel Spur, so covering the southern flank for an attack upon the German position on Orange Hill and about Monchy, the First Army (north of the Third Army) was to continue the battle, attacking east of Arras. *18/19TH AUG.*

In the early morning hours of 21st August, at 4-55, the IVth[1] and VIth Corps of the Third Army, attacked the enemy line north of the Ancre, from Miraumont to Moyenneville—a frontage of about 9 miles, and by nightfall British troops had reached practically the general line of the railway—Achiet-le-Petit, Logeast Wood, Courcelles and Moyenneville were all captured and east of the last two places the railway had been crossed.[2] *21ST AUG.*

The positions required for the main operations thus fell to the IVth and VIth Corps (the Vth Corps assisting by clearing the north bank of the Ancre about Beaucourt) as well as over 2,000 prisoners.

The IIIrd Corps of the Fourth Army attacked eastwards on the morning of the 22nd, capturing Albert, and the British line between the Somme and the Ancre was advanced well to the east of the Bray—Albert Road. *22ND AUG.*

On the 23rd the main attack was launched, on a front of 33 miles, from the junction of the British and French Armies north of Lihons to the Mercatel Spur, in which neighbourhood the Hindenburg Line from Quéant and Bullecourt joined the old Arras—Vimy defensive line of 1916. *23RD AUG.*

Over ground which had so often witnessed costly and terrible struggles, across the same terrain which Sir Douglas Haig's troops had moved in the German Retirement in 1917, and in the British Retirement in 1918, the Divisions advanced "with a persistent, vigorous and relentless determination, which neither the extreme difficulty of the ground, nor the obstinate resistance of the enemy, could diminish or withstand."

South of the Somme, Herleville, Chuignolles and Chuignes,

---

[1] In this attack the 62nd Divisional Artillery supported the 37th Division of the IVth Corps. The gun positions of the 310th and 312th Brigades, R.F.A., were between Essarts and Bucquoy, familiar names to all ranks of the 62nd Division.

[2] The Battle of Albert—21st August/23rd August.

23RD AUG. were taken : about Albert, Tara and Usna Hills fell to the IIIrd and Vth Corps ; the eastern banks of the Ancre, in the neighbourhood of Hamel, were gained by troops of the 38th Division ; progress was made by 17th and 21st Divisions along the left bank of the Ancre, north of Thiepval.

" North of the Ancre, the attack of the VIth Corps was opened at 4 a.m., at which hour the 3rd Division took Gommecourt, with 500 prisoners. During the morning the attack spread along the front of the IVth Corps also. The enemy's main line of resistance was stormed and, penetrating deeply beyond it, our troops captured Ribeaucourt, Ervillers, Boyelles and Boiry Becquerelle, together with over 5,000 prisoners and a number of guns. Under the constant pressure of our attack the enemy was being disorganized and showed signs of confusion. Our troops were now astride the Arras—Bapaume Road and closing down upon the latter town from the north and north-west. The position of the German Divisions in this pronounced salient on the Thiepval Ridge was becoming perilous."[1]

At nightfall on 23rd August the Battle of Albert ended.

At this stage of the Advance to Victory, the 62nd came again into the battlefield, for during the 23rd[2] the Division had received orders to return to the VIth Corps that night, and relieve the 3rd Division about the railway, east of Courcelle, on the 24th August.

Very tired, and greatly in need of reorganization, the 62nd Division had arrived in the IVth Corps area, with Divisional Headquarters at Pas, on the 5th August. From the 6th to the 12th reorganization and platoon training occupied all units of the Division. It was during this period that another well-tried and hard-fighting Battalion of the Division—the 2/5th West Yorks. Regt.—was disbanded. The Battalion Diary of 9th August contains the following entry : " 62nd Divisional letter A/303/67 of 8/8/18 received. The letter confirms the rumour that this Battalion is to be disbanded owing to the lack of reinforcements. The news is a terrible blow to us all. The ' esprit de corps ' of the Battalion was at a very high standard. The N.C.O.'s. and men are to be divided (a) to complete the 8th West Yorks. Regt. to an establishment of 900 (b) augment the various Yorkshire Regts. in the Division. The disposal of the

---

[1] Official Despatches.

[2] The location of the Division was as follows : Divisional Headquarters —Pas. Of the three Infantry Brigades, the 185th was in the Vauchelles area, the 186th in Pas and the 187th at St. Leger. Headquarters, 62nd Division, R.A., were also at Pas, but the 310th and 312th Brigades R.F.A. were with the IVth Corps, supporting the attack on Achiet-le-Grand, Bihucourt and Irles.

officers is not yet settled......At 2-15 the C.O. (Lieut.-Colonel 23RD AUG. R. H. Waddy, D.S.O.) paraded the Battalion and told them the sad news." The blow fell most heavily upon the officers for, whereas the N.C.O.'s. and men were to stay with their beloved Division, the majority of the officers, at this late period of the war, when victory was almost within sight, were transferred to other Divisions. On the 12th General Braithwaite inspected the Battalion. The G.O.C. expressed his regret that they were to be broken up, but emphasized the fact that the Battalion was one of the smartest and best-fighting Battalions in the whole Division. At 11-20 a.m. on the 13th the 2/5th West Yorks. ceased to exist.

The 2/5th West Yorks. were replaced by the 2/20th London Regt., which had arrived at Mondicourt from Palestine on the 10th August, and went into billets in Thievres. The London Battalion was commanded by Lieut.-Colonel W. St. A. Warde-Aldam.

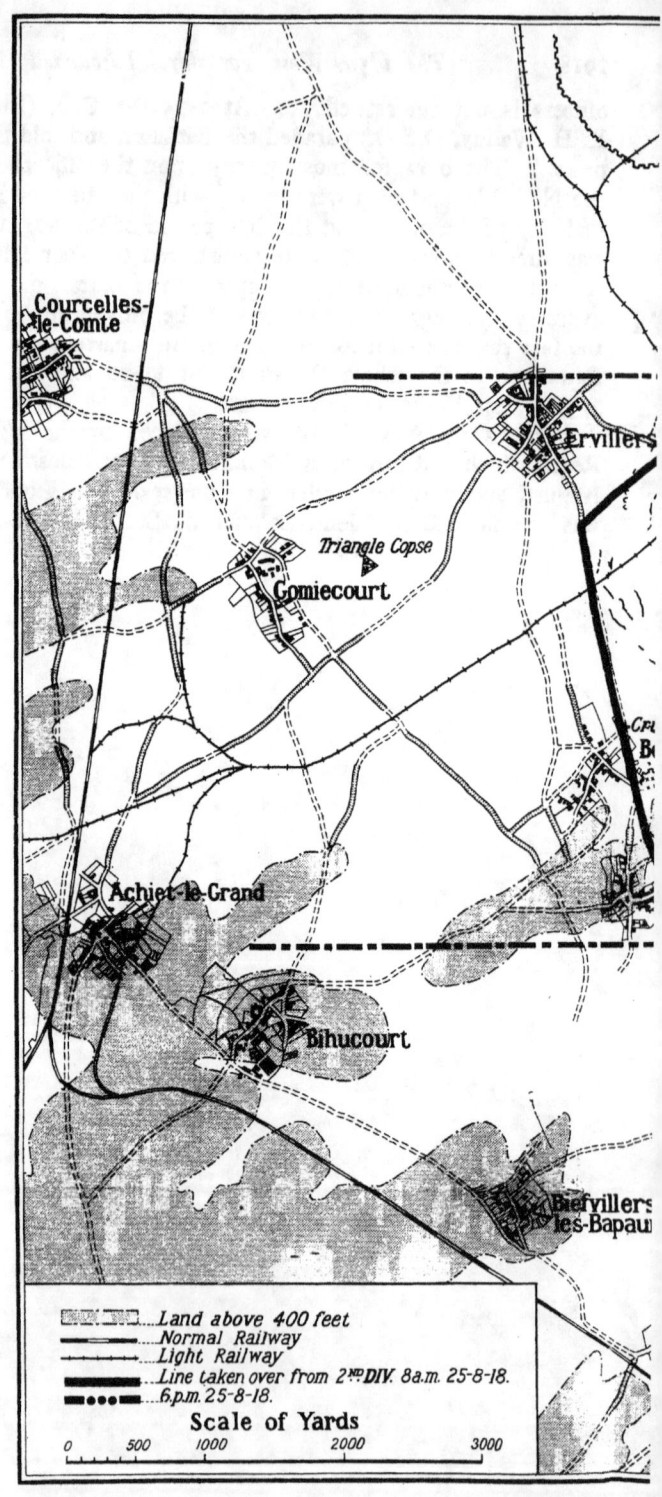

THE CAPTURE

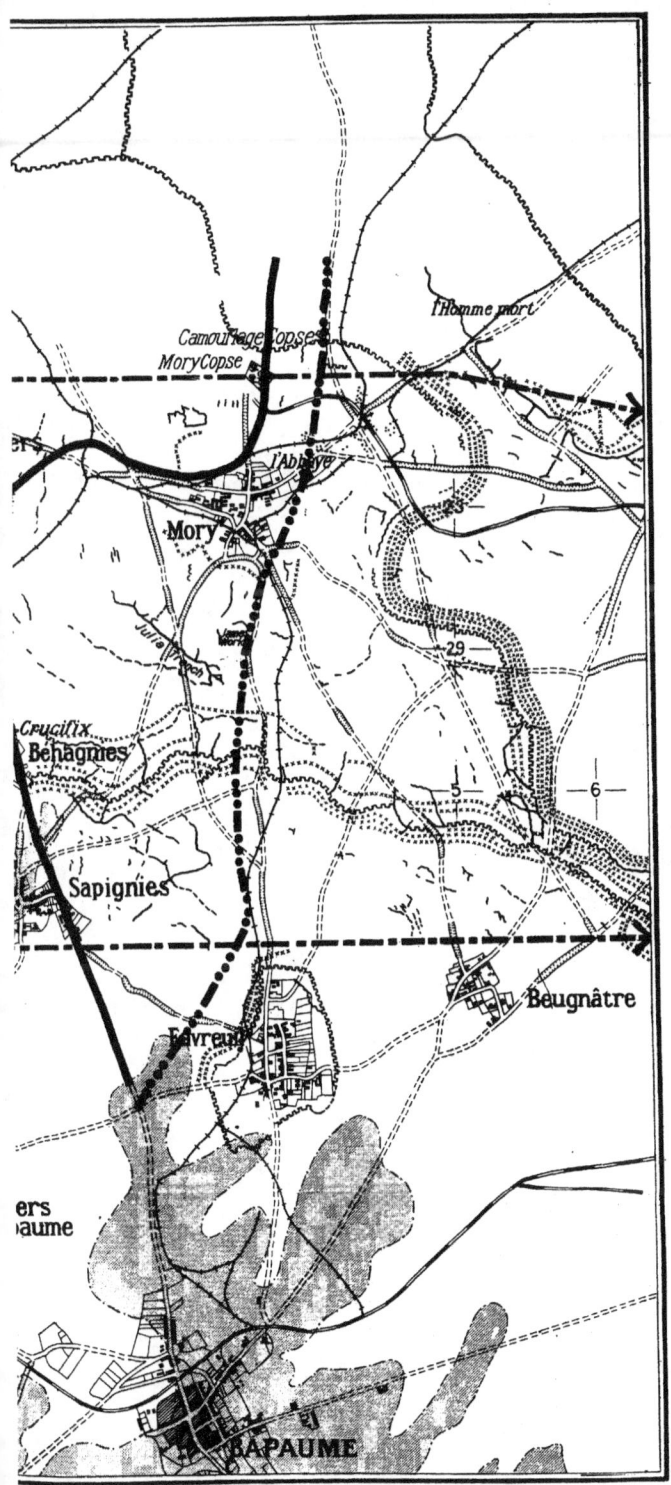

Chapter XX.

1918.

MORY

AT 12-30 a.m. on 24th August orders received from VIth 24TH AUG. Corps Headquarters stated that the advance was to be continued on Vaulx—Vraucourt on the 25th. Headquarters of the 62nd Division were then at La Bazeque, and at 2-15 a.m. confirmation of moving orders, issued the evening before, were sent out to all units to move forward at 7-30 a.m. and relieve the 3rd Division. The three infantry Brigades were to be distributed in the following areas:—185th and 187th Brigades in the valley east of Courcelles (in A.18—A.23) and the 186th Brigade in the valley west of Courcelles (A.14—A.15).

The 186th Infantry Brigade and two Battalions of the 187th were conveyed by lorry as far as Adinfer, but the remainder of the Division marched.

The Division was well on the move when another telegram from VIth Corps Headquarters was received at 10-30 a.m. postponing the relief of the 3rd Division until dusk and ordering the three Brigades to be halted west of the Achiet-le-Grand Railway. Duplicate orders were immediately sent out with orders to all Brigadiers to bivouac the troops west of Courcelles : 185th and 187th in the valley west of the village about A.14 and A.15 and 186th Brigade about A.13 and A.14.

At 1 p.m. warning was issued to the 187th Infantry Brigade to prepare to relieve the 99th and 6th Infantry Brigades of the 2nd Division, west of Mory and in front of Ervillers. The 185th Infantry Brigade was to move east of the Achiet-le-Grand Railway in support and the 186th to the valley west of Courcelles.

During the afternoon the 99th Infantry Brigade (2nd Division) attacked and captured Mory Copse, and the G.O.C., 187th Infantry Brigade, who was at 99th Brigade Headquarters, was able to complete his arrangements for taking over the line. The warning order was confirmed at 6-15 p.m. and the relief began.

24TH AUG.

The relief of the 99th and 6th Infantry Brigades of the 2nd Division was a difficult matter, as units of both these Brigades had been engaged in an attack during the afternoon and, in consequence, had become somewhat mixed up during the operations. But eventually the 5th K.O.Y.L.I. on the right relieved the 2nd South Staffords and 17th Royal Fusiliers (of the 6th Infantry Brigade), east of Ervillers, and the 2/4th York and Lancs. Regt. (Hallamshires) took over the line on the left from the Rifles, Fusiliers and King's (of the 99th Infantry Brigade), which included Mory Copse and thence ran westwards, north of Mory Village to the left flank of the 5th K.O.Y.L.I.; the 2/4th K.O.Y.L.I. were in 187th Brigade Reserve, west of Ervillers.

Meanwhile, at 7-45 p.m., VIth Corps Headquarters had rung up 62nd Headquarters, the Corps line being down, asking for a staff officer to be sent over to the 2nd Division with a message to the G.O.C. of the latter; the Corps Commander wished Sapignies and Béhagnies captured that night " at all costs " in order that the 62nd Division might attack through the 2nd Division on the morning of the 25th.

Following these instructions the G.O.C., 186th Infantry Brigade, was ordered to take up a position on the ridge between Achiet-le-Grand and Gommecourt, thus supporting the 5th Infantry Brigade (2nd Division), which had been ordered to capture the two villages. If the attack launched by the 5th Infantry Brigade was not successful, the 186th Brigade was ordered to complete the capture of Sapignies and Béhagnies.

The 2/4th Duke of Wellington's and the 2/4th Hants. moved off to take up their positions, the former on the right north-east of Achiet-le-Grand and the latter on the left south-east of Gommecourt, the inner flank of both Battalions joining up about the junction of the light railway, half-way between Gommecourt and Bihucourt. The 5th Duke of Wellington's were in Brigade Reserve, west of Courcelles, the 185th Infantry Brigade, also in the valley west of Courcelles, in Divisional Reserve.

SEE MAP NO. 14.

Thus the Division was once more disposed for battle on the Western Front. The general attack had been ordered to take place on the following morning, Zero hour being 9 o'clock. The IVth Corps, on the right of the VIth, had been directed on Bancourt and Beugnatre; the VIth Corps, with the 62nd Division on the right, and the Guards Division on the left, were to capture Vaulx-Vraucourt and Longatte and Ecoust St. Mein, respectively.

Whether by design or sheer coincidence the 62nd Division had   24TH AUG. come back from the Marne battlefield to a field of operations the terrain of which, at least in the early stages of the battle, was more or less well known to it. Achiet-le-Grand, Gommecourt, Sapignies and Béhagnies were all names (the *villages* were very little more at this period) of places, familiar in those early months of 1917 to the newly-arrived 62nd Division, when the Yorkshiremen were following up the retreating enemy to the Hindenburg Line.

East of Mory, and south-east to between Beugny and Frémicourt, ran part of the old Third Army Line, over which the enemy had swept in the holocaust of March, 1918, just five months previously. Thick belts of old wire, rusty and torn in places, still protected (inversely) the battered and tumbled trenches, many of which, however, were capable of being turned to good account.

The 187th Infantry Brigade had been ordered to capture the high ground east and south-east of Mory, across which these old defences ran, while further south the 186th Infantry Brigade was to act similarly in obtaining a footing in, and holding, the old Third Army Line on the right of the 187th Brigade.[1] Each Brigade was to be supported by a Field Artillery Group,[2] to be directly under the G.O.'sC. both infantry Brigades. Machine-gun Companies were also attached to each Brigade.

Of the 186th (Brig.-General J. G. Burnett) and the 187th (Brig.-General A. J. Reddie) Infantry Brigades, the 5th Duke of Wellington's (Lieut.-Colonel J. Walker) and 2/4th York and Lancs. Regt. (Lieut.-Colonel L. H. P. Hart), on the right and left respectively, were the attacking Battalions.

The attack of the 5th Infantry Brigade (2nd Division) on   25TH AUG. Sapignies and Béhagnies was completely successful and at 4-30 a.m., on 25th, Colonel Walker received verbal orders from Brigade Headquarters to move forward and assemble for the main attack to be launched at 9 a.m. Two hours later the 5th Duke's moved off from the valley west of Courcelles and assembled just west of Béhagnies.

The scheme of attack of the 5th Duke's was for B Company on the right and C Company on the left to advance through the villages of Sapignies and Béhagnies (respectively) and take up a position on a north and south line, about 1,300 yards east of the

---

[1] These objectives are more clearly shown in the map: that of the 187th Infantry Brigade being the high ground about the figures 23 and 29 and the objectives of the 186th Infantry Brigade the ground in the vicinity of 5 and 6.

[2] The 62nd Divisional Artillery was still with the IVth Corps.

25TH AUG. villages and some 400 to 500 yards west of the Favreuil—Mory road. D Company on the right and A on the left were then to pass through B and C Companies and capture the final objective, a portion of the Beugnatre—Vraucourt Road, running through the old Third Army Line between the Square Numbers 5 and 6. Two Companies—C and D—of the 2/4th Duke of Wellington's Regt. (Lieut.-Colonel P. P. Wilson) were attached to the 5th Duke's for this operation and were sent forward to concentrate behind the attacking Battalion.

The attack was carried out under a barrage. The forming-up operations had been successfully carried out and at 9 a.m. (Zero hour) the 5th Duke's moved forward on a two-company front towards Sapignies and Béhagnies. At Zero hour no news had reached the C.O. of the Battalion as to whether the two villages were clear of the enemy, and orders had, therefore, been issued to the troops to be prepared to clear those places. But no opposition was encountered, the 2nd Division having done its work thoroughly, and on the two attacking Companies emerging from the eastern exits of the village, the existing outpost line of the 5th Infantry Brigade was found to be on the line of the Bapaume—Ervillers Road.

In spite of very considerable machine-gun fire from Favreuil and Mory, which swept the whole of the ground over which the attack was advancing, causing heavy casualties, the whole of the first objective was gained by 10-30 a.m. D and A Companies of the 5th Duke's now passed through B and C, but just east of the light railway running between Favreuil and Mory the advance was brought to a standstill, for both flanks of the Battalion were now exposed; on the south the 37th Division had failed to capture Favreuil, and north, the 187th Infantry Brigade had not advanced in line with the 186th Brigade.

For the left of the attack had not gone forward with that almost clockwork regularity which had characterized the advance of General Burnett's Brigade.

The very difficult conditions under which the 187th Infantry Brigade had relieved the 99th and 6th Infantry Brigades of the 2nd Division had made it impossible for General Reddie to reorganize his Brigade in time for the main attack at 9-30 a.m. On reporting this to Divisional Headquarters he was given instructions at 5-30 a.m. to fix his own Zero hour when all his arrangements for the attack had been made. At 7 a.m., the G.O.C., 187th Infantry Brigade, held a conference at Battalion Headquarters, 5th K.O.Y.L.I., intending to alter Zero hour to 10-30 a.m. But the message to attend

ERVILLERS.

the conference did not reach the C.O., 2/4th York and Lancs. Regt. 25TH AUG. in anything like good time, for telephonic communication was bad, and it was 8-30 a.m. before Colonel Hart arrived at 5th K.O.Y.L.I. Headquarters, having left instructions with his Battalion (failing the receipt of further orders) to advance at 9 a.m. according to the original intention. As it was impossible for the C.O. of the Hallamshires to get in touch with his Battalion and cancel the attack, the 5th K.O.Y.L.I. (Lieut.-Colonel F. W. Peter) were ordered to support the right flank of the former by pushing forward patrols south of Mory; the 2/4th K.O.Y.L.I. (Lieut.-Colonel C. A. Chaytor) were also ordered to move up east of Ervillers and be prepared to advance through the Hallamshires and push the attack home to the high ground in 23 and 29. Time was too short, however, to arrange a creeping artillery barrage, and the guns were ordered to concentrate on suspected strong points east of the objective, and form a steady barrage on the flanks of the attack. To add to the confusion, the Guards on the left had been informed that the 187th Infantry Brigade was going to attack at 10-30 a.m. instead of 9 a.m., and had, therefore, postponed their attack until the former hour.

Before Colonel Chaytor could get back to his Battalion, the attacking Companies had gone forward—A on the right and C on the left. The absence of the creeping barrage on the Battalion front, and also in front of the Guards, seemed a curious omission, but the Hallamshires had been in many an awkward predicament before and no one thought of holding up the attack. Each attacking Company had a frontage of about 250 yards.

From the south-east and from the direction of l'Homme Mort the deadly fire of many enemy machine guns swept the front of the advance. In spite of heavy losses, however, the Hallamshires pushed forward. That the Battalion had been formed up in its assembly position, enabling the original Zero hour (9 a.m.) to be adhered to, reflected great credit on the C.O. and his officers and, had the Guards, on the left, attacked simultaneously with the Hallamshires, greater progress might have been made. As it was, A Company was held up after advancing between 400 and 500 yards and C Company on reaching a line between 300 and 400 yards from its assembly position. D Company was now sent for to reinforce the two attacking Companies, but even with this addition, it was impossible to carry the line further forward. At 10-30 a.m. the 2/4th York and Lancs. Regt. held a line running north and south, approximately 300 or 400 yards east of Mory Copse.

25TH AUG.   Meanwhile, the 2/4th K.O.Y.L.I. had moved forward in support of the attack of the 2/4th York and Lancs. Regt.; three Companies were disposed in the Sunken Road, running between Mory and Mory Copse, and the fourth Company in some old trench-works east of the road. By 2 p.m. the units of the 187th Infantry Brigade held the following positions :—5th K.O.Y.L.I.—two Companies in the Sunken Road, south-west of Julia Trench, and two just east of James Work; 2/4th K.O.Y.L.I.—three Companies in the Sunken Road, between Mory and Mory Copse; 2/4th York and Lancs. Regt. were approximately in the Sunken Roads, east of the 2/4th K.O.Y.L.I. and south of Camouflage Copse.

Presumably, Mory Village was cleared of the enemy by the 5th K.O.Y.L.I., but there are no records to this effect, for the Diary of that Battalion, on the 25th August, contains only the following entry : " Battalion attacked and occupied Mory and valley running south from Mory." That is all !

At 5 p.m. the enemy put down an intense barrage all along the Divisional front and as far west as Sapignies and Béhagnies. The barrage was followed at 6-15 p.m. by a powerful counter-attack. The S.O.S. was sent up both by the 186th and 187th Infantry Brigades and the guns promptly opened fire on the enemy. The 2/20th Londons, of the 185th Infantry Brigade, were also moved up to the vicinity of Ervillers, in close support. The heaviest attack fell on the right Brigade, where the right flank of the 5th Duke of Wellington's Regt. was not in touch with the left of the 37th Division (IVth Corps), the village of Favreuil still being in the possession of the enemy. (An attack on Favreuil had already been ordered, but the enemy's counter-attack was made just before Zero hour, 6-30 p.m.).

About two Companies of the enemy attacked frontally from the Vraucourt—Beugnatre Road, coming down the slope of the hill towards C and A Companies of the 5th Duke's. Heavy rifle and Lewis gun fire was opened on the advancing Germans who, as the bullets tore through their ranks, hesitated. A German officer was seen trying to get his men on, though his efforts were apparently in vain. Presently he dropped to the ground. The enemy's hesitation then turned to action and in a few minutes the remaining Germans were running helter-skelter for their own trenches. Thus the enemy's attack in this part of the line failed.

On the right flank of the Battalion, however, the situation was much more serious. A large force of the enemy, estimated at five

Battalions had concentrated in the thickly-wooded northern parts 25TH AUG. of Favreuil village. From this position he attacked the right flank of the 186th Infantry Brigade. Captain C. G. H. Ellis, who commanded the right flank Company (D) of the 5th Duke's, quickly realizing the danger, threw back his line slightly to face south-east, thus forming a defensive flank, against the threatened attack.

Met by an accurate rifle and Lewis gun fire, and being caught by the Divisional artillery in the northern end of Favreuil, the enemy suffered very heavy losses. The loud explosions of bursting shells and the sharp crack of rifles were punctuated by shrieks and groans issuing from the wood north of the village. Every attempt by the enemy to advance was broken up and finally the attack died down and by 5 p.m. Captain Ellis had resumed his former position.

But it is impossible to separate the repulse of the enemy from the north of Favreuil by the 5th Duke of Wellington's from the attack on the village by the 37th Division and a Company of the 2/4th Duke of Wellington's, for about 3 o'clock in the afternoon a message reached the G.O.C., 186th Infantry Brigade, stating that the attack by the IVth Corps on Favreuil, which had been unsuccessful in the morning, was to be renewed at 6-30 p.m.; also that the IVth Corps Commander, having asked the 62nd Division to co-operate by enveloping the village from the north, General Burnett was ordered to assist, though not allowing the attack to interfere seriously with his own operations.

One Company (A—Capt. N. Geldhard) of the 2/4th Duke of Wellington's Regt. was, therefore, moved from the Gomiécourt Ridge to the south-eastern corner of Sapignies, from which it was to advance from the north-west on Favreuil. Two mortars of the 186th T.M. Battery took up gun positions also in the south-east corner of the village, to cover the attack.

At 6-30 p.m. the operation began. "A" Company of the 2/4th Duke's, advancing in two waves, two platoons in each, deployed so quickly for the attack, and moved so rapidly towards the north-western exits of Favreuil, astride the Sunken Road between the latter village and Sapignies, that the trench mortars were not brought into action. On the right of the Company, the Battalions of the 37th Division (IVth Corps) attacked due east from the Arras—Bapaume Road, *i.e.*, across the front of attack of A Company. Hostile machine-gun fire, in action in the Sunken Road on the line of advance, swept the ranks of the Company, but the right platoons, pushing a Lewis gun forward, put the German machine-gun out of

R

25TH AUG. action, about thirty of the enemy coming down the road, with their hands in the air, crying out " Kamerade ! " After further fighting on the high ground north-west of the village, two more parties of Germans, one of fifty and the other of sixty, surrendered. But by now A Company of the 2/4th Duke's had become mixed up with the 13th K.R.R.C. of the 37th Division, and the Company Commander therefore placed himself under the orders of the latter unit. The 2/4th were then ordered to protect the left flank of the Rifles, whilst the latter were advancing into the village. This move was successfully carried out and the K.R.R.C. penetrated Favreuil and worked northwards. Throughout the night of 25th, A Company, of the 2/4th Duke's, remained with the 37th Division.

In the Divisional Diaries, the repulse of the enemy's counter-attack, by the 5th Duke of Wellington's Regt., and the attack on Favreuil by the 37th Division and one Company of the 2/4th Duke's, are given as separate actions, but taking the two Zero hours of attack—6-15 p.m. *by* the enemy and 6-30 p.m. *on* the enemy, it is almost certain that these two actions clashed and that the discomfiture of the Germans was also due to the action of the IVth Corps, aided by the 2/4th Duke's.

On the northern flank of the Divisional front, *i.e.*, the 187th Infantry Brigade, the enemy's heavy artillery barrage succeeded in gradually forcing back the Hallamshire's Posts in the Sunken Road and about the light railway junction, north-east of L'Abbaye ; the troops holding the defensive flank along the railway south of L'Abbaye were also temporarily forced out of their positions. They fell back on the Sunken Road running north from Mory Village to Mory Copse. The enemy was using large quantities of " sneezing " gas shells and shrapnel, and many men were temporarily put out of action as the effects of the " sneezing " gas made the wearing of gas masks practically impossible. It was at this period that the 2/4th K.O.Y.L.I. came into action. Heavy machine-gun fire accompanied the Hallamshires as they fell back towards the Sunken Road. The O.C., A Company of the K.O.Y.L.I. (Lieut. G. E. Spencer), then lying in the Sunken Road, hearing the heavy firing gradually drawing nearer, jumped up on to the bank and discovered that the forward posts of the Hallamshires had been driven in and the enemy was advancing rapidly. A section of Lewis guns promptly came into action, and covered by this fire, Lieut. Spencer led his Company in a bayonet charge against the enemy. The left Company of the K.O.Y.L.I. (B Company, under Lieut. Holland) and the men of the 2/4th York and Lancs., who had been driven in, also joined in the charge, and the enemy was forced to retire, the vacated posts on the right being re-established.

Simultaneously with the attack on the right of the Hallamshires, *i.e.*, the Sunken Road and Light Railway about L'Abbaye, the enemy attempted to work round the northern exits of Mory Copse. These Germans were seen by the O.C. of a section of B Company, 62nd M.G.C., who had eight guns in a trench north of the Copse. The O.C., D Company, K.O.Y.L.I. (Capt. Skirrow), had also detected the attempt of the enemy to outflank the left of the 187th Infantry Brigade. The Section Machine Gun Company opened fire and inflicted heavy losses on the enemy and Capt. Skirrow led his Company forward to the attack. A number of Germans had actually penetrated Mory Copse, but taking two platoons, the O.C., D Company, charged into the Copse. Capt. Skirrow personally knocked out the crew of a machine-gun with his revolver and, getting in touch with troops of the Guards Division advancing from the north, he and his men cleared the Copse and drove the enemy back. A large number of prisoners was captured. All along the line the enemy was by now thoroughly demoralized and the British barrage which now began to take heavy toll, completed his discomfiture. From statements made by prisoners, the enemy had lost 50 per cent. of his attacking force. Throughout the night of 25th/26th August, consolidation of the line, and the carrying forward of rations and water, occupied the troops. The 2/4th K.O.Y.L.I. took over the front line from the 2/4th York and Lancs. (Hallamshires), the latter taking up supporting positions in rear and about the Sunken Road, north of Mory Village.

Thus, at nightfall on 25th August, substantial progress had been made by the Division and preparations were being made to continue the advance on the following morning.

Appendix I.

ORDER OF BATTLE OF THE 62ND (W.R.) DIVISION ON ARRIVAL IN FRANCE
In January, 1917.

General Officer Commanding : Major-General W. P. Braithwaite, C.B.

A.D.C. : Lieut. G. H. Roberts.
„ Second-Lieut. J. C. Newman.
G.S.O. : 1. Lieut.-Colonel Hon. A. G. A. Hore-Ruthven, V.C., Welsh Guards.
„ 2. Major W. G. Charles, Essex Regiment.
„ 3. Captain J. A. Batten Poole, 5th Lancers.
A.A. and Q.M.G. : Lieut.-Colonel R. M. Foot, C.M.G., late Royal Innisk. Fus.
D.A.A. and Q.M.G. : Major H. F. Lea, late Yorkshire Regiment.
D.A.Q.M.G. : Captain F. J. Langdon, late The King's.
C.R.A. : Brigadier-General A. T. Anderson, R.A.
C.R.E. : Lieut.-Colonel F. Gillam, R.E.
A.D.M.S. : Colonel de B. Birch, C.B., R.A.M.C. (T).
D.A.D.M.S. : Major T. C. Lucas.
A.D.V.S. : Major F. J. Taylor.
D.A.D.O.S. : Lieut. R. M. Holland.
A.P.M. : Major G. D'Urban Rodwell.

185th Infantry Brigade.

G.O.C. : Brigadier-General V. W. de Falbe, C.M.G., D.S.O.
Brigade Major : Major R. E. Power, The Buffs.
Staff Captain : Captain W. A. C. Lloyd, 2/7th West Yorkshire Regiment.
2/5th Battalion West Yorkshire Regiment : Lieut.-Colonel J. Josselyn.
2/6th Battalion West Yorkshire Regiment : Lieut.-Colonel J. H. Hastings.
2/7th Battalion West Yorkshire Regiment : Lieut.-Colonel Hon. F. S. Jackson.
2/8th Battalion West Yorkshire Regiment : Lieut.-Colonel W. Hepworth, V.D.

186th Infantry Brigade.

G.O.C.: Brigadier-General F. F. Hill, C.B., C.M.G., D.S.O.
Brigade Major: Major C. A. H. Palairet, The Fusiliers.
Staff Captain: Captain W. O. Wright, 5th The King's Own.
2/4th Battalion West Riding Regiment: Lieut.-Colonel H. E. P. Nash.
2/5th Battalion West Riding Regiment: Lieut.-Colonel T. A. D. Best, D.S.O.
2/6th Battalion West Riding Regiment: Lieut.-Colonel J. Mackillop.
2/7th Battalion West Riding Regiment: Lieut.-Colonel W. Clifford, D.S.O.

187th Infantry Brigade.

G.O.C.: Brigadier-General R.O.B. Taylor, C.I.E.
Brigade Major: Major R. B. Bergne, The Leinster Regiment.
Staff Captain: Captain F. M. Lasseter, 4th Yorkshire Light Infantry.
2/4th Battalion K.O.Y.L.I.: Lieut.-Colonel E. Hind, V.D.
2/5th Battalion K.O.Y.L.I.: Lieut.-Colonel W. Watson.
2/4th York. and Lancs. Regiment: Lieut.-Colonel F. St. J. Blacker.
2/5th Battalion York and Lancs. Regiment: Lieut.-Colonel P. Prince.

Royal Artillery.

C.R.A.: Brigadier-General A. T. Anderson, R.A.
Brigade Major: Captain W. G. Lindsell, M.C.
Staff Captain: Captain A. J. Elston.
A.D.C.: Lieut. R. A. T. Anderson, R.A.

310th Brigade, R.F.A.:
Lieut.-Colonel G. R. V. Kinsman, D.S.O., R.A.
A/310th Battery: Major W. R. Cockayne.
B/310th Battery: Major L. B. Bigg.
C/310th Battery: Major R. C. Williams, D.S.O.
D/310th Battery: Major L. M. Webber.

311th Brigade, R.F.A.:
Lieut.-Colonel A. Gadie, T.D.
A/311th Battery: Major E. R. L. Fraser-Mackenzie.
B/311th Battery: Major C. W. Campbell.
C/311th Battery: Major W. Browne.
D/311th Battery: Major J. L. Gow.

312th Brigade, R.F.A.:
Lieut.-Col. E. P. Bedwell
A/312th Battery: Major C. F. Bennion

Royal Artillery—*Continued*:

B/312th Battery : Major F. A. Arnold-Forster.
C/312th Battery : Major G. R. Fleming.
D/312th Battery : Major F. H. Lister, D.S.O.
62nd Divisional Ammunition Column :
Lieut.-Colonel F. Mitchell.
No. 1 Section : Captain J. Fraser.
No. 2 Section : Captain T. C. Kewley.
No. 3 Section : Captain R. G. Rice.
No. 4 Section : Captain C. S. Walker.

Royal Engineers.

C.R.E. : Lieut.-Colonel F. Gillam, R.E.
Adjutant : Captain G. D. Aspland.
461st Field Company, R.E. : Major W. A. Seaman.
457th Field Company, R.E. : Major L. St. J. Colley.
460th Field Company, R.E. : Major E. J. Walthew.

Signal Service.

62nd Division Signal Company : Captain R. V. Montgomery, Somerset Light Infantry.

Medical Units.

2/1st W.R. Field Ambulance : Lieut.-Colonel W. Lister.
2/2nd W.R. Field Ambulance : Lieut.-Colonel C. W. Eames.
2/3rd Field Ambulance : Lieut.-Colonel W. S. Kerr.
2/1st Northern Casualty Clearing Station : Lieut.-Colonel W. A. Wetwan.

62nd Division Sanitary Section.

Captain Moss C. B. Blundell.

Army Service Corps.

62nd Divisional Train : Lieut-.Colonel H. H. Wilberforce.
525th Company, A.S.C. : Major P. A. Wright.
526th Company, A.S.C. : Lieut. S. G. Shaw.
527th Company, A.S.C. : Lieut. W. N. Roberts.
528th Company, A.S.C. : Captain H. P. Peacock.

Divisional M.T. Company.

62nd Divisional M.T. Company : Major H. J. C. Hawkins.

Mobile Vet. Section.

2/1st W.R. Mobile Vet. Section : Captain P. Abson, A.V.C.

Appendix II.

EXTRACT FROM "LONDON GAZETTE," 8th May, 1918.

Maj. (A/Lieut.-Colonel) Oliver Cyril Spencer WATSON, D.S.O. (R. of O.), late K.O.Y.L.I.

For most conspicuous bravery, self-sacrificing devotion to duty, and exceptionally gallant leading during a critical period of operations.

His command was at a point where continual attacks were made by the enemy in order to pierce the line, and an intricate system of old trenches in front, coupled with the fact that his position was under constant rifle and machine-gun fire, rendered the situation still more dangerous.

A counter-attack had been made against the enemy's position, which at first achieved its object, but as they were holding out in two improvised strong points, Lieut.-Colonel Watson saw that immediate action was necessary, and he led his remaining small reserve to the attack, organizing bombing parties and leading attacks under intense rifle and machine-gun fire.

Outnumbered, he finally ordered his men to retire, remaining himself in a communication trench to cover the retirement, though he faced almost certain death by so doing.

The assault he led was at a critical moment, and without doubt saved the line. Both in the assault and in covering his men's retirement, he held his life as nothing, and his splendid bravery inspired all troops in the vicinity to rise to the occasion and save a breach being made in a hardly tried and attenuated line.

Lieut.-Colonel Watson was killed while covering the withdrawal.

Appendix III.

EXTRACT FROM "LONDON GAZETTE," 4th June, 1918.

No. 203590 Pte. Thomas YOUNG, 9th Bn. Durham Light Infantry (High Spen, co. Durham).

For most conspicuous bravery in face of the enemy when acting as a stretcher-bearer.

He showed throughout the whole course of the operations a most magnificent example of courage and devotion to duty. On nine different occasions he went out in front of our line in broad daylight under heavy rifle, machine-gun and shell-fire which was directed on him, and brought back wounded to safety, those too badly wounded to be moved before dressing he dressed under this harassing fire, and carried them unaided to our lines and safety; he rescued and saved nine lives in this manner.

His untiring energy, coupled with an absolute disregard of personal danger, and the great skill he showed in dealing with casualties, is beyond all praise.

For five days Pte. Young worked unceasingly, evacuating wounded from seemingly impossible places.

Appendix IV.

Vme Armée.

Q.G., le 30 Juillet, 1918.

Etat-Major 3me Bureau.

No. 1863/3.

ORDRE GENERAL NO. 63.

Au moment ou le XXII. C. A. Britannique est appelé à quitter la Vme Armée, le Général Commandant l'Armée lui exprime toute la reconnaissance et toute l'admiration qu'ont merité les hauts faits qu'il vient d'accomplir.

A peine débarqué, tenant à l'honneur de participer à la contre offensive victorieuse qui venait d'arrêter la furieuse ruée de l'ennemi sur la Marne, et commencait à le rejeter en desordre vers le Nords, précipitant ses mouvements, réduisant à l'extreme la durée de ses reconnaissances, le XXII. C. A. s'est jeté avec ardeur dans la melée.

Poussant sans répit ses efforts, harcellant, talonnant l'ennemi, il a, pendant 10 jours successifs d'âpres combats, fait sienne cette vallée de l'Ardre largement arrosée de son sang.

Grace au courage héroique, et à la tenacité proverbiale des fils de la Grande Bretagne, les efforts continus et répétés de ce brave Corps d'Armée n'ont pas étés vains ;

21 officiers, plus de 1,300 soldats prisonniers, 140 mitrailleuses, 40 canons, enlevés à l'ennemi, dont 4 divisions ont été successivement malmenées et refoulées,

la haute vallée de l'Ardre réconquise avec les hauteurs qui la dominent au Nord et au Sud.

tel est le bilan de la participation Britannique à l'effort de la Vme Armée.

Ecossais de la Montagne, sous le commandement du Général Carter-Campbell, Commandant la 51me Division !

Enfants de Yorkshire, sous le commandement du Général Braithwaite, Commandant la 62nd Division !

Cavaliers Neo-Zelandais et Australiens !

Vous tous, officiers et soldats du 22me C. A., si brillament commandé par le Général Sir A. Godley, vous venez d'ajouter une page glorieuse à votre histoire.

Marfaux, Chaumuzy, Montagne de Bligny, ces noms prestigieux pourront être écrits en lettres d'or dans les annales de vos regiments.

Vos amis Francais se souviendront avec émotion de votre brillant bravoure, et de votre parfaite cameraderie de combat.

Le Général Commandant le Vme Armée,

'Berthelot.'

Appendix IV.
TRANSLATION.
Q.G., July 30th, 1918.
ORDER OF THE DAY NO. 63.

Now that the XXII. British Corps has received orders to leave the Fifth (French) Army, the Army Commander expresses to all the thanks and admiration which the great deeds that it has just accomplished deserve.

The very day of its arrival, feeling in honour bound to take part in the victorious counter-attack which had just stopped the enemy's furious onslaught on the Marne, and had begun to hurl him back in disorder to the North, the XXII. Corps, by forced marches and with minimum opportunity for reconnaissance, threw itself with ardour into the battle.

By constant efforts, by harrying and by driving back the enemy for ten successive days, it has made itself master of the Valley of the Ardre, which it has so freely watered with its blood.

Thanks to the heroic courage and proverbial tenacity of the British, the continued efforts of this brave Army Corps have not been in vain.

21 officers and 1,300 other ranks taken prisoners, 140 machine-guns and 40 guns captured from an enemy, four of whose Divisions have been successively broken and repulsed; the Upper Valley of the Ardre, with its surrounding heights to the North and the South, reconquered; such is the record of the British share in the operations of the Fifth Army.

Highlanders under the orders of General Carter-Campbell, commanding the 51st Division; Yorkshire lads under the orders of General Braithwaite, commanding the 62nd Division; Australian and New Zealand Mounted Troops; all officers and men of the XXII. Army Corps, so ably commanded by General Sir A. Godley, you have added a glorious page to your history.

Marfaux, Chaumuzy, Montaigne de Bligny—all those famous names will be written in letters of gold in the annals of your regiments.

Your French comrades will always remember with emotion your splendid gallantry and your perfect fellowship in the fight.

'Berthelot,'
le Général Commandant,
la Vme Armée.

INDEX

Anderson, Brig.-Gen. A. T.
  7, 24, 67, 73, 79, 216
Arras Rest Area : Dec., 1917-Mar., 1918, 123 ; reduction of Battalions in Infantry Brigades, 124 ; 9th D.L.I. join 62nd Division 125
Balguy, Brig.-Gen. J. H. .. 4, 7
Bangalore Torpedoes 46
Barton, Lt.-Col. B. J., 77, 145, 151
Bastow, Lt.-Col. H. V. .. 179
Beaumont Hamel, 15 ; 62nd Div. relieves 32nd, 16 ; first hostile raid on Div., 19 ; good work by 187th Bde., 25 ; Orchard Alley occupied .. 27
Beever, Lt.-Col. 6
Best, Lt.-Col. T. A. D. 49, 78, 87
Birch, Col. de B. 4
Bissett, Major F. W. L. .. 163
Blacker, Col. F. St. J., 23, 49, 50, 151, 156, 162
Bradford, V.C., Brig.-Gen. R.B. 72, 78, 86, 89, 120
Braithwaite, Major-Gen. Sir W. P., 7, 16, 17, 67, 75, 90, 91, 102, 120, 139, 140, 149, 157, 169, 178
Brigades, Artillery :
  310th : 7, 9, 10, 11, 15, 37, 57, 72, 75, 76, 96, 107, 126, 183, 215, 216, 225
  311th : 7, 9, 10, 11, 15, 19, 37
  312th : 7, 9, 10, 11, 37, 57, 72, 75, 76, 96, 107, 126, 183, 215, 216, 225
Brigades, Infantry :—
  185th : 7, 9, 11, 12, 16, 17, 21, 22, 24, 25, 27, 28, 31, 34, 38, 39, 41, 42, 46, 48, 50, 52, 54, 55, 56, 60, 62, 64, 67, 71, 77, 82, 83, 92, 95, 103, 106, 108, 112,113, 114, 115, 118, 121, 124, 125, 133, 137, 138, 140, 141, 145, 152, 153, 159, 160, 165, 166, 172, 173, 175, 179, 182, 186, 190, 191, 193, 195, 203, 206, 207, 209, 215, 229, 231

Brigades, Infantry—contd.
  186th : 7, 9, 11, 12, 16, 17, 21, 22, 24, 25, 26, 27, 31, 34, 37, 38, 46, 48, 50, 52, 54, 55, 56, 60, 72, 78, 86, 92, 95, 96, 102, 103, 106, 108, 112, 113, 114, 115, 116, 118, 120, 121, 124, 125, 127, 133, 137, 138, 141, 144, 152, 154, 155, 157, 161, 165, 166, 172, 173, 176, 182, 186, 190, 191, 193, 195, 201, 203, 205, 206, 207, 209, 214, 229, 230, 232
  187th : 7, 9, 11, 12, 16, 18, 21, 22, 24, 25, 26, 31, 34, 38, 46, 48, 51, 52, 54, 55, 56, 60, 71, 77, 81, 83, 85, 92, 95, 103, 106, 108, 112, 113, 114, 115, 117, 118, 124, 125, 133, 135, 136, 140, 141, 145, 151, 153, 157, 159, 165, 166, 170, 172, 173, 176, 179, 181, 184, 185, 190, 193, 195, 202, 203, 204, 205, 206, 214, 229, 232
Brook, Major F. 101
Bullecourt : First attack on, 37, 40, 41 ; attack by 2/7th W. Yorks., 41 ; second attack 42, 43
Battle of, May, 1917, 45 ; dispositions for attack, 48, 49 ; failure to capture, 51, 52 ; causes of failure, 53 ; deeds of gallantry, 53, 54 ; final attack, 54 ; Bullecourt captured, 56 ; casualties of Div. 57
Burnett, Brig.-Gen. J. G. 144, 161, 162, 195, 209, 231
Cambrai, Battle of, 1917, 69 ; scheme of operations 70, 71 ; preparations for attack, 73 ; the German defences, 74, 75 ; disposition of 62nd Div., 77, 78 ; attack opens, 79, 80 ; Havrincourt entered, 81 ;

Index

Cambrai, Battle of—contd.
 " Blue Line " captured, 83 ;
 " Brown Line " captured, 84 ;
 Graincourt captured, 89 ;
 Hindenburg Support Line captured, 89 ; record advance by 62nd Div., 90 ;
 Div. congratulated, 93 ;
 attack on Anneux, 98 ;
 Anneux Chapel captured by 2/4th Duke's, 99 ; end of first phase, 107 ; Special Order of the Day, 108, 109 ;
 attack on Bourlon Wood,111, 112; disposition of Div., 115;
 Bourlon Village reached, 117;
 Div. relieved, 119 ; total casualties of Div. 119
Chamberlin, Lt.-Col. F. G. C., 49, 78
Chaytor, Lt.-Col. C. A. 178, 233
Collinson, Col. H. 218
Coombe, Major R. 78
Coombe, Major L. J... .. 145
Croix de Guerre awarded to 8th West Yorks. 209
Crouch, Lt.-Col. E. .. 125, 193
Dale, Major, A. P. 31
Devonshire Regt. :
 1/5th Bn., 168, 179, 189, 198, 207, 211, 219
Duke of Wellington's Regt. :
 2/4th Bn., 3, 17, 34, 35, 37, 49, 78, 86, 87, 88, 89, 96, 97, 98, 99, 101, 103, 112, 115, 117, 119, 135, 138, 145, 147, 148, 152, 158, 190, 191, 192, 205, 206, 207, 210, 230, 232, 235, 236
 2/5th Bn., 3, 17, 27, 34, 35, 37, 49, 50, 51, 52, 55, 78, 86, 87, 88, 89, 96, 97, 101, 102, 103, 112, 115, 116, 117, 119 ; amalgamated 125
 5th Bn., 125, 135, 138, 141, 145, 146, 147, 148, 151, 152, 154, 158, 159, 190, 191, 196, 197, 198, 200, 206, 231, 232, 234, 235, 236
 2/6th Bn., 3, 10, 15, 18, 34, 35, 37, 49, 51, 78, 86, 87, 88, 89, 96, 97, 102, 103, 112, 113, 115, 116, 117, 119 ; disbanded 125
 2/7th Bn., 3, 18, 34, 37, 49,

Duke of Wellington's Regt.
 —contd.
 55, 78, 86, 87, 88, 89, 96, 97, 100, 101, 102, 103, 112, 115, 117, 119, 126, 127, 135, 138, 144, 145, 147, 148, 150, 153, 154, 157 ;
 disbanded 167
Durham Light Infantry :—
 9th Bn., 125, 139, 145, 146, 152, 153, 158, 182, 193, 194, 195, 199, 200, 201
Eames, Lt.-Col. C. W. .. 4
Eden, Lt.-Col. A. G. .. 76, 215
England, Lt.-Col. N. A.
 179, 200, 211
Ford, Lt.-Col. S. W. 49
Gadie, Lt.-Col. A. 37
German Offensive, Mar., 1918 :
 Condition of opposing Armies 130 ; German plan of attack, 131 ; disposition of 62nd Div., 133 ; offensive opens, 134 ; 62nd Div. transferred to Third Army, 135 ; march to Bucquoy, 137 ; defence of Bucquoy, 143 ; disposition of Div., 145 ; Div. attacked, 146, 147 ; Div. sorely pressed 147, 148 ; Gen. Ironside's machine gunners, 149 ; five enemy attacks repulsed, 150 ;
 Pte. Young, D.L.I.,wins V.C., 152 ; gallantry of 2/4th K.O.Y.L.I., 155 ; attack on Rossignol Wood, 156 ; Col. Watson's death and award of V.C., 156 ; further attack on Rossignol Wood, 160 ; tribute to Brigadiers and C.O.'s, 161 ; casualties of Div. in March 162
Gillam, Lt.-Col. F. 39
Gordon, Major A. O. 126
Grieve, Lt.-Col. M. 6
Guinness, Col. H. W. 4
Hampden, Brig.-Gen. Viscount 77, 144, 162, 179, 209
Hampshire Regt. :—
 2/4th Bn., 168, 192, 205, 206, 209, 210, 219, 230
Harrison, Lt.-Col. G. N.
 126, 182, 217
Hart, Lt.-Col. L. H. P., 49, 77, 159, 178, 231, 233

Index

	PAGE
Hastings, Lt.-Col. J.	49
Hindenburg Line, 20, 21; advance to, 31; Miraumont, 33; 62nd Div. squeezed out of the line, 35; casualties of Div., Mar, 1917	36
Hoare, Lt.-Col. C. H.	77
Ironside, Gen.	149, 150
James, Lt.-Col. A. H., 49, 77, 144, 152, 161	
James, Lt.-Col. C. K., 49, 77, 143, 152, 159, 161, 162, 167	
Josselyn, Lt.-Col. J.	42, 49
Kerr, Lt.-Col.	4
K.O.Y.L.I. Regt. :—	
2/4th Bn., 3, 23, 24, 25, 49, 50, 81, 82, 104, 113, 115, 118, 151, 156, 178, 182, 185, 186, 204, 205, 206, 230, 233, 234, 236, 237	
2/5th Bn., 3, 23, 24, 49, 50, 81, 82, 83, 104, 113, 115, 117, 118; amalgamated	125
5th Bn., 125, 151, 156, 178, 182, 184, 194, 195, 204, 230, 233, 234	
Lassetter, Col. H. B.	5
Lea, Lt.-Col. H.	217
Lister, Lt.-Col.	4
Lough, Lt.-Col.	76
Machine Gun Coy. 62nd, 126, 140, 144, 145, 163, 182, 217	
Mainwaring, Col. H. G.	4
Maitland, Lt.-Col. A. E.	77
Marne, The, general situation, 171; Div. leaves for, 172; Battle of Tardenois, 175; disposition of Div., 176; concentration of Div., 177; move to assembly positions, 179; Forest of Rheims, 180, 181; attack begins, 183; attack on Marfaux, 189; attack on Bouilly Ridge, 193, 194; attack on Bois du Petit Champs, 196, 197, 198; Cuitron captured, 201; Divisional front reorganised, 203; capture of Bligny and Montaigne de Bligny, 209; Div. relieved	215
Molesworth, Lt.-Col.	6
Molyneux, Major	191
Montgomery, Major R. V.	151

	PAGE
Musketeen (Automatic Rifle) Bn.	53
Nash, Lt.-Col. H. F. P.	49, 78, 120
Newman, Lt.-Col. C. R.	140
" Pelican Troupe "	169
Perry, Lt.-Col. B. H. H.	151
Peter, Lt.-Col. F. W.	178, 233
Pioneers (9th D.L.I.) join Div.	125
Power, Lt.-Col. R. E.	49, 77
Reddie, Brig.-Gen. A. J.	178, 231
Shearman, Major	157
Sherlock, Lt.-Col. D. J. C.	121, 215, 216
Stewart, Major R.	179
Sloman, Col. H. S.	4, 6
Taylor, Brig.-Gen. R. O. B.	77
Thackeray, Lt.-Col. F. S.	78, 144, 147
Trench Warfare : 29/6-19/11/17 59; Noreuil-Lagnicourt Sector taken over, 61; fine patrol work, 62; successful raid by 2/6th W. Yorks., 65; hostile raid repulsed, 66, 67; active defence, 165, 166; raids and counter raids	167
Trotter, Major-Gen. Sir J. K.	4, 7
Victory, Advance to, Review and tribute by Gen. Berthelot, 221; situation at end of July, 1918, 222, 223; attack on Mory, 231; Mory captured	234
Waddy, Lt.-Col. R. H.	77, 144, 213, 227
Walker, Lt.-Col. J.	125, 161, 200, 231
Warde-Aldam, Lt.-Col. W. St. A.	227
Watson, V.C., Lt.-Col. O. C. S.	151, 156, 161
Watson, Lt.-Col. W.	49, 51
West Yorkshire Regt. :—	
2/5th, 3, 17, 19, 31, 38, 41, 42, 49, 50, 52, 54, 64, 81, 83, 84, 104, 106, 115, 118, 134, 137, 143, 144, 150, 152, 153, 167, 179, 182, 186, 188, 190, 206, 207, 213, 214; disbanded 226,	227
2/6th, 3, 17, 31, 38, 43, 49, 50, 51, 52, 54, 64, 80, 81, 83, 84, 104, 106; disbanded	125
2/7th, 3, 17, 31, 38, 41, 42, 43, 49, 51, 52, 54, 55, 62,	

Index

West Yorkshire Regt.—contd.
64, 79, 83, 84, 104, 115,
117, 119, 134, 137, 143,
144, 152, 153, 154; disbanded 167
2/8th, 17, 31, 38, 41, 42, 43,
49, 51, 52, 54, 64, 79,
83, 84, 91, 104, 106, 118;
amalgamated 125
8th, 125, 134, 137, 144, 145,
147, 150, 152, 159, 160,
167, 179, 182, 186, 190,
200, 201, 202, 207, 209,
211, 212, 213

Wilberforce, Lt.-Col. H. H. .. 217
Williams, Major R. C. .. 28
Wilson, Lt.-Col. P. P. 210, 232
York and Lancaster Regt. :
2/4th, 3, 21, 22, 23, 49, 51,
83, 104, 106, 113, 115, 118,
152, 158, 159, 160, 178,
181, 184, 185, 186, 193,
194, 204, 231, 233, 234, 237
2/5th, 3, 23, 24, 35, 49, 51,
83, 85, 103, 106, 113, 115,
117, 118; disbanded .. 124
Young, V.C., Pte. T... .. 152

www.ingramcontent.com/pod-product-compliance
Lightning Source LLC
Chambersburg PA
CBHW061931220426
43662CB00012B/1874